'Entertaining and very, very funny. It's also a brilliant introduction for the classical novice' *Independent*

'Hunter has a great eye for biographical absurdity (and he's a pro at strategic swearing) but he also really wants to listen, to understand the music. He is passionate about sound. He gets to the stage where he can't imagine a life without classical music; that's the real story in the end. It makes you want to listen. Go with him and you will get a breathless, very entertaining sense of the history and sociology of this rich art, and a much clearer understanding of Mozart's fondness for sticking a finger up his own backside' *Guardian*

'Hunter has hit on a page-turning formula . . . a Bill Bryson for the *Kerrang!* generation' *Sunday Telegraph*

'Hunter is as good as it gets' *The Times*

'A philistine he may be, but he turns his ignorance into a blitzkrieg of witty observations and raucous rock 'n' roll metaphors . . . he never loses his edge, and this is what makes *Rock Me Amadeus* such an entertaining and irreverent read' *Irish Times*

'Hunter has the growling mongrel spirit of his late Gonzo namesake, mixed with the rabid fanboy attitude of the best *NME* writers, back when that organ was a force to be reckoned with. *Rock Me Amadeus* is vulgar, irreverent and shameless, and it should be on every music lover's shelf' *Irish Examiner*

'Hilarious, engaging and educational' *What's On In London*

'Hunter approaches his task with a doggedness that verges on the obtuse' *Sunday Times*

'Hunter's instant connection with Bach is unexpectedly touching, and his outsider's view of classical music points up its rampant cosiness and occasional absurdities. A giant tick in Hunter's plus column is that he never confuses trimmings like these with the music itself . . . hilarious' *Gramophone*

ABOUT THE AUTHOR

Seb Hunter is a writer, musician and occasional broadcaster. He is the author of the critically acclaimed *Hell Bent for Leather*. He lives in Hampshire with his wife and young son.

To subscribe to Seb's fortnightly newsletter *The Bitterest Pill: Classical Music One Step at a Goddamn Time*, register free at www.sebhunter.com/TBP

Rock Me Amadeus

When Ignorance Meets High Art, Things Can Get Messy

Seb Hunter

PENGUIN BOOKS

PENGUIN BOOKS

Published by the Penguin Group
Penguin Books Ltd, 80 Strand, London WC2R ORL, England
Penguin Group (USA) Inc., 375 Hudson Street, New York, New York 10014, USA
Penguin Group (Canada), 90 Eglinton Avenue East, Suite 700, Toronto, Ontario, Canada M4P 2Y3
(a division of Pearson Penguin Canada Inc.)
Penguin Ireland, 25 St Stephen's Green, Dublin 2, Ireland
(a division of Penguin Books Ltd)
Penguin Group (Australia), 250 Camberwell Road, Camberwell, Victoria 3124, Australia
(a division of Pearson Australia Group Pty Ltd)
Penguin Books India Pvt Ltd, 11 Community Centre, Panchsheel Park, New Delhi – 110 017, India
Penguin Group (NZ), 67 Apollo Drive, Rosedale, North Shore 0632, New Zealand
(a division of Pearson New Zealand Ltd)
Penguin Books (South Africa) (Pty) Ltd, 24 Sturdee Avenue, Rosebank, Johannesburg 2196, South Africa

Penguin Books Ltd, Registered Offices: 80 Strand, London WC2R ORL, England

www.penguin.com

First published by Michael Joseph 2006
Published in Penguin Books 2007

1

Typeset by Rowland Phototypesetting Ltd, Bury St Edmunds, Suffolk
Printed in England by Clays Ltd, St Ives plc

ISBN: 978-0-141-02293-2

'I don't know anything about music. In my line, you don't have to.'
Elvis Presley

0. Losing My Religion

My name is Seb Hunter, and I'm an addict.

My vice is popular music.

And I'm old enough to know better. I still buy the *NME* every week, and I have to hide it underneath my *Guardian* so the newsagent doesn't take me for a paedophile. As well as this early-adolescent staple, every month I buy *The Wire*, *Uncut*, *Mojo*, *Record Collector*, *Word*, a few guitar magazines, *Classic Rock* and even *Q*. I read them all, cover to cover. The occasional music magazine that I don't buy I stand in your way and read in WH Smiths anyway.

I spend the majority of my disposable income on popular music. As well as going to gigs, I buy, on average, four or five CDs every week, both old stuff and new releases, and I rake the internet half a dozen times a day for the latest popular music news. If the drummer out of Stereophonics breaks a wrist mid-tour, I know about it within an hour, even though I loathe Stereophonics, and have not bought, nor ever will buy, any of their music.

One unfortunate side-effect of this is that I still dress like an indie-obsessed university student circa 1992. After being clocked that I'm well beyond teenage, I'm looked at oddly in the street. Shouldn't he have grown out of looking like that by now? I confuse and frighten schoolchildren. I don't even have the excuse of being in a band any more – I'm happily married – so nor am I attempting to snare chicks. The only place in the world I'm still cool is at certain popular music venues, after a couple of drinks, in the dark.

None of this is particularly unusual. My ilk and I are a recognizable flock in the great Venn diagram of social tribes. A sallow cluster of twilight-chasing thirty-somethings, our tedious, repetitious tales have been cast many times over. What's unusual in my case is that I am about to renounce the whole caboodle. Turn my back on everything I know and love and say farewell to pop.

I don't know much about classical music, although I have, on occasion, pretended to. In the company of somebody grown-up, listening to the radio, they might cock their head and muse, softly, 'Isn't this Grieg?'

I'd feel compelled to cock my head too, and thoughtfully reply, 'Mmm, you might be right.'

'Or, perhaps, Debussy?'

'Yessssss. Maybe even . . .' I would pause, appreciatively, '. . . Chopin?'

'Don't be absurd.'

'Yes, right, sorry.' Then they'd turn the radio off, so that the oily DJ couldn't go on to prove them mistaken. But they only said something in the first place because they felt the need to reassert their cultural, moral and discriminatory superiority anyway, so I should have known better than to attempt to join in. But I so want to join in. Why, just because I like popular music, should I be so comprehensively watermarked as an intellectual retard? There's been enough popular music around now for the likes of me to have remained entirely within its walls; indeed, I'm pretty sure I can carry on with it for the rest of my life and not have to push too hard at the edges. There's been so much to satisfy and entertain us that there's been no need to investigate our snooty, superior cousins, down there in the *glassed-off* basement in HMV.

I want to know what's down there. I want to know what's

going on behind those doors, now that I'm just about old enough to be trusted not to spontaneously start moshing, or breakdancing or – good Lord – singing along. When I was growing up, classical music was the ultimate aspirational art form: you had to try and raise your game in the presence of it. Classical was, we were solemnly informed, the absolute pinnacle of human expression; no explanation necessary – just trust us on this one. I want to know if it's worth all the effort. Because effort seems to be a big part of this; they've made getting into classical music *difficult on purpose*; they've made it look like the most boring thing in the whole world so that we never come sniffing. They want to keep us out. Well, I'm sorry, but I want to come in. I love music, you see. And I've reached a stage in my life where it's time to try and love classical music too, even if it doesn't particularly want to love me back.

So my suitcase is packed, and I'm ready to say my good-byes. In just a few hours' time I'm going to be moving through to the anti-matter: the adult, empyreal world of classical music. My mission is to feel as passionate about classical as I do about pop, and I've decided that the only way to properly achieve this is to stop listening to popular music altogether, at least until I come to the end of my voyage. I'm going to start at the Beginning of Musical Time and consume, one by one, the mystical riches conferred upon me from raw frontline exposure to symphonic choral braggadocio. Concerto modulation and diatonic magnificats. Harmonic variations on polytonal madrigals. Fucking *opera* for chrissakes. I can hardly wait to be blown away by virtuoso performances from the greatest orchestras on earth playing the most venerated composers' most lauded masterpieces in the world's most humbling concert halls. Before breakfast. After breakfast, I'll sit at Mozart's old harpsichord and, having sufficiently soaked up the heady, powdered-wig-like vibes, knock out an aria or two by myself. Then, having enjoyed a sophisticated lunch in a baroque Wolfgangstrasse Kirchenhaus with a batty impassioned composer with a sweaty comb-over, I'll weep silent, bitter tears over a Honegger piano concerto before – after a meditative half-hour on a higher plane of Viennese consciousness – drifting off to a peaceful contemplative sleep, closer than I've ever been to a deep and profound understanding of the complexities of the Human Condition. It's that simple.

So, I sit here and I take a deep breath. As a concept it sounds pretty straightforward. I'm not scared yet – I'm almost excited. But then I think I'm probably in deep denial of what all this is going to take: rock 'n' roll only needs three chords; classical music just has *too many notes*.

Classical music, it's a pleasure to meet you. My name is Seb Hunter and I'm ready to go cold turkey. I've come to join you. Please, let me in.

Maybe it's time to grow up a little bit.

The Classical Eras

11th–15th centuries: Medieval

15th and 16th centuries: Renaissance

17th century: Baroque

18th century: Classical

19th century: Romantic

20th century: Modern

1. The Music of the Spheres

Disibodenberg monastery ruins, Staudernheim,
Germany, October 2003

The sun's coming down in cables.

This cold, watery October sunlight filters through the wind-twisted canopy as the grass below flattens into spectral partings and gullies. The ground is stubbled with stone: mossy blocks of rubble scattered in lines; long curves; crooked heaps lying in weed-scarred shadows. Orange leaves swirl in from above, speckling my sunbright blindness. The hilltop is empty; I'm the only person up here. I slowly rotate, checking. Only when I'm absolutely sure that I'm completely alone do I allow my knapsack to slide down my arms to the ground. I kneel, unzip its primary compartment and withdraw a small black Sony compact disc player and a large pair of Technics headphones. I don't need to load a disc, as I specifically did that early this morning with this moment firmly in mind. With fingers slow and numb from the chill autumnal wind, I steadfastly urge the volume control to its peak. Then I plug in the headphones and arrange them comfortably bulbous on my head, holding my thumb ready over the silver button with an arrow on it that means *play*.

First, though, I cast a final, nervous glance around the ruins. Amid the thick twisting creepers that defend the edges of the hill, a few high walls teeter on, meekly awaiting their final collapse. You can just make out – from the remaining inches-high blocks – the border of the old church walls, curving broadly round to the remains of a flat back wall. Within this empty space stands the altar; although only the altarpiece remains, it's still in its original position but with new supporting concrete legs, wide, squat and vaguely incongruous on this ruinous perch of grass. Yet it still stands proud. I look at it for a long time, then take a photo. I check the photo. It looks all right. I take one more for luck. I put the camera back in my pocket. The headphones are itchy, so I readjust them. I take a long time adjusting the bass and treble settings. My thumb hovers reluctantly over the play button. I'm stalling here, aren't I? I have a sneaky wee behind a split tree. I drink some water. I check my mobile phone still has reception. It doesn't – very grown-up. I push my hair behind my ears and cough self-importantly. I check my zip's done up.

I press play. I hear a nun.

There's no instrumentation. The nun sings:

Columba aspexit	The dove peered in
per cancellos fenestre	through the lattices of the window
ubi ante faciem eius	where, before its face,

8

| *sudando sudavit balsamum* | a balm exuded |
| *de lucido Maximino* | from incandescent Maximin |

I press stop and whip off the headphones. I can feel myself blushing; I'm deeply embarrassed for myself. What the hell am I *doing* here on this freezing-cold hillside in the middle of bloody nowhere, listening to a nun singing some bullshit in Latin at full blast? This laboured attempt at profundity suddenly feels quite awe-inspiringly ridiculous. I feel like an idiot. The dove peered in through the lattices of the window my arse. I have a sudden urge to cry and run back down the hill.

No! (I exclaim to myself.) *You cannot give up now. You've come so far – all the way to Germany. Persevere. Listen to the nun. Press play once more.*

O Maximine!	O Maximin!
mons et vallis es	you are the mount and the valley
et in utroque alta	and in both you seem a
edificatio appares	high building
ubi capricornus exivit	where the goat went
cum elephante	with the elephant
et Sapientia in deliciis fuit	and Wisdom was delighted

I trudge around listening to it with my hands in my pockets. Other nuns join in. Then some monks. They're all chanting the same line, there isn't any harmony, it sounds like an endless arbitrary vocal elevator. I read along with the words that are helpfully reproduced in the CD booklet.

The voices sound like they're suspended in the air between my ears, shimmering with a pure, holy light. The music's making me feel a bit like a dove now, actually – light, fluffy; quite friendly. I imagine where the goat went with the elephant – to the high building to visit Maximin. I begin to feel rather spiritual and superior. It's a nice feeling. I am calm. The gossamer whorls of the nun and monk voices rise and fall with the breeze as I glide gently through the ruins, my hair blowing voluptuously behind me.

Viscera tua gaudium habuit	Your flesh has known delight
sicut gramen super quod ros cadit	like the grassland touched by dew
cum ei viriditatem infudit	and immersed in its virility
ut et in te factum est	the same as with you

It even rhymes in translation! Heh heh heh, I chortle to myself, humming along with the voices. Maybe this is going to be easier than I thought!

I shimmy all round the hill for forty-five minutes.

But I've got ahead of myself.

In the Beginning . . .

The Earth was created 4.6 billion years ago. Its music was organic; it came from nature; from birdsong, bubbling brooks, wind in the trees, the howling of wild cats and the melodious roar of grumpy woolly mammoths.

5 million years ago: by walking upright, mankind gradually emerged from primates.

1.5 million years ago: we became Neanderthal (sloping foreheads), then discovered fire.

200,000 years ago: Homo Sapiens (vertical foreheads) emerged, from Africa.

The Stone Age: we learned to make tools from flint and animal bones. We painted and decorated our caves, then learned farming.

The Bronze Age: we learned metalwork and mining. We made bronze by mixing copper and tin. We also invented the wheel, which soon led to the plough, which made vegetables easier.

The Iron Age: we started making everything out of iron.

Up to this point, music has had a minimal influence on the evolution of mankind. But you'd still call it music. Cavemen banging stones, whacking bones, thumping lumps of bronze against cave walls, trees, probably themselves too, in ritual, excitement, frustration, sexual frenzy, communication and eventually just habit. And at some point they probably began singing along too. The problem that faces us now is that there's no record of any of this stuff. We can only speculate as to the very earliest levels of Cro-Magnon musicianship. The ambient profundity of *Now That's What I Call Grunting* and *The Greatest Megalithic Dinosaur-Chasing Album, Ever* are denied us.

It went on like this for a very long time.

The foundations of modern Western music are deeply muddy. So muddy, in fact, that academics still argue about this today. Did modern music rise out of the ashes of Rome? Greece? Egypt? Manchester? The lack of musical notation makes nailing down any of this impossible, but all of these ancient civilizations had primitive musics of their own; the Greeks, for example, played the double aulos, a kind of twin-necked flute. The Romans had the lyre, a shoddy portable harp. The early Christian church, however, relied solely on the human voice; chants used for general prayers, recitation of sacred texts, and other things along these lines. These were entirely functional – there were no 'composers' involved in their creation; they were just another form of worshipping. They were passed down through the ecclesiastical generations, without much thought going into structure, melody or lyrics. The important question with regard to the beginnings of classical music is when did these chants turn into genuine, proper music to be actively listened to and appreciated, rather than just prayed along to like sheep?

Who knows.

But three things worth mentioning happened during the Middle Ages:

1) Anicius Manlius Severinus Boethius (480–524) was the most cultured and revered gentleman of his era, which his name reinforces. His *Fundamentals of Music* suggested that music could be broken down into a simple science of numbers. Boethius said there were three different types of music: Cosmic (from the planets, elements and seasons), Human (the union of body and soul, only humans can't hear any of it) and Instrumental (everything we can hear). Boethius also wrote the classic *Consolations of Philosophy* while he awaited execution for overtly philosophical thoughts.

2) Gregory the Great (540–604), an enthusiastic singer, gave us the term Gregorian Chant. Gregorian chanting is as above: boring single-note mumbling in churches.

3) Somebody wrote the *Carmina Burana*. You'd recognize this if you heard it; it's the cheesy doom music you hear in films (*The Omen*) and adverts (Old Spice). An all-new sexed-up version was written in the 1930s, though its original authorship is disputed.

But then, in western Germany in 1106, a well-bred eight-year-old girl was handed over to a monastery as a tithe (basically a present). There she was locked up in tiny cell-like quarters wearing a hair shirt, straw, chains and with very strict rules for forty years, until the day her ruthless abbess,

Jutta von Sponheim, suddenly died, and her muse was – at last – set free. This woman, Hildegard von Bingen (1098–1179), was, to all intents and purposes, the world's first-ever composer.

My job is to go to Bingen to investigate.

The Cosmic Egg

Bang – I was out of the traps! No more pop music now for months, maybe even, my interior monologue hissed at me malevolently, *years*. This large, icy concept loomed over my quiet (pop farewell) hangover as I lurched out to Heathrow through bright fog on the Piccadilly Line. It was eight in the morning, and I was feeling uneasy about everything; consumed by thirst, doubt and worries about whether or not I was up to the challenge.* This upbeat mood was compounded by contemplation of my journey ahead: a plane to Frankfurt, then a couple of trains west along the Main and the Rhine to Bingen, where I hoped to find somewhere cheap to stay for a few nights while I threw myself into the Dark Ages during the day.

As I waited for my plane at Heathrow, I sat on a high stool, drinking coffee and trying to write travel-writerly observations in my notebook. I wrote a few lame, pointless descriptions of my fellow travellers, then resorted to writing things like 'well it's nice weather I suppose', 'come on, chin up' and 'coffee: 5/10', before sliding into 'really in the mood for some Dylan' and 'classical music mags in Smiths look scary, especially *Classic FM* one – too much smiling'. This had been my first real test: whether or not to buy the brand

* My conclusions gathered blackly around 'probably not'.

new (how do airports always manage this?) edition of *Mojo* magazine. It was one of those hermetically sealed issues that you can't just browse through in the shop, so I couldn't even just have a quick flick through it. I stood, thrown, by the racks. I hadn't bargained for this one, I didn't have a rule for it. In the end I decided that buying a music magazine without being able to listen to any of the music mentioned inside was like buying a porn mag and not being able to masturbate: completely pointless. I bought a paper instead, which I folded up and squeezed into my medium-sized knapsack. Also in there was:

Hildegard of Bingen: The Woman of Her Age by Fiona Maddocks,

A History of Western Music (5th edition) by Donald Jay Grout and Claude V. Palisca (heavier than a telephone directory, I swear),

Hildegard von Bingen: In Portrait (double BBC DVD),

A Feather on the Breath of God: Sequences and Hymns by Hildegard of Bingen (CD),

Gregorian Chants (CD, free from a petrol station),

Medieval Music (CD, free with *The Sunday Times* in 1994),

portable CD player and headphones,

laptop computer to play the DVD,

speakers for the laptop,

digital camera,

micro-cassette recorder (in case I needed to interview anybody),

notebook and pen,

a German 'Show Me' phrasebook (you find the phrase you need then hold up the book – the lettering is very large),

some clothes,

sanitary items.

You can see how seriously I'm taking this. All I needed now was some piercing insight, a little historical empathy and plenty of witty incidents along the way. In anticipation of these, I selected a special page in my notebook, and wrote 'WITTY INCIDENTS' at the top. I had prepared myself in this regard by reading a book by the heavyweight king of travel writing, Bill Bryson. Unfortunately he seemed to have rather a lot of witty incidents. I shuddered at the terrifying thought of a Bryson/me witty incident showdown and decided to put that idea on hold for the time being.

As I headed for my allocated gate, I felt my mood slowly improve. The sunshine, the caffeine and the prospect of the inevitable amusing escapades had bolstered my spirits considerably. And then, to my delight, I spotted a group of Southampton fans milling blearily around the desk at Air Romania. They were heading out for the second leg of our first-round UEFA Cup match against Steaua Bucharest. *What a brilliant omen!* I thought to myself, smiling encouragingly at them all. Unfortunately, we lost 1–0 and were knocked out.

But a second good omen was just around the corner: peering out into the glare at my gate, I saw that the Lufthansa plane we were going to be flying in was named *Bingen-am-Rhein*. Of the hundreds of German towns my plane could've been named after, I was flying on the one named after my own final destination! Here was a proper omen. I excitedly photographed the nose of the plane a few times, hurried on board and entered the two omens under 'witty incidents'. 'All Lufthansa planes have grey leather seats,' I also noted, though not under witty incidents. The rest of the flight was sadly uneventful. 'Cheese sandwich: 3/10', etc.

Bingen-am-Rhein isn't a nice place. It doesn't even try to be nice, or bother to pretend. Its location, though, is ectacular – right on the corner of the Rhine and Nahe rivers, in the picturesque heart of the historic German Rhineland. I'd been expecting an old-fashioned German tourist town, all welcoming Gothic lettering and wafting meaty aromas, red waistcoats and drooping facial hair. But it was just fat wandering smokers with toy dogs, and a crap concrete shopping street with eight utility bargain stores and a thick railway line running along the edge of the river. Bingen clearly doesn't give a fuck what you think – it's too busy being grey and disconsolate. Downhearted in the cold dusk, I booked into a low grey hotel that overlooked the Rhine and the railway, where I was made to pay for my entire stay in advance – they'd obviously rumbled the cut of my jib – and sent up to the second floor, where I rustled on my single bed staring blankly out at the heavy traffic of cargo barges grinding up and down the river. There was no minibar, so I went to sit on the toilet.

Modern Bingen is probably best known for not being anything like Rudesheim, the charming, heavily gabled, tourist-friendly town over on the opposite side of the Rhine. Rudesheim makes you feel welcome, wanted; it has gift shops, restaurants and bars, with waiters rumbustiously nudging you inside. Bingen doesn't. It has a supermarket without any shopping baskets and a high-tech Volkswagen dealership. But Bingen was where I needed to be; here was the epicentre of the Medieval music; I didn't have time for distractions, or for anything fun, or nice. My first evening in the Rheinhotel Starkenburger Hof was spent wrestling with my room's faulty radiator and reading up on the life of Hildegard. The most surprising thing, I soon learned, was that her music wasn't what she's most famous for. Historically, she's probably better known for being a psy-chedelic, visionary nun. Not only that, but she was also,

I discovered, an artist, a poet, a physicist, a herbalist, a physiologist, a nurse, a keen biologist, a powerful ally of the pope and a natural born leader of nuns generally. Despite my small, cold Starkenburger Hof room, I felt myself warming to her tale.

After her loving parents dropped her off at the gates of the monastery for the rest of her life in 1106, Hildegard did nothing for thirty-two years. Under the watchful eye of her abbess, Jutta, Hildegard dutifully fulfilled her largely pointless role as a cloistered nun. Most of her time here in the Disibodenberg monastery, 40 kilometres down the Nahe river from Bingen, was spent imprisoned in a tiny room, her only access to the outside world being a small hole in the outer wall, which was occasionally unplugged so that she could offer chippy religious advice to passers-by. Hildegard would spend most of her time at prayer, or learning Latin, or at prayer, or knitting for the monks who lived over on the other, nicer, side of the monastery.

At a time when the average life expectancy was only around fifty, Hildegard arrived at the ripe old age of forty having achieved nothing in her life other than having shouldered much harsh devotional solitude. However, as soon as mean Jutta died, the true Hildegard finally stepped forward to confess that for her entire life she'd been suffering powerful, ecstatic visions, sent directly from God. She described these revelations to her timid assistant monk, Volmar, who wrote them all up on goat-skins while Hildegard, her soul freed at last, busily spewed and frothed at the mouth. News of Hildegard's hotline to God spread far and fast; her chewy outpourings soon came to the attention of the pope – who was delighted, and sent Hildegard some supportive messages. This disembodied hoopla, however, came with a hard physical price. The visions made her physically sick;

often wreaking so much agony upon her writhing, emaciated frame that she lay regularly at death's shadowy door. As well as describing the visions to Volmar in great detail – which were soon published as her first bestseller, *Scivias* ('Know the Way'), in 1151 – she illustrated them herself.

Hildegard's art is packed with confidence, definition and colour; it looks weirdly contemporary – a bit like psychedelic 1960s pop art especially the 13th Floor Elevators.*

In each painting she portrays herself in the bottom left-hand corner, wax tablet in hand, recording the various fright-scenes that materialize before her. These days, Hildegard's visions are attributed to migraines and self-imposed starvation. Personally, I suspect it was a bit of that, and maybe too much monastery homebrew; perhaps even the odd hallucinogenic herb plucked from out of the convent cabbage patch. Slip inside this monastery.

* Whom I have absolutely not been listening to.

As her fame spread throughout Europe, noble families increasingly dropped by to hand their daughters over too; thus the convent ranks steadily grew. Then, in 1147, against the wishes of the local monks, Hildegard left Disibodenberg to set up her own convent, taking eighteen nuns upriver to a remote, isolated hill overlooking the two great rivers of the Rhine and the Nahe, where she founded the Rupertsburg Abbey, here on the site of modern-day Bingen. And it was here that she properly got down to work.

Throughout her life, Hildegard was obsessed with the categorization and compilation of the natural world. One of her later works, *Physica*, was a kind of contemporary medical encyclopedia. Here are a few genuine examples of some twelfth-century ailments, along with Hildegard's suggested cure:

Clouded sight: rub liver of turbot into the eyes.

Rotting gums: rub your mouth with powdered salmon bones.

Epilepsy: either eat small cakes made from mole's blood, duck's beak, goose's feet and flour for five days until it goes, or drink some water marinated with a dead mouse.

Indigestion: drink water with a dried lion's liver in it.

Jaundice: tie a punched bat to your groin, then watch it die.

Scrofula: pounded hamster liver soup or mashed earthworms should sort you out.

Feeling a bit horny: rub unguent of sparrowhawk and fat on to your penis, but not too vigorously, all right?

In another later work, *Causae et Curae*, Hildegard supplied pages of detailed advice on sexual matters. Being an erotic medieval agony aunt was yet another string to add to her already bulging psychedelic bow.

I found all this very interesting, though to be honest, rather distracting from my subject – after all, I was supposed to be here for the music, not these Renaissance nun antics. Hildegard was obviously talented, but what did any of this have to do with the tunes? Did she really have the spare time, amid her exciting celebrity lifestyle, to sit down and invent classical music as well? Yes. And not only that, but she also wrote the world's first ever concept album while she was at it.

Hot on the Trail of the Music

I woke on my first day proper in Bingen feeling energized and raring to go. In the deathly Starkenburger Hof dining room, I greedily wolfed down a bowl of gerbil-cage muesli served with tepid chemical milk, covertly eying my fellow diners for amusing descriptions or incident. They were all fat and smoked cigarettes while they ate. They stared at me openly. Soon, a large woman wearing a giant embroidered apron emerged from a side door. I think she said, 'Egg.'

'An egg would be really nice, thank you, that's so kind,' I replied. She disappeared and came back with an egg. I ate it quickly and headed back to my room to listen to the *Gregorian Chants* CD. I was already having the time of my godforsaken fucking life.

Knowing that I was going to be stuck in an alien musical rut for so long had given me the jitters. It probably doesn't sound like a big deal to you, but to me this was proper heavy shit, and, internally, I'd blown its significance out of all proportion. I was feeling bitter about the whole miserable project before I'd even properly got started, so it felt good now to be finally applying my ears to the task in hand. I loaded the *Gregorian Chants* CD into my laptop and listened to it all the way through three or four times. I lay back on the plasterboard bed, closed my eyes and let the voices wash through my consciousness. My consciousness replied by finding it difficult to concentrate. I am also finding it quite hard to describe. I mean, it's just a bunch of guys chanting in Latin, you know? What else can you say? It sounds sad, mournful, gloomy – it's profoundly depressing. Some of it sounds slightly less depressing, but that might have been the parts where I wasn't concentrating. But, aware of its 24-hours-and-counting pop aridity, my brain was thankful for anything – this was music after all – and, despite the fact that my desire to hear some Bob Dylan had now escalated alarmingly, I'd prepared myself well for any early knee-jerk 'wanting what you can't have' psychological pangs. The best bit of the *Gregorian Chants* CD is when the sound of church bells joins in on track 5, 'Gloria', although this felt a bit like cheating; the CD compilers were well aware of how tedious the monks were getting, so they decided to add a bit of external textural colour. Well, it works. The bells are good, they distract from the monks. Jingle jangle, ding dong. Track 10, helpfully entitled 'Monastery Bells', doesn't even bother with any chanting, it just cuts straight to the spires. They ring unaccompanied for three and a half minutes – it's like standing directly outside Salisbury Cathedral but without the gagging old women's perfume. The monks come back in on track 11, 'Wandregisilus', this time accompanied by an organ, which is yet more cheating, as there's no way organs had been invented yet. As I listened on, sensuously licking congealed egg from around the corners of my mouth, I felt myself being slowly transported; I even began to recognize some of the melodies as they came back round again. It felt like I'd broken through an important psychological barrier: I didn't totally hate it, it was all right, I was getting my sonic rocks off after all – an incy-wincy, teeny-weeny little bit. Then, suddenly, there was a loud knock on the door. I opened it and there stood a chambermaid. We stood in the doorway listening to the monks and the bells and the organ.

'I am cleaning your room,' she said.

'Can you come back later? I'm quite busy.'

'I am cleaning your room.'

'Can you give me five minutes?'

She shook her head and pushed past into the bathroom. In a mild panic, I hurriedly filled up my knapsack, listening to her cough and flush my toilet violently. I trudged through draughty corridors, down the stairs and out into the cold.*

There's only one thing in Bingen that concedes to the fact that Hildegard ever existed at all: a museum on top of a sewage pipe. I crossed the railway line and headed along the riverbank towards it. It was housed in a big old converted electricity generator, and a bald man wearing glasses stood on the steps outside holding a steaming silver tankard and smoking a cigarette. He said straight away, 'So you want to see my museum?' He was tall, and camp.

'Am I too early?'

'Ha! Go in please!' He gestured overtly.

I held my camera up to his face. 'Can I take *photographs*?'

'Usually no, but because it is you, then maybe this time it is, yes.'

---

* Note to self: too much trudging already.

He tried to shake hands, but absolutely no way.

Inside, it was warm and spacious. White models of Hildegard's monasteries sat inside glass cases, and plaques telling her story tastefully lined the walls. Monk-humming discreetly filled the air. I wasn't surprised to find myself the only person here. I knew most of the stuff on the plaques already, and though the enlarged, light-mounted Hildegard paintings were good, the thing that surprised me most was the music. Although it was the standard monkish carp, this didn't sound anything like what I'd heard on the *Gregorian Chants* CD; it sounded more human. And instead of it provoking pathological boredom, I found it rather sensual and stimulating. It sounded alive; it was warming, nourishing, from somewhere near the heart. The bald man came back in and walked loudly over to where I was standing.

'Do you have a reason why I should not charge you the full price for the entry?' he said. 'Are you a student or a thing like this?'

'No.' I handed him three euros. 'Although I am interested in Hildegard,' I said. 'Where is the Rupertsburg monastery? I would like to visit it.'

'You cannot do this, as Rupertsburg does not exist at this time. It is only now a railway track and a door in a wall, and I cannot recommend you are going there,' he warned. 'This is *nothing*.' Misinterpreting my secret relief as disappointment, he continued, 'Please do not worry! You must go to the monastery ruin site at Disibodenberg. There it is beautiful, and good location, and you can meditate, like this, and walk for two hours, maybe three hours, if you like. I have a map with the trains and so on, and so forth.'

Fifteen minutes later I was sitting on a train flicking through an expensive glossy book on the history of the Rhineland that he'd forced me into purchasing. 'Reminding you of your visit to this region,' he pressed. 'The writing is also English.'

There were some old pictures of boats and things. I got off the train where I'd been told, at a station in the middle of nowhere called Staudernheim, and looked around. There was a boarded-up hostelry and a closed ticket office. No signs for anything. The sun shone cold. I ambled up a narrow road and came to another road, and then a bridge. I was surrounded by rolling countryside and woodland. I saw some low buildings in the distance and strolled hopefully towards them; they led to a couple more, and then I thought maybe I'd arrived in the centre of Staudernheim, I wasn't sure. There was no one around to ask where the fuck I was supposed to be going, so I just carried on walking up the hill, until ten minutes later I saw a bleached old sign that said *Klosterruine*, which sounded like maybe that was it, so I followed the sign up and around another hill into some vineyards, and then, half an hour later, I was there. The entrance to the monastery ruins was automated. I clanked through the gates and carried on up, past some sheep and a man standing by a wheelbarrow, smoking. Then I spotted the ruins and I've caught up with where I was at the beginning of the chapter, wandering around the place listening to Hildegard on my headphones. Just as I was about to head back down to the station, I spotted a tiny white tubular building on the very edge of the site, overlooking a village far below. It was a discreet little commemorative chapel, dedicated to Hildegard – a *Hildebunker*. Inside was a small stone altar strewn with flowers, candles, a picture of a saint, and dozens of small coloured pebbles. Moved, I picked a daisy from outside and placed it with the other flowers on the altar, while the monks cantillated lustily through my cans. *It's time to go*, I thought, so I did.

During her lifetime, Hildegard composed approximately eighty monophonic (one melody line – no harmonies) songs, hymns, sequences (similar to hymns I think), strophic psalms (no idea), antiphons (no, sorry), and a concept album called *Ordo Virtutum* ('Play of Virtues'). She was, arguably, the first person to break out of the strictly liturgical constructs of church music and 'compose' music for its own sake. Hildegard saw music as a bridge to the harmonies of heaven; what Boethius had called the Music of the Spheres. Although the music she wrote was fundamentally religious – show-offy prayers set to music really – the very fact that she dared to actually 'write' anything at all was, just by itself, revolutionary. That records still exist of the music she wrote is also pretty amazing. The problem musicians face today is interpretation. In the twelfth century they didn't have pianos or tuning forks or anything like that, so they had to just fish a note out of the air and start on that. And in what style are these various rudimentarily transcribed melodies supposed to be sung? There's no such thing as a definitive performance of this stuff. The only remaining nuns in the area, over on the other side of the Rhine near Eibingen in the modern St Hildegard Abbey, sing her music very merrily indeed. Are they right, or are they just trying to cheer themselves up?

Personally, I genuinely enjoyed the sequences and hymns on the *Feather on the Breath of God* CD. I was surprised by how much I liked it. When I arrived back at the Starkenburger Hof later that evening, I sat on my bed and wrote passionately in my notebook: 'frighteningly, instantly transcendental – sounds like it's moving with the wind – almost like it's constructed *out of* the wind – the light – the elements. Historical context alone is awesome. It has an epic, feelgood fatalism – lightfootedness – a pure, soft, spectral truth. Finding it hard to stay with it, to adapt my brain to its rhythms, the sparsity of it, my ears are too ratty for this. Unlearn! Unlearn! This is a sexual disrobing! – casting aside of the lumpen frippery of the destination politics of modern music! This is cold-hearted minimalist spiritualism. It has layers – unpeely layers, sun layers, night layers, rain layers, wind layers, morning layers – it's decadent! – allusions of flesh – hidden secrets – doesn't this raw sensuality contradict its pious aspiration?!?!?! Humility makes it more erotic! – this does not make the performers tragic, it makes them iconic!! *I think it makes them Sex Gods!!*'

The St Hildegard Abbey wine was delicious.

Still in Bingen

My first thought upon waking the next day was: *Oh, please God, not this again.* I lay listening to the barges groaning up and down the river while a train rattled by under my window. Another day of this bollocks, then, I thought to myself, reaching for a glass of water and knocking it over. Down in the deathly Starkenburger Hof dining room, things were much the same as yesterday.

'Egg,' said the woman with the embroidered apron. The fat smokers stared.

I ate the egg. I ate the muesli. I ate a warm pineapple yogurt. I ignored a decorous platter of smoked tongue. I withdrew to my room and sat on the bed and put the *Hildegard of Bingen: In Portrait* BBC DVD into my laptop, put on my headphones and settled down uncomfortably to watch it.

Jesus.

It was really, really terrible. This was a full-on costumed dramatization of Hildegard's concept album *Play of Virtues* in a church, with a different rapturous singing nun representing each virtue, featuring occasional cameos from a slimy Italian-looking guy who was supposed to be the Devil. Back in the day, Hilde's assistant monk Volmar played him. *Play of Virtues* apparently features eighty-two separate melodies; I sat through all of them. The performance's only saving grace was that I quite fancied the nun who played 'Knowledge of God'. It went on for seventy minutes but felt like seven million. I don't want to talk about it any more.

I was officially in a grump. I left the Starkenburger Hof and caught a ferry over the Rhine to go and explore the opposite bank, glaring at my fellow old-age pensioners on the lower deck as we threaded through the river traffic. In Rudesheim I stood on a street corner eating a currywurst, watching a bunch of Japanese tourists buy sackfuls of regional merchandise. I listened to more Hildegard through the headphones, still trying to acclimatize to it, only now the monks were properly starting to piss me off. *Get used to it*, I muttered to myself angrily through the rich chunks of wurst. I spent the rest of the day wandering up the vineyards on the broad north riverbank. I learned that Germans don't say hello when out walking. I took a photograph of myself on the gigantic Kaiser monument that overlooks the valley. I imagined what life must've been like here during the twelfth century. Shit. I walked the few kilometres back down to the small town of Eibingen, the site of Rupertsburg's sister convent, which Hildegard had also founded but never actually stayed at. It was boring. I went into the modern church erected on the original site. It was a church. No amusing incidents presented themselves. I walked, knack-ered, back into Rudesheim and sat in a darkened bar and ordered a beer. A heavily moustachioed waiter wearing a leather waistcoat brought it over. This was a little more like it. I opened my notebook on to a fresh page and tried to think through all the things that I'd learned.

It felt like I'd crept into classical music under the radar. Despite Hildegard's awesome claims to fame, I'd been sur-prised at the complete lack of a tourist trail in her name. I'd had to dig out everywhere by myself. But then, I realized, none of the important places she stayed at or founded were still standing, so what's this trail supposed to consist of exactly? I felt glad that I'd started here, though, no matter how dull I found most of the music. Bingen, and of course Hildegard, would for ever be my anchor. Now I understood the shape music was in at this point in time. I could see how far it had to go, and I was excited about discovering its next development, whatever – and wherever – that might prove to be. I hoped it was nowhere near here, though. I also felt lucky to have avoided any pop/classical snobbery so far, since I'd been the only person actually here. It felt like a lunar landscape; no live performances or concerts or deep end to throw myself into. But this had been a grounding, a cleansing of the palate before I got to any mucky stuff, like harmonies or musical instruments. And I was feeling pretty proud of myself for going three days without listening to any pop music. It hadn't been easy, but I was getting through it OK. My senses will have better stimulation next time, I thought to myself.

*

I've decided to give each composer some ratings, to help me contextualize their various sociological components. I'm going to give them all a sex, drugs and rock 'n' roll rating out of ten, plus a brief description of why. I'll also try to provide a few of my own personal listening recommendations plus a matching 'Ambulance Rating'. The key is: 🚑🚑🚑🚑🚑 = amazing; 🚑🚑🚑🚑 = very good; 🚑🚑🚑 = pretty good; 🚑🚑 = poor; 🚑 = shit.

Hildegard of Bingen gets:

Sex: 5. In *Causae et Curae*, she talks with vivid ferociousness about ejaculation, sperm and orgasms. It's completely filthy. She also scores highly for the sheer sexual frustration she must have felt throughout her lifetime.

Drugs: 8. Mystic hallucinations and copious psychedelia abound.

Rock 'n' roll: 2. Things can only get better.

Seb suggests:

A Feather on the Breath of God by Gothic Voices (Hyperion) 🚑🚑🚑🚑

(The original and the best – at time of writing, I have now heard this over 200 times ☹.)

Canticles of Ecstasy by Sequentia (Deutsche Harmonia Mundi) 🚑🚑🚑

(This is supposed to be good too, but I thought one Hilde CD was enough to be going on with.)

I do not recommend my *Gregorian Chants* CD 🔊

Hildegard died from natural causes in 1179, at an extraordinary eighty-one years of age.

*According to this statue, Hildegard looked
exactly like Victoria Principal.*

2. The Sonic Switch

I thought it was a bit strange that the only language music was being composed in so far was already a dead one – i.e. Latin. Why weren't people performing (or composing) any music in their own languages? I found out that, actually, they were, only it was taking place well below the sightlines of the church. Over on the secular side of the tracks was a breed of bastardized court jesters that called themselves jongleurs. These were wandering minstrels, bards who travelled the countryside in dishevelled circus troupes, singing, dancing, telling jokes and dragging scrawny wild animals (probably bears) behind them through the mud – while juggling. Jongleurs were untrustworthy social misfits, and their lives were exhaustingly hand-to-mouth; but, as they became commonplace throughout Europe in the tenth century, they managed to achieve semi-professional status, able to provide tuition in the dark arts of hand-me-down primeval folk rock. Theirs were songs of wine and women and general sarcastic japery – popular with proles, but heartily disapproved of by the pious auteurs slowly emerging from the parishes.

In the thirteenth century, a higher class of wandering minstrel appeared on the scene: the troubadours. These guys were a distinct cut above the crusty old-age travellers of the jongleurs; they were fey and aristocratic, tedious upper-class nonces in feathery velvet caps, whose ranks included the occasional prince, even the odd king. Thousands of these troubadours flounced around the south of France singing songs of chivalry on lutes, reciting self-pitying poetry about themselves, or tragic, unrequited love (involving themselves). Though there was a repertoire of troubadour standards, it wasn't unusual for them to compose a few ditties of their own, which they wrote in their own vernacular French instead of nasty Latin.

In northern France, this song-and-dance routine was developed yet further, by a bunch of guys called trouvères. Trouvères came a little after troubadours, and were slightly cooler. They also sang in French, they also sang about unrequited love, they also recited lovelorn poetry and wore dumb hats, but, importantly, they also sang songs that took this piss out of the troubadours. In fact a large amount of trouvère material focused on satire, parody, doing impressions of and laughing at troubadours.

Germany followed heartily, with Minnesingers and Meistersingers, who were exactly the same as the trouvères only more earnest in their lyrical approach. Italian and Spanish minstrels appeared too; there were even a couple of plucky minstrel Brits. Though details are sketchy as to exactly how these travelling musicians performed their material, we do know that it was still unexciting. It's certainly possible that they accompanied themselves with lutes, harps or hurdy-gurdies, but, as with Hildegard's stuff, contemporary interpretation varies wildly.

Despite these roaming dudes, the world remained stuck on the single note. The chant droned on. You still couldn't get a decent version of 'London's Burning' going. Harmony lurked in the shadows. The polyphonic revolution warily approached.

The sonic switch was the *troper*.

On the Trail of the Winchester Troper

My mother's house, Winchester, Hampshire, October 2003

I had arrived at a bad time. White-hot controversy was coursing through the city, polarizing residents and whipping the local press into frothing, apoplectic rage. It was all about a newly published book called *Crap Towns*. To the stunned dismay of its populace, Winchester had been voted the fifth-crappest town in the whole of Britain. The book had noted its 'priggish complacency', its 'odious arrogance' and the endemic late-night violence in the city centre. Winchester was dazed, in shock, reeling with the punches. 'Doesn't *every* town aspire to be priggishly complacent?' it metaphorically whined. 'And us? Crapper than Basingstoke?!' spat the *Winchester Extra* editorials and the swollen *Hampshire Chronicle* letters page. *Beautiful, historic Winchester? Crap? Hahahahaha YOU MUST BE BLINKING CRACKERS*.

Etc.

My mother was particularly angry, especially when I appeared to be defending the book over a distinctly frosty lunch.

'But *Winchester*?' she hissed in mock amazement. I had noticed already that just saying 'Winchester' in quizzical italics was the townsfolk's stock reply to the charges.

'Well, it was compiled from votes from the public,' I evenly replied.

'People actually voted against *Winchester*?'

'No they voted for it, as the fifth-crappest town in the country.' I was enjoying rubbing it in, but my mother's face was purple with barely suppressed fury.

'So I suppose you think Winchester is "crap" now too, do you?'

'I can see why people might think that, yes, definitely.'

My mother's eyes widened further. My stepfather, originally from Grimsby – a much more deserved inclusion, according to my mother – sniggered into his bread and butter.

'And don't you start,' she rounded on him. 'I've had enough of this from you already over the years, and I don't want to hear it again now, thank you very much.'

My stepfather continued to eat quietly.

But I wasn't here just to wind up my mother. Not long back from Bingen, I'd read about the ancient lost art of 'troping'. A trope is an extra melodic line added to a chant or plainsong; it could be either tacked on at the beginning of a verse, like a fancy intro, or, as it soon became, a simultaneous *harmony to the main melody*.

At last!

And not only that, but the most famous of these mysterious tropers was the *Winchester* Troper; this guy was from my own home town and I'd never even heard of him! Another brilliant omen. It would also, I realized, be cheaper to research than Germany.

After my mother had calmed down about Winchester being the official fifth-crappest town in the country (making it crapper than Wolverhampton, Slough, Reading – even Portsmouth), I asked if she'd heard of the Winchester Troper. She hadn't, but she was intrigued. I told her everything I knew, which took about fifteen seconds.

'So where are you going to start?' she asked.

'I'll try the cathedral,' I replied. 'I might as well.'

'Right. I'm coming with you.'

'Oh, no, you don't have to . . .'

'No, I'm definitely coming with you.'

'Oh, good.'

My stepfather discreetly cleared the dishes from the table.

'And I don't want any swearing in this book please,' she warned as she thrust on her coat.

'How could I possibly swear in a book about classical music?'

'I know what you're like.'

'I promise there won't be much swearing.'

'You see? *Much.*'

Eventually we left the house and headed towards the cathedral. It was pouring down with rain, and I'd been so flustered by my mother's decision to come along too that I'd completely forgotten to bring my notebook, a pen, my camera, or anything useful like that. It has to be said that I wasn't holding out much hope for our outing; I just wanted to get this over and done with.

I don't know what I was expecting to find in Winchester Cathedral exactly; maybe a wee statue or a side chapel dedicated to the Troper that I could investigate; perhaps even some of his original sheet music. A few years ago they built a massive gift shop and a coffee shop next to the main entrance, so at the very least I hoped to find some troping CDs.

My mother and I arrived, sodden, at the iron cathedral doors, to discover that you have to pay £3.50 to get in. We agreed this was outrageous. I rooted in my pockets for change, but my mother had already approached the man on the cash desk.

'This is my son,' she told him. The man was tall, with

grey hair, glasses and an official Winchester Cathedral tie. 'And he . . .' she beckoned me over to the desk '. . . is writing a book!'

Oh no, not that, don't say anything like that.

She put an arm around me. 'Isn't he lovely? He's writing about . . . what is it dear? The Winchester Trunker? Anyway, this trunker was *very important*. So I think we should probably get a discount, seeing as we're here for research purposes.' She turned and beamed at me. 'It's a book all about classical music, isn't that fascinating? I'm a concession, by the way, that's half price.'

The man turned and stared. I stood there wet and unshaven, with long straggly hair. High above my mother's eyeline, the two of us exchanged mutual hatred.

'Two adults please,' I said, holding out a damp tenner. My mother continued to beam. Specifically to spite me, he let us in for free, and we scuttered under a red rope and into the dark towards the cathedral library. My mother was bloody *triumphant*.

'You see?' she delightedly whispered. 'You *see*?'

We didn't find the Troper in the library, nor any mention of him, nor anything actually. We were told in no uncertain terms that if we wanted to look at any of these books we should have made an appointment with Mr Fairweather months ago. My mother tutted – justifiably – at my complete lack of foresight. However, she hadn't been dissuaded – we investigated every last tomb and cavity in the cathedral, and each member of staff we subsequently came across she grilled about the trunker. Half an hour later, we were still none the troping wiser, so we disconsolately trudged over to the gift shop to search the CD racks. There were hundreds of CDs; the selection would've done a medium-sized HMV proud. We unearthed shitloads of stuff, but none of it featured the Troper. We stood and waded through *Church Bells of England, Favourite Anthems from Winchester, Winchester Cathedral Organ Spectacular, Oh Come Let Us Adore Him – Hymns and Psalms from Winchester, Sacred Choral Music Volumes 1 and 2, I Sing of a Maiden – Winchester Cathedral Choir, Winchester Cathedral Organs, Music from Renaissance Portugal (?), Favourite Gregorian – 60 Minutes of Peace and Calm, Chants from Salisbury Cathedral, Gregorian Chants from Canterbury Cathedral.*

Who'd have thought there'd be so much of this shit? This clever trip to Winchester was turning into a dead-end after all. However, just as we were about to leave, my mother suddenly lurched high into the dusty top left corner of the display, bringing down one final, empty case.

'The trunker!' she exclaimed. The American tourists milling around us shifted uneasily. 'I've found him!'

I grabbed the CD. She *had*. Whoah. *Christmas in Royal Anglo-Saxon Winchester.* And underneath, as clear as day, '. . . from the Winchester Troper.'

I'd got the bastard. My mother was a genius! A master sleuth! We hugged, and I bought some authentic Winchester Cathedral mead for drinking while I listened to it, and we swaggered back to the house like conquering heroes.

Back home, we settled down for a serious listening session. My stepfather was roped in too; my mother placed him on the chaise-longue, put a blanket over his shoulders, and he fell asleep instantly. The music began, and I watched him with envy. It was two monks singing monophonic Latin in a church. My mother and I sat and listened to the first two tracks. We shuffled uneasily while my mother mouthed a few kind but unconvincing platitudes. The Troper was a goddamn fraud. My mother even started to look 'trope' up in the dictionary, so disillusioned was she by the monks' interminable mumble. I eyed the mead.

But then, fifteen minutes into the CD, it happened. The voices split. One monk went downhill and the other one went up. It sounded like the splitting of the motherfucking atom.

'They did it!' cried my mother. 'They troped!'

'Shit!' We sat bolt upright in our chairs.

It was genuinely cool. This was the first harmony I had heard in over three weeks! It was as if the sound had suddenly switched to 3D. The two voices came on like a rainbow river of tropical sonic refreshment. The monks' voices coiled around each other; the new colours warmed the room like a candle. I felt an instant emotional empathy

L–R: Stepfather (comatose), mother (posing), me (I'd hardly call that posing).

with the singers; and though the melodies were along the same boring lines as usual, this new alchemical friction made the whole thing sound as fresh as rain. We tried, in our excitement, to wake up my stepfather, but he was completely away with the fairies.

Soon, however, we were bored. These occasional tropes were diverting enough for a while, but their duelling magic rapidly waned, and we felt our heightened senses plopped back down into a cold, damp medieval church again. With the doors locked. My mother said that she was looking forward to me getting to Schubert, and I said yes, me as well. We switched the music off and my stepfather slowly raised his head.

The Winchester Troper is the first known composer of polyphonic music. He was an Anglo-Saxon man named Wulfstan, and he was the cantor (lead singer) of Winchester Cathedral choir. That's all we know. And as for his actual pair of troping manuscripts, I have since learned that one is in Oxford, and the other's in Cambridge, and they're both virtually impossible to decipher, so I'm glad that my mother and I didn't find them in Winchester Cathedral after all. This lack of biographical detail means that we don't know exactly how Wulfstan arrived at this sensational new concept of harmony. There is speculation, however, that he had been experimenting with differing plainchant octaves when, one dark night, one of his choir's voices accidentally slipped off the rockface, then it was *BLAM*, you know? And before you knew it: Simon and Garfunkel.

Troping was abolished – for being too fancy-pants – in the sixteenth century. Oh, how Wulfstan must've chuckled in his grave: the horse had *way-bolted*, dude.

The New Art

It's raining hard. Churchbells thunder. Footsteps clatter over metal grilles. Gallic voices pitch and grumble. Thick coats are clumsily folded. Small wooden chairs scrape flagstones. Incense wafts damply through the gloom. Smokers cough. Discreet loudspeakers crackle. Service sheets flap about. My wife Faye and I are sitting halfway down on the right-hand side of the inner nave, chomping on Werthers. We're here for an experiment. Expecting a pleasant and relaxing weekend in Paris, Faye has been forced to attend Catholic High Mass, and, considering we were out last night until 3 a.m., she's handling this with surprisingly good humour. I'm not. My feet are soaked, I've got terrible heartburn, and last night's dinner is repeating on me incessantly. Also, I'm a serious goddamn atheist. But this experiment is bigger than my petty prejudices – we're standing here in the hope of getting genuinely enlightened via serious historo-scientific comparison. I can smell my own feet, but it doesn't matter.

In 1320, the minor French composer Philippe de Vitry wrote an impassioned treatise on how new and revolutionary and *different* modern music was turning out to be, compared to the monophonic dirges we've been learning about so far. This new, premature and frankly wishful way of looking at the latest musical developments became a bona-fide movement, called *Ars Nova* (New Art), a phrase that came to be used to describe virtually all classical music from the fourteenth century. It meant that polyphonic music now had its own rules and regulations – a disciplined system that

could be written down, instead of the hopeful troping it had
been so far. A bit like this:

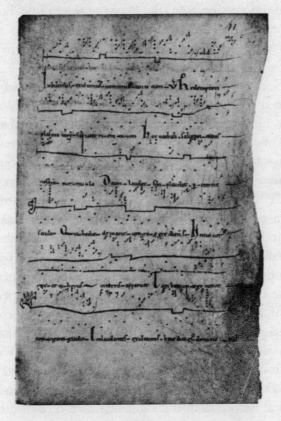

Catchy.

The leading composer of the *Ars Nova* was a man named
Guillaume de Machaut. Born in 1300 in Champagne in
northern France, Machaut studied to become a cleric and
was appointed secretary to the King of Bohemia, whom he
served with holy distinction all around Europe until the king's
grisly death at the Battle of Crécy in 1346. Machaut then
became a jobbing cleric under a succession of pre-eminent

aristos, writing secular songs as well as great big lairy religious pieces for the church. His secular songs were a natural progression from the music of the troubadours and trouvères; his poetic prowess matching the complex rigours of his melodies. This intellectual, visionary approach to music – plus an almost complete dominance over his peers – has led to Machaut being universally recognized as the first 'real' composer; certainly classical's first 'big name'. (Sexist historians prefer to ignore Hildegard.) Machaut's most famous piece is the *Messe de Notre Dame* ('Notre-Dame Mass') – the first ever complete polyphonic version of an ordinary Catholic Mass. Sounds like exciting stuff, right?

Today's experiment in Paris is a straightforward comparison between a contemporary Notre-Dame Mass, and Machaut's fourteenth-century *Messe de Notre Dame*; the same thing taking place in the same building, only with a 650-year gap in between. I am able to perform such an experiment because I recently picked up a really useful album: a performance of Machaut's *Messe* put together by two (probably) bearded guys, Dr René Clemenic and Mr Colin Mason. As well as the Mass, the CD features some of Machaut's secular songs too; in fact it features all the music you'd hear inside Notre-Dame, plus minstrels and beggars playing outside the cathedral beforehand. It's a genuine slice of musical fourteenth-century Parisian life. This was brilliantly educational, especially since I'd only bought this CD because it was the cheapest Machaut I could find in the record shop. It should be easy, and interesting, to contrast and compare the fulsome vividness of a High Mass in both the fourteenth and twenty-first centuries. Let's enter our imaginary Tardis, and begin.

Fourteenth century: Let there be drums! Machaut's secular instrumental 'Quant je suis mis' kicks things off with a natty rolling beat thumped out on a giant drum. The excitement building outside Notre-Dame is palpable, as a reedy flute-type thing breaks through with a nursery-rhyme melody and bags of peasant charm. It's a light, Eastern-flavoured melody, like perky snake-charming music. Other cheap instruments join in; it's damnably merry! But suddenly the leper crowd is hushed, as the King of Navarre breaks in with a song of his own. Its ethereal, buzzing intro (which sounds uncannily like Led Zeppelin's 'In the Light' off *Physical Graffiti*) leads to a plaintive warble that continues for five and a half minutes. Impressive.

Twenty-first century: Fifty yards from the cathedral's main doors sits a tramp in a wheelchair, playing 'Yellow Submarine' on a blackened acoustic guitar. It's raining heavily, and he's blithely ignored by the cagoule-clad crowd of Japanese tourists taking photographs (of the cathedral, not him).

Fourteenth century: Another Machaut instrumental, 'Dame à qui m'ottri'. This one starts with a melody played on an elastic band, before the minstrels pipe up with drums and everything. Soon a fiddle-type instrument plays a jig, backed with some clacking castanets. Everybody's getting nicely psyched for the service. A song from a Burgundy beggar follows, called 'C'est Guignolot de St Lazo' (I can translate this: it means 'It's Guignolot, from St Lazo'). Again, this one sounds extremely similar to the Zep's 'In the Light', until, inevitably, the beggar starts to sing. The message here is probably: don't forget about poor people.

Twenty-first century: Sod the poor people, they're getting in my way. No, you can't have any euros, piss off.

Fourteenth century: This next section is subtitled 'Entry into the Church'. Our entry is heralded by a cosmic blast of organ (which appears to have been invented). The medieval congregation files in to this musical red carpet; the vibes are pretty sombre. The organ plays mournful descending chords but with a suitably uplifting edge, and it ends on a huge major chord, which means it's probably time for . . . some hymns. 'Ave Maris Stella'. The congregation enthusiastically sing along with the cantor ☺.

Twenty-first century: All is confusion in the Notre-Dame porch. A flustered church warden is trying to siphon the genuine congregation into the seated area, while nudging the continual wave of tourists away around the sides. Everyone is dripping wet. The organ is blasting so loud that a deep feeling of disorientation pervades. Some tourists accidentally end up in the congregation area, and shuffle confusedly down the ranks of chairs until they're standing smack bang in the middle of the action. They half-heartedly begin to unfasten their multicoloured waterproofs while being hissed at by middle-aged French women. Faye and I take up discreet positions on the right-hand side. The organ galumphs on. The vibes are poor.

Fourteenth century: Machaut's *Messe* begins in earnest. A brief splash of organ, then the choir kicks off alone, and *KABOOM*, a giant fist is punched through space and time, the air has exploded like a water balloon, my ears are being savaged by orgasmic daggers, it's too much! This is a seriously psychedelic avant-Baroque version of something off the Beach Boys' *Smile*. Gawd! There are voices coming from everywhere! Blitzkrieg! This is the best thing I have heard so far by a mile – I'd *buy* this. The fourteenth-century congregation have probably fainted!

Twenty-first century: Our own Mass begins. A boys' choir pipes up. It sounds weighty and quadraphonic through the mounted speakers. We stand. Up by the altar, some robed old men wander about. The multicoloured displaced tourists raise camcorders.

Fourteenth century: In amongst the careering harmonies fly little verbal hiccups, called 'hockets'. They're like old-fashioned doo-wops: continuity devices that add cool little staccato rhythms. So far, the fourteenth century is absolutely miles better.

Twenty-first century: We hush, as a grizzled bishop raises his arms up at the altar. He clears his throat (the loudspeakers carry his phlegm beautifully), then begins to solemnly intone in French. The three-fifths-full church eventually replies with a shoddy Amen, then the organ bleats out a couple of pumping stabs and we all sit down. Nothing happens for approximately ten minutes except for further scurrying latecomers.

Fourteenth century: 'Gloria in Excelsis'. Mournful, weeping holding-harmonies slither through the church like black satin ribbons; dusting the oxygen like a funereal maypole. But then, suddenly, the King of Navarre bursts back in with 'Du tres douz non la virge Marie'. He lurches through the song sounding completely shitfaced.

Twenty-first century: The gnarled bishop begins his sermon. Two short women shuffle into the row behind us; they smell strongly of sweat. Halfway through the sermon, the misplaced tourists with the camcorders finally get up to leave, filming their retreat as they go. We tut.

Fourteenth century: More hymns. Then the 'Credo'. Solemn. Delicate. Profound. The King of Navarre keeps his mouth shut.

Twenty-first century: Queues for communion, then more hymns. The etiquette here is unclear; is the congregation supposed to join in with the choir, or not? Some do, most don't. The fragrant women behind us sing the occasional line; in fact they continue to sing randomly throughout the rest of the service, at all the wrong times; even when it's just the bishop gargling by himself.

Fourteenth century: A secular song from Machaut. 'Dame, vostre doulz vivaire', which means, I think, 'Woman, Your Distress Is Amazing'.

Twenty-first century: Sit down, stand up, wait standing up for ages, sit down then stand up again. Pray. The bishop raises his crooked arms into the air, and his deputies follow suit – it's like when everyone's being a tree in primary school drama lessons.

Fourteenth century: The peasants slowly file out of the cathedral, accompanied by 'Astra Polorum', a pretty eleventh-century French hymn which I am unable to translate – something about a car.

Twenty-first century: Our phlegmatic bishop leads the choir down and out through the congregation. He winks at those he recognizes as he hobbles amongst us. The organ quakes back into life as Faye gives me a 'happy now?' look. I attempt to give the impression that I don't know what she means. We shuffle back out into the rain, then go and eat a big *croque-monsieur*.

Conclusion: God is dead.

*

I did not attempt to foist any further Medieval music antics upon Faye over the remaining duration of the weekend. We went to the Louvre, and I bought some shoes and a tin helicopter made by African children.

Guillaume de Machaut spent the latter half of his life as a priest in Rheims, fêted throughout Europe for his poetry as well as his music; Chaucer is believed to have regarded his work very highly. At the same time as Machaut's French revolutions, the *Ars Nova* was also afoot in Italy, with its *trecento* music (don't worry, *trecento* just means 'from the 1300s'). The first great Italian composer was Francesco

Landini (1325–97), a blind organ builder from Florence. I have mildly investigated him, and I can safely report back that his music wasn't very interesting – it was much like Machaut's, only without his intensive zany Beach Boys harmonies. However, we can't entirely discount Italian music from this period; against their nature, they had sorted contemporary music into three different types, all of which became building blocks for important things to come. They were:

The Madrigal: fancy song.
The Caccia: dirty song.
The Ballata: disco.

These three distinct strands were the basis for all *trecento* music, and all feature in Landini's work, most notably in the *Squarcialupi Codex* (I'd thought that was a film starring Ernest Borgnine). Most of the notation that survives from this period comes directly from these huge, richly illustrated, ancient bound volumes of manuscripts called codices; the *Squarcialupi Codex* alone features 354 musical works by various different composers of the time. There's also the *Montpelier Codex*, the *Bamberg Codex*, the *Los Huelgos Codex*, the *Alexandria Codex* and the *Robertsbridge Codex*.* That's enough codices.

Late fourteenth-century Italian musical heads were turning towards the simple delights of the melodies themselves; it was as if their holistic powers had been unearthed for the

* The only time there's been a film about one was in 1993, with the Russian *Codex of Disgrace*, starring Boris Shcherbakov, who went on to star in a Russian version of *The Wizard of Oz* a year later, then in a film called *Do Not Pester Men!*

very first time; composers were falling over themselves in search of ever-sweeter lilts. They polyphonized these with pretty little basslines and harmonic overlays, like sprinkled tonal sugar; the church's influence over music was gently loosening, and, at last, music was falling into the hands of music lovers. It was an exciting time; the beginning of the end of the church's dominance of cultural life; the Medieval era was coming to an end, to be replaced by a new and progressive humanist age, of which polyphony was the most spectacular manifestation to date except, perhaps, for the arrival of the orange. And maybe the Black Death as well.

But the *Ars Nova* didn't have it all its own way; naysayers gathered on the sidelines, trying to get this frilly flim-flam back into a stripped-down, ecclesiastically minded, 'Praise the Lord, remember?' religious context. This new music 'displeases many!' raged the scholar and cleric Jacques de Liège. 'Wherein does this studied lasciviousness in singing so greatly please, by which, as some think, the words are lost, the harmony of consonances is diminished, the value of the notes is changed, perfection is brought low, imperfection is exalted, and measure is confounded?!?'

'Sacré bleu!' exclaimed Machaut and de Vitry. And, 'Zut alors!'

Methadone

Back home from Paris, I was slightly gutted to find the new edition of *The Wire* magazine waiting for me on the door-mat. Worse, it also came with a free CD of fabulous left-field electronica. Wearily, I prepared to file it away for listening to in a decade or whatever, but then Faye came up with an idea.

'Why don't I listen to it on headphones instead,' she suggested.

'Brilliant, yeah, cheers.'

For fuck's sake, eh?

'No, shush. I'll listen to it through headphones, but then sing it back to you. So you won't have to break your stupid pop ban, but you'll still be able to hear how it goes . . .'

I looked at her. It was sheer bloody genius.

Five minutes later we were ready; sitting facing one another on the sofa; Faye wearing my Technics headphones, and me ready with the tape recorder, because I had decided to bootleg her performance. Faye pressed play and I pressed record, and we waited.

'Dum, tish, dum, tish, dum, tish, dum, tish,' she said.

I nodded.

'Dum, tish, dum, tish . . . oh . . . ,' she paused.

'Please, keep going.'

'Derrrrr, derrrrrr, dum, dum dum.'

I nodded.

'Dum, tish, dum, tish, dum, tish, derrr.'

I nodded.

'Derrrrrrrrrr, derrrrrrrrrr, derrrrrrrrrr, dummmmmm, dum-dum whoo!'

I appreciated the drama of the exclamation mark. Perhaps this was the chorus.

'Dum, tish, dum, tish, dum, tish.'

Maybe it wasn't the chorus. Maybe it was the brid . . .

'DUMMMM, DERRRRR, DUM-DE-DUM . . .' She clapped her hands. 'DUM! DUM! KRRRRRREERRRRK DERRRRRRRRRRrrrrrrrrrrrrrr . . . plop, plop, ploppy, plop, ploppy, plop-plop DERRRR DERRRR . . .' More clapping.

I nodded.

49

'Dum, tish, dum, tish, dum, tish.'

OK.

'Whooo, whooo,' Faye nodded vigorously. 'Tish, whoooooooo!' Then she mumbled 'bum' for about two minutes, ending with an impressive fade-out:

'Bum, bum, bum, bum, bum, bum . . .'

'Brilliant,' I complimented. She took a deep breath and a sip of tea.

'You liked that one?'

'Yeah.'

Track 2 was similar, only with longer periods of inactivity, which I angrily discouraged. By track 3, the recitation was minimalist, to say the least; Faye stared into the middle distance, gently humming under her breath. I waved the tape recorder under her nose and she guiltily sat up and hummed slightly louder, but I think we both realized that we'd taken this idea as far as we could.

*

Wulfstan the Winchester Troper scores a general 10 for enabling us to realize that harmony was born in glorious Hampshire.

Guillaume de Machaut scores:

Sex: 3. In his late sixties, despite having lost an eye and suffering terrible gout, devout Machaut fell in love with a teenage countess called Peronelle de Armantières, and they wrote each other hundreds of adoring, lust-filled letters. These inspired many of Machaut's later songs; I'm not surprised, the dirty old dog. Could it, indeed, have been Madame Armantières who inspired 'Woman, Your Distress Is Amazing'?

Drugs: 3. All those leftfield harmonies and hockets must've come from somewhere.

Rock 'n' roll: 7. All those leftfield harmonies and hockets sound fantastic!

Seb suggests:

La Messe de Notre Dame by the Clemenic Consort and René Clemenic (Arte Nova Classics) 🚐🚐🚐🚐

(I consider this a classic classic. Whenever I put this on, as soon as I hear the first few bars, inside I go *Yeah!*)

The Mirror of Narcissus by Gothic Voices (Hyperion) 🚐🚐

(I don't actually recommend this, but it cost me sixteen quid, so I feel obliged to mention it.)

Guillaume de Machaut died in Rheims in 1377.
Francesco Landini died in Florence in 1397.*

---

* Boris Shcherbakov is alive and well and living in St Petersburg.

3. More than Words

As I've been writing this, I've been getting increasingly
worried about a potential Achilles heel in the project: my
basic powers of musical description. So far it's been OK;
I've either taken the piss or compared things to Led Zeppelin
or the Beach Boys; but as we start to click through the
centuries, and the music gets more complex and involving,
it's not going to take long before I'm hoisted by my own
petard. So, before I describe my 'hilarious' mix-up between
John Taverner (1490–1545) and John Tavener (1944–), I
thought it was a good idea to try and investigate some of
the more tried and tested ways of describing classical music,
so that by the time I hit, say, Bach, I'll be properly up to
speed with the lexicon, and you'll be impressed by my deft
usage of the word 'sonority'.

Here in my local Martins the Newsagent there's a long
wall of newspapers and magazines; they stock everything
from the *Angler's Times*, to – let me just check – *Best of
Over-50s Readers' Wives Volume 3, Issue 6.* In among these is
the usual thick seam of music magazines; about six-odd
'grown-up' ones, ten garish teeny-bopper fanzines and about
seven specialist technical instrument guides. On my third
sweep through, right at the top at the back, wedged between
Knave Volume 5, Issue 11 and a *Reader's Digest* special edition
on Great Victorian Buildings, I finally spot a copy of *Classic*

FM Magazine. I take it down from the shelf and peruse the cover. It comes with two free CDs, under which is a large photograph of singer Lesley Garrett plus bursting cleavage. Then I notice that behind it on the same shelf sits a solitary copy of *BBC Music Magazine*; this also comes with two free CDs, plus a photograph of singer Cecilia Bartoli showing some whopping, mechanically elevated cleavage. As I queue to buy them both, it's difficult to avoid the conclusion that classical music readers have a real thing going for as much free music as will fit inside the cellophane wrapper, plus an old-fashioned fondness for big, bouncy, bold-as-brass knockers. I feel a bit pervy as the newsagent bleeps them through the till and decide to ask him for a bag.

Ample.

Back home, I start on the magazines; beginning with the *Classic FM* one, since Ms Garrett's cleavage is the biggest. The first thing that strikes me is how many photographs of David Mellor there are in it. There seem to be hundreds of pictures of him; standing there hunchbacked with his hideous fucking teeth, dumb glasses and greasy flick; holding a stupid pile of CDs. This isn't a good start at all – I'm tempted to burn the magazine immediately, but, after the initial shock has waned, I calm down and look through the rest of the issue, carefully avoiding the many further pictures of David Mellor. (I soon realize that he's the magazine's resident 'expert' on, Christ, pretty much every goddamned thing imaginable.)

It's not a bad magazine, actually. Because of the 'housewife's choice', dumbed-down, Prozac approach to classical music pioneered by Classic FM, I'd been half expecting some sort of devilled cross between the *Radio Times*, *Heat* and *Good Housekeeping*, which, actually, is exactly what it's like. There are lots of bite-sized, illustrated with a chucklesome cartoon-type articles on stuff like 'A List of Liszt', 'Shoppin' for Chopin' and 'Don't Be a Maus: Listen to Strauss'. It's got charts and celebrity questionnaires (Nigel Kennedy), an album of the month and a star letter ('I was overwhelmed by the recent Classic FM concert at the Royal Albert Hall . . .'). It has a piece on the opera version of *Pop Idol* (winners: fat chicks), a piece on Ms Garrett (in jeans), lengthy programme listings for their radio station (but not the opposition's) and a piece on a hunky young American cello player called Zuill (lustrous curly chestnut hair). There are hundreds of full-page adverts for velvety CD box-sets and digital radios and comfortable space-age reclining chairs. It's a lifestyle magazine. It smells lovely. It has an in-depth article on how they make pianos. It has eleven photographs of David Mellor.

The reviews section is different; it's twenty-two full-colour pages of serious medium-brow criticism. This is what I'm here for: to attempt to plagiarize the writing styles of the *Classic FM Magazine* journalists. They use words like 'exquisite', 'mesmeric', 'contemplative', 'improvisatory' and 'idiom'. 'Surpasses', 'Bruckner's', 'entrancing', 'sense of . . .', 'sentimental', 'agility'. This is like those sets of wordy fridge magnets you get. 'Fauré's', 'big-boned', 'requiem', 'dazzles', 'Lieberson's', 'unhinged', 'squalor'. 'Susan Graham's', 'accompaniment', 'drips', 'horrific', 'interpretative', 'acrobatics'. 'Nigel Kennedy', 'sucks', 'hard', 'on', 'Satan's', 'monster cock'. Oops.

The *BBC Music Magazine* is an altogether more serious beast. For a start, its pair of free CDs – unlike Classic FM's photo of a Christmas bauble and photos of Nigel Kennedy et al. – both feature sombre oil paintings of vases of flowers, without a single bauble in sight. Impressive. Inside the magazine, the highbrow mood continues, with gritty articles on the Tenerife Opera House, the uncertain future of British choirs (pro choirs are ruthlessly elbowing the amateurs out the way; state schools have stopped doing choirs – damn them; Sainsbury's have stopped sponsoring the Choir of the Year award – *damn them*), the Kazakhstan classical music scene (healthy but underfunded), lengthy programme listings for Radio 3 (but not the opposition's) and, erm, 'Composer Cuisine' – six great composers and their favourite recipes. But you can tell the BBC magazine is classier by its star letter: a complaint about a Union Jack faux-pas at the Last Night of the Proms in – get this – *1985*. *Feel the girth*, Classic FM!

And it has way more in-depth reviews, fewer vulgar photographs and far fewer adverts for stairlifts. To tell the truth, I'm intimidated. These guys (and occasional gals) really, truly know what the hell they're talking about. They know what all the instruments are, and exactly how they should be played and everything. One of the first things I'm learning is that *understanding the performance* is absolutely vital; just describing the way the music comes across isn't going to be sufficient. The very angle at which the bows touch the strings can be the subject of huge conjecture; the character of the theme of the tonal structure of the Expressionistic nuances in the bass is what we're talking about here, dude. Beads of sweat prickle my forehead; I've so much to learn, and these guys are spraying it around with their goddamn fingertips. It's nice in a way, though; I read them and I trust them implicitly; it's not like in the pop music press where sometimes a critic's apparent misjudgement can single-handedly ruin your entire day's equilibrium; here, it's only the calm, weighty fundament, firmly prescribed in a deep, mahoganized burr. When I'm told that a certain £100+ velvety box-set is 'inordinately rewarding', I can feel its bronzed notes settling comfortably into my guts, oozing through and enriching my impoverished empty soul from now until the day I keel over.

There's also a publication called *Gramophone*. *Gramophone* is serious; much too serious to joke about – I'd be assassinated. *Gramophone* reeks of withering, middle-aged testosterone; it's strictly Men Only. When it, too, began to cover-mount CDs to keep up with the competition, there was uproar and panic from its debased and violated readership. Scores of men in tucked-in checked flannel shirts committed grisly communal suicide using letter-knives. *Gramophone* is so hardcore that newsagents have to pass a test before they're even allowed to stock it, so there's no way I'd ever be able to purchase a copy; I had to surreptitiously borrow one from my step-father; and even he made me wear gloves to read it. When I say 'read it', I can't really tell you much about its contents, as I didn't understand a single word of what was going on. It's small type; very dense; deeply impenetrable. They

appeared to be frowning upon a number of societal developments – maybe something to do with micro dB levels on
laserdisc sub-woofers. There are about thirty pages of techie
hi-fi porn towards the back. It's frightening stuff (though I
secretly enjoyed it). They don't 'review' records so much as
forensically demolish them over nine or ten columns. Not
terribly welcoming, I must say. I didn't understand – literally
– anything at all between its covers, not even the advertise-
ments. I don't even know what a gramophone is. I handed
it back to my stepfather, and he disappeared back into his
study and locked the door behind him. Soon after, I discerned a lone, mournful cello.

Now I wish I hadn't read those magazines. I feel dwarfed
and belittled by their grace of erudition and fathomless
depths of understanding (despite the fact that half of it's
showboating skull-polish). If you want to cut to the chase
and get on with some deep classical marinade, you shouldn't
bother with the rest of this; just head directly for your local
noiseagent – you also get the cleavage, Mellor and Christmas
carols sung by inexpensive Eastern Europeans.

In a humiliated panic, I broke my chronological code of
honour and listened to two of the free CDs. They were
both Christmas-themed, and, once again, the class divide
between the rival publications reared its marketing head.
Classic FM's *Best of Christmas* has 'Silent Night', 'For Unto
Us a Child is Born' and 'Santa Claus is Coming to Town',
and sounds like a good old-fashioned Le Piat d'Or/
Warninks-fuelled Xmas knees-up, whereas *BBC Music Magazine*'s demure *Christmas Music* has 'L'adorazione dei Magi'
and 'Une cantate de Noël', and evokes rivers at dusk, winter
bonfires and banging the mud off your boots after an icy
stroll through the fields with Marmaduke.

Classic FM Magazine's 'Best Buy' for December is *The*

John Tavener Collection. John Tavener is the contemporary composer who looks like irritating art critic Brian Sewell crossed with Brian Eno circa 1973. Among other things, he wrote some music for Princess Diana's funeral, which, after telling my mother that I quite liked it, I subsequently received a tape of that Christmas. I could only manage two listens, because each time I put it on I was so overcome by a sudden and profoundly suicidal depression that I had to hurriedly chuck the tape under the stairs. Tavener's music is the classical equivalent of Noel Edmonds; it's blacker-than-black, remorseless, unrelenting misery from beginning to end. It's almost hysterically bleak, gloomy, foreboding, oppressive, dispiriting, desolate and wretched; it somehow manages to sound like a twisted parody of itself. The four-star review in *Classic FM Magazine* praises Tavener's 'unique idiom', and calls it 'genuinely uplifting' (read: 'upsetting'). Which just goes to show that I haven't quite got the hang of all this yet.

The mistake it's easy to make is mixing up the Johns: Tavener and Taverner. In my research I'd been finding it hard to believe that a man who was born in 1490 had been able to contribute a specially commissioned piece of music for Diana's funeral in 1997. I'd been spatchcocked by that one, good and proper. All became clear after a kind chap I met at a wedding sent me a couple of Tavener CDs, explaining the difference between the two similarly named composers. Because of the kindness of this man at the wedding, I decided to try and listen to Tavener one last time.

You know how it feels when you're sitting on a train, and it inexplicably stops in the middle of nowhere for three-quarters of an hour, and you've forgotten to bring a book or a magazine or newspaper with you, and all you can see out of the window is a steep cutting or the walls of a tunnel?

That's how it felt listening to John Tavener again. And then, when the train suddenly lurches forward, and your heart leaps? That's how it felt in the gaps between the tracks. Then the train shudders to a halt again and the engine wheezes back down, and the air-conditioning shuts off too, and you stare forlornly back out of the window.

I'm afraid that John Tavener's Ambulance Rating, on the basis of the CDs the kind man at the wedding burned for me, is a mere 🚑. John, maybe relax a little next time, yeah? Lighten up. Then you might be in line for a second mini ambulance. 'I'm not very interested in music,' he has been quoted as saying, 'it's a mystery to me.' I am paraphrasing him slightly here, but I think it makes his position quite clear.

The Fifteenth Century: Composers of the Early Renaissance

This sounds grim, doesn't it? What is it about that word 'Renaissance' that reduces people like me to incoherent, shambling wrecks? I only have to hear the word to break into sweaty jitters. 'Renaissance' is one of those spectacularly adult arrangements of letters, like 'equity', 'coagulate' or 'Tom Waits'. A couple of people have asked where I'm up to with this book.

'I've got to the Renaissance.'

And the atmosphere is suddenly artificial and serious.

'Ah . . . the *Renaissance*.'

'Yep.'

We stare at the carpet.

'Ahhhhhhh.'

'Heavy.'

'The *Renaissance*.'

'Yep.'

'That was quite something.'

'Wasn't it just?'

They walk away fast, and I wish to God I could go with them.

However, like ridicule, it's nothing to be scared of.

A Renaissance Primer

What? Renaissance means 'rebirth'. Europe experienced a flowering of the arts and science in the fifteenth and six-teenth centuries, ushering in a new-found progressive humanism and rationality; it marked the transition between the Medieval era and the Baroque.

Why? Because everybody was fed up having going to church so much.

Where? It spread from Italy to the whole of Europe; eventually even to Britain.

How? With art (Michelangelo), philosophy (Erasmus), science (Galileo), robust appreciation of the Classics (the Classics), music (Palestrina), printing (Gutenberg) and less all-pervasive religious dogma, generally.

How much did it cost? 700 million pounds (estimated).

Am I now in full possession of all the facts about the Renaissance? Yes.

In the early 1400s, there was a sudden, dramatic flurry of composers, a string of like-minded individuals, all of whom learned a little bit from the one that had come before. It was a bit of a compositional Renaissance tag team. The first one was Frenchman Guillaume Dufay. Dufay was one doped-up, super-smooth snake-oil salesman. Listening to his 'Mass for Saint James the Greater' is a deeply syrupy experience, especially coming after the dry, Modernist sonic rampages of Machaut. Right away it's clear that the Renaissance had acted fast and got right up Dufay's colon, flaying his insides with peach-smoke and self-pity. My initial 'Mass for Saint James the Greater' listening notes included the following remarks:

'elegant'
'stagey'
'hot bald men under yellow lights in robes'
'slithery reptiles (like *Jungle Book* snake)'
'melancholic tears plus glassy sniffles in a tepid breeze outside the castle'
'(self-satisfied) rivers'
'weeping over trodden-on strawberries'
'Kinder Egg'

I think the most important thing to note about Dufay is that his music doesn't sound arcane; it has a familiarity; I can relate to these sounds; they have contemporary resonance, unlike, say, Hildegard, which sounds fabulous but alien and otherworldly to my dumbed-down senses. Maybe the reason for the above slur of adjectives is that I was able to emotionally contextualize the music I was listening to for the first time. Though whether 'big symmetrical Xmas cake made out of candyfloss' counts as adept criticism is unlikely. I think, looking at this harder, that sex must come into this somewhere; and if not sex exactly, then certainly some unashamed sensuality. Which makes sense, seeing as here in the fifteenth century, art music wasn't about just religiosity any more, it was properly off, full steam ahead on its mission to map out the specifics of the human heart, soul and mind, arriving eventually of course, at its *ass*. This, I realize now, must be the beginning of the sound of the great MDMA thaw that came to be known as the Renaissance.

Dufay came from Cambrai in north-west France, and, as was now increasingly common, wrote both religious and secular music. He joined the pope's private choir in Rome in 1428, then ten years later headed for Florence, where high-flutin' nobleman Piero de' Medici nicknamed him 'The Greatest Ornament of Our Age'. Then he went home to Cambrai, where he remained, hanging around the cathedral being smug and ornamental until he died in 1474, though not before specifying that his own music must be played at the funeral, particularly his motet 'Miserere tui labentis Dufay' ('Have Mercy on Your Dying Dufay' – oh please). His will survives to this day. It was absolutely enormous.

The next Early Renaissance composer was Dutchman Johannes Ockeghem. Born in 1420 in the village of Ockeghem, Ockeghem was, by all accounts, a very nice chap, as well as having a quite exceptional singing voice. Indeed, surviving reports are mercilessly consistent in their praise. 'You could not dislike this man,' said fellow musician Francesco Florio, 'so pleasing is the beauty of his person, so noteworthy the sobriety of his speech and of his morals and his grace.' It got purpler: after his death in 1497, the next composer in line, Josquin Desprez, set a memorial poem – written by the aptly named Guillaume Cretin – to music in his honour:

> Death, terrible satrap,
> has trapped your Ockeghem in his trap,
> true treasurer of music and chef d'œuvre,
> learned, handsome in appearance, and not stout.
> It's a great pity that the earth should cover him up.

Moving.

Ockeghem didn't compose much, but when he did, we're talking high-grade chansons. His music wasn't as greasy as Dufay's, it had more muscle and was a bit more complicated. Musical scholars today praise his 'personal refinement' and his 'fine bass voice', which he used to good effect on his own repertoire, especially the modern classic 'Missa L'homme Armé' ('Mass of the Man Holding a . . . Gun'). Ockeghem died to the sound of the further thousands of musical poems composed in his honour.

Next, we find Josquin Desprez, who was French and grumpy. He too hung around with kings and noblemen and had sycophantic poems written in praise of his globe-straddling talents ('Josquin is the master of the notes – the notes do whatever Josquin wants!'). As did composer number four, Antoine de Brumel, another sensational Frenchman from around Chartres, who moved around the different courts of Europe so fast and furiously that he picked up a reputation for being a bit of a fly-by-night wanker. Fifth, Jacob Obrecht from Ghent. Obrecht was choirmaster at the Guild of Our Lady in Bergen op Zoom before heading over to St Donatian's in Bruges in the service of Duke Ercole the First, in Ferrara, until he died of the plague in 1506. It's straightforward.

The biographical detail is slipping, I know. This lack of depth isn't really good enough, but I don't seem to be able to help it. I've been meticulously looking into the seemingly identical lives of these Early Renaissance guys for a couple of weeks now, and I'm finding it hard to get anywhere near excited about any of them.

Dufay, Ockeghem, Desprez, Brumel and Obrecht all:

wrote polyphonic High Masses. Your bog-standard High
    Mass consists of a Kyrie (good catchy intro, and usually

the only time you'll hear a proper tune), a Gloria (glory
to God in the highest, etc.), a Credo (I believe I can fly),
an Alleluia (power ballad), a Sanctus (holy, holy Jesus),
then an Agnus Dei (squealing frenzy of galumphs);
served a French king or three. Then an Italian duke. Then
a . . . etc.;
were the pope's mate;
sang like heavenly angels. Behold, for Dufay openeth his
mouth and doves doth fly out and mortal scums are
besmitten by the holiness . . . etc.;
thought musical instruments were the work of the Devil;
wrote nauseating poems about one another;
wore velvet hats;
were boring.

The music's been the worst thing: try as I might, I can't tell
any of these guys apart. *All* this music sounds like weeping, over-self-satisfied, trodden-on Kinder Eggs outside the
castle. Night after night, day after day I've sat and listened
through Gloria after Agnus Dei after Sanctus, waiting for
my ostrich brain to finally click into appreciative place, but
it's not happening. Why the hell not? All of it – every last
damnable cantus firmus – leaves me 100 per cent stony cold
emotion-free. Endless swirling dirges of pretty dovetailing
choral muzak with half-decent reverb. There are no tunes.
There's no drama. There's no pacing. There's nothing – so
far as I can discern – stylistically distinct about any of this
stuff; it sounds completely interchangeable. You'd put this
music on if you were twenty-two and your new girlfriend
was round at your flat for dinner for the first time; it would
be on quietly in the background while you cooked pasta,
talking bollocks and glugging red wine too fast, listening
neither to her nor to the music, instead blushing a lot and

accidentally dunking your untucked shirt in the sinkwater. You get laid with remarkable ease because this alleged grown-ups' music has implied that you're spiritual. And that you really like foreplay, honest.

I need to find out how it manages this. I need to get inside the slop; get to the bottom of it. In fact, I think I need to consult an expert, as clearly it's me who's at fault here, not these poor venerated guys. For the first time on the journey so far, I feel genuinely beaten. I'm not getting it. None of this is enjoyable.

A Helping Hand

Six months ago, I was having a few drinks with my old friend Doug, explaining my plans for this book. He was very polite, although the more I talked, the more gradually incredulous his demeanour became. He shifted on his stool.

'Whoah, now hold your horses,' said Doug. 'It sounds like you're biting off more than you can chew. Have you thought through what all this is going to involve? It's a seriously monumental subject, and it's more than likely that you're going to need some help with it. A shoulder to cry on, to say the very least . . .'

For a moment I was worried that he was about to suggest himself. Doug's a big fan of disco dancing, you know?

'No. I don't think I will,' I replied, cocky and untested and with my insides straining with lager. 'I've got to do this all on my own, you see? That's the whole point.'

'In fact, you're going to need absolutely shitloads of help,' he rudely continued.

'There are books. There are places to go. There's the *music*, Doug,' I said like I thought permed Brit conductor

Simon Rattle might say it – patronizingly pleading, with my arms in the air.

'No, listen to me. I know the perfect person to point you in the right direction.'

'Look, I appreciate your taking an interest, but really, I'm not going to need any pointing; I don't need any help with this – period. It's going to be . . .'

'Crap.'

'No, not crap. It'll be *educational*, man.'

'But wouldn't it be nice if you had a mentor?'

I looked at him – rather blurrily – with new-found respect. A mentor, eh? That sounded rather grown-up and soulful; it sounded like less work; it sounded like an extremely fine idea.

'Who is this "mentor" you have in mind?'

'Ah. Well. She's some serious shit. She's, like, the Queen of All She Surveys.'

My heart beat slightly faster. 'Not *the* queen?'

'No, you cock. Her name is Fiona Maddocks. I used to work with her. She knows absolutely everything there is to know about classical music. Fiona's one of the biggest names on the classical scene.'

I was familiar with this name already. Ms Maddocks was the author of the excellent biography of Hildegard of Bingen that I'd read while in Germany; indeed, I plundered it for interesting facts which I then put into this book. Amazingly, Doug (who works in publishing) used to work as Fiona's editor; in fact he'd actually edited the Hildegard book! Here was yet another cracking omen. My eyes gleamed.

'Do you think she'll be my mentor?'

'I doubt it, she's quite sensible.'

'But this was your idea. I suggest you hand over her email address right this minute.'

'First, you have to promise me that you're not going to harass her, or be weird. I don't want you ruining my reputation.'

'OK I promise. Give me the email address.'

'Let me speak to Fiona first, just to check that she doesn't mind you getting in touch.'

So I was to be subjected to a vetting procedure. I scowled at Doug over the table.

Fiona *was* excellent. We emailed one another and she agreed to be my mentor; to give me tips intermittently: whenever I got stuck, or confused, or upside-down, or suicidal. And Doug was right: Fiona sure knows her classical music. As well as writing the acclaimed biography of Hildegard, Fiona also founded (the superior) *BBC Music Magazine*. Nowadays, amongst other things, she writes for the *Evening Standard*; her CV is extremely intimidating; I was too frightened even to read to the bottom of it.

Nevertheless, after civilized introductions, I emailed Fiona with my list of recent woes, and then, a couple of days later, she replied. First of all, she gave me a bossy telling-off about my dislike of the Early Renaissance.

'Why should you like it?' she wrote. 'Do you like all art? Or theatre? How enthusiastic are you about the Chester Mystery plays compared with the York cycle, or do you really just like Stoppard? How often do you read Beaumont and Fletcher or Philip Sidney?'

Oh man. Who the fuck were all these? All I knew was that Tom Stoppard is frequently angry and looks like Dr Who.

I was soothed, though, by her gist. Why should I be getting stressed out about liking everything? Surely only a fool would claim to love all they'd ever listened to? Finally, artistic appreciation, Fiona reminded me, is subjective. She advised me to chill out and not to worry about it; there were plenty of cool things coming up; in fact, the very next man on the list was the true boss-man of the music of the Early Renaissance: the genuinely bowdlerizing figure of Giovanni Pierluigi da Palestrina.

'He was Italian,' wrote Fiona, helpfully. Yes, I can see that.

I immediately wrote back to inform Fiona of my intention to travel to Florence to investigate him.

'Yes very good,' she replied. 'But if you're investigating Palestrina, why aren't you going to Rome?'

I see.

Rome Wasn't Burned in a Day

Rome, eh? *Bellissima*.

Although I'd been to Italy many times in the past, I'd never made it to Rome before. I'd been to Siena, which was nice; Venice, which was very nice; Milan, which wasn't so nice; Bari (surprisingly nice); and Brindisi (grim as fuck). And some other places in between. I've got a bit of a love/hate thing going with the peninsula. On the one hand, it's stunning; the climate is marvellous, the countryside is beautiful, the art and architecture are a delight and the food and wine are in perfect harmony with the laid-back pace of life. But, on the other hand, it's got Italians, who I've always found rude, dishonest, vain, sexist, shallow and remorselessly slimy. And I haven't got past passport control yet.

So when it became clear that my next destination was going to be Rome, the first thought that popped into my head was that I was too scared to go by myself. So I called my best friend Owen and asked if he fancied coming with me. Owen is a handsome bachelor and an accomplished Shakespearean actor, and at the time of my call was in the middle of an intense and protracted period of 'resting', so I kindly offered to pay for his ticket and board. In order to feel better about himself, he delayed his reply for several days, claiming to be waiting on some important calls from his agent. And so it was, after a whole week of blatant lying, he finally informed me that yes, he was now free to come away for a few days. But that I should make sure that our hotel had a gym, as Owen was in the middle of a new keep-fit regime, which as well as regular gym sessions involved eating nothing but nuts, melons and fish. I informed him that we were going to be staying in a cheap, two-star hotel, and that it was exceedingly unlikely they'd even have towels, yet alone a gym. He replied at haughty length but I pressed delete immediately, since he'd also transcribed his complicated melon requirements.

We touched down at Rome's Fiumicino airport late on a Sunday afternoon. In the plane on the way over we'd arrived at the miserable conclusion that neither of us spoke any Italian, or knew anyone in Italy, or knew anything about Giovanni Pierluigi da Palestrina, or were going to be any practical use in this country whatsoever. Though this was quite depressing, at least it meant that we were on a curiously level playing field; we raised plastic glasses to our ignorance, hoping for enlightenment.

'This might be our own, personal renaissance,' suggested Owen.

'Maybe.'

'Just imagine . . .'

'Yes.'

It was a heady flight. Rome already seemed to be weaving its magic.

Excited in the toilets at Heathrow.

Our hotel was five minutes from the station, and shabby. Never mind a gym, it took us a fair while to work out where the front door was. Children playing in the street pointed and laughed as we wandered about. Inside, though, was classy; shiny brown marble and free sweets in a bowl, and our second-floor twin room was just about big enough to fit us both inside. We even had our own window, which Owen yanked grandly open, and then closed again because it was quite cold. The television and the toilet worked all right, so the hoops an establishment must have to jump through to attain that mythical third star must be frightening indeed. We dumped our stuff and hit the town; as before the next morning's investigations, we felt that first it was time to party reasonably hard, though not too hard, as it was Sunday, and we wanted to respect the Catholics, and – hey – our livers too.

Several hours later, we found ourselves slightly tipsy in a

gigantic Renault Bar – as in the French and not Italian car manufacturer. The ceiling was a hundred feet up and the walls were mammoth video screens showing freak-sized supermodels straddling runway-proportioned catwalks and monster collages of bouncing, muslin-covered breasts, thick eye make-up and giant octopus-sized pouting. It was border-line disturbing, and annoyingly compulsive. This was the sort of place you might expect (possibly short-sighted) grand prix drivers to frequent; or not-quite supermodels; or porky DJs. Well, they might, were this not on Rome's equivalent of the High Street, and had it not goons like me and Owen sitting inside, looking around for them.

A hyper-trendy low-lit bar glistened along the back wall, and, strangely, a Renault Clio sat on display at the far end, where we were sitting. There were also a couple of teenage girls in here. They left.

'A Renault Clio?' said Owen. 'Is that the best they can manage? You'd think they might be able to stretch to a racing car or something.'

'Or a Mégane.'

'Or a . . .' but we didn't know any more Renaults.

The waiter served us with contempt. Owen picked at a bowl of nuts.

'You must be pleased about the nuts,' I said.

'Not really.' Our two drinks had just cost him almost twenty pounds. The waiter wouldn't come over and serve us a second time. I ate the ice in the bottom of my glass, and then we walked back to the hotel in silence, replete with Rome's bewitchery.

The next morning we were woken early by shouting and what sounded like gunfire in the street outside. Knowing we had lots to try and fit in, we chucked on some snazzy outfits and hit the fragrant bitumen at pace, heading for the station to pick up a copy of the Rome version of *Time Out*, in which we hoped to find details of all the concert halls featuring selections of Palestrina's greatest hits tonight – or, at a stretch, tomorrow night also. The newsstand guys all shrugged – no one had heard of it. We went into the tourist information office instead and waited politely while a lady who looked like Spice Girl Mel B finished a long personal call on her mobile.

'Yes, what?' she said finally. We told her what we were after, and she reluctantly printed a list of all the classical music concerts taking place in Rome over the next few days. One piece of paper came out. It had one concert on it – a Mozart one.

'Is this all there is?'

She shrugged.

'Just one concert in the whole of Rome?'

She shrugged. The four Japanese queuing behind us coughed politely.

'Could you check for opera, too?' asked Owen.

Opera?

Owen and Mel B looked at me – I think my hair might have been standing on end. Out came another sheet of paper; this time with two concerts on it. One was Mozart, the other was Monteverdi, who, apparently, did operas.

'Perfect,' said Owen, folding the paper.

'Perfect? Opera? What in God's name are you talking about?'

But, again, it was me who was off the pace, because Monteverdi was around at about the same time as Palestrina. This just meant that our quest had rounded out a little bit. Although possibly a little bit too far.

'*Il Combattimento di Tancredi e Clorinda*. At the Teatro dell'Opera di Roma,' pronounced Owen, risibly. 'Tomorrow night. Eight o'clock.'

'Jesus wept,' I groaned.

'Zig-a-zag-ah!' exclaimed Mel B.

Giovanni Pierluigi da Palestrina was, you might say, the Superman of the Renaissance. This isn't because of his music – which was pretty super too – or even a remarkable foretaste of Nietzschean philosophy, but because he single-handedly saved polyphonic music from going to the dogs (or Protestants, as they're known in Rome – but then maybe not).

He was born in the town of – you guessed it – Palestrina, a hill town on the outskirts of Rome, in about 1525. Legend has it that when, as a child, hiking into Rome city centre to flog his parents' home-grown vegetables, Palestrina began to sing as he threaded through the winding streets with his hefty, rotting load, his piping infant voice happened to prick the ears of the passing choirmaster of Santa Maria Maggiore church, who scooped him off the streets and into the ranks of his celebrated choir. Here Palestrina remained for several years, before, homesick, returning to Palestrina to be church organist there instead. This would have been the end of his tale, had it not been for the timely election of the Bishop of Palestrina as the new pope: Julius III. Julius immediately installed his local organist Palestrina as the resident maestro at St Peter's in the Vatican, which was extremely controversial, as, compared to everyone else there, Palestrina was *shit*.

Palestrina, delighted but out of his depth, was desperate to thank Pope Julius for this leg-up; though what could he – but a humble musician – possibly possess that might be of any use to a pope?

Palestrina began to compose. He'd give Pope Julius his songs as a present.

His songs were terrific.

Pope Julius was delighted with Palestrina's efforts: a

couple of compact polyphonic Masses. In fact, he was so pleased that he immediately over-promoted Palestrina again, this time to the Sistine Chapel choir. *Here we go again*, thought Palestrina glumly. But then some weird shit happened. Everything changed. Palestrina's name was about to pass over into legend.

What happened was the Reformation. In the sixteenth century, the unity of the Europe-wide Catholic church was destroyed by the rising tide of 'reformed' – Protestant – churches. They'd had enough of what they perceived as gross abuse of church wealth and power; Luther, Calvin, Henry VIII; accursed reformers, all – though Henry wasn't so fussed about the details as the rest.

The Reformation led to the dreaded Counter-Reformation: The Empire Strikes Back. Subtle interrogation techniques, pioneered by the Spanish Inquisition, were rolled out through the continent, to the dismay of the many Protestants fond of their private parts. This in turn led to the Thirty Years' War, which finally ended up with the perpetual Catholic/ Protestant schism that we all know and love today.

In the middle of this mess, struggled music, being pulled from both sides. The Protestant church embraced music's growing secular complexity; a move that made it easier for Rome to come down hard on the other side: that fancy music was sinful. Plus, it's so damn complicated that we can't understand the words any more. The Counter-Reformation favoured a return to undiluted, pure liturgical plainchant and proposed the complete abolition of polyphony. It seemed that classical music was about to be put back – literally – hundreds of years.

Damn.

But then Pope Julius remembered the holy polyphonic Masses that Palestrina had recently composed for him.

Surely they hadn't been so bad? Maybe this nice chap Palestrina could show the way forward? Pope Julius called Palestrina into his office and spoke to him quite frankly:

'Ah, Palestrina, forsooth.'

'Yes, Lord Pope?'

'I like your tunes. They are nice.'

Palestrina bowed.

'However, we might have to ban them, as the Council of Trent (the committee in charge of these sorts of decisions) wants to go back to Gregorian chanting . . .'

'Oh no!'

'Yes. However, as I'm the pope, we've got one last chance. If you can write some polyphonic music which is really, really holy and nice, we'll play it to the Council of Trent and see if they'll change their mind.'

'So it's like a test?'

'Yes.'

'OK then, I'll try.'

'Thank you. You are dismissed. Amen.'

'Amen.'

A few weeks later, Palestrina came back with his *Missa Papae Marcelli*. The Council of Trent listened to it carefully, making detailed notes on its precise levels of holiness. When it had finished, there was a long, tense silence. The clock ticked loudly.

'Oh, all right then,' boomed the chairman. 'Carry on.'

Pope Julius, Palestrina and everyone else were delighted. Palestrina had *singlehandedly saved classical music*.

Worn out by the stressfulness of this situation, Pope Julius III died. And then, three weeks later, his successor died too. Palestrina was fired from the Sistine Chapel for breaking their strict vows of celibacy, and moped back to Palestrina (the town) to play the organ again. But hey.

Owen and I stood in the Sistine Chapel, mouths agape, mulling over this amazing story. How many of the hundreds of people in here knew about the near-catastrophe that had befallen music in this exact location, nearly 500 years beforehand? Probably none. In fact I didn't know either, as I only found out about it afterwards. Instead, tourist heads craned towards Michelangelo's frescoes. As did ours.

'I think I've cricked my neck,' said Owen. 'I can't seem to move my head.'

He staggered over to a bench and sat down on a female American student. I apologized as she squirmed away, trying to explain that Owen has a history of chronic back trouble.

'Was she attractive?' asked Owen, head bent backwards.

'Yes, quite.'

'Get her back.'

'She appears to be complaining to her tutor.'

'OK, next room.'

Nine hundred rooms later, we fell out into the white-gauzed Roman winter sunlight of the exit courtyard, utterly exhausted. I never wanted to see another fresco, painting, marble statue, old map, bust, vase, or giant Renaissance tapestry, ever, ever again. I was completely culturally filleted, and Owen was still having problems with his head.

'I need a drink,' he groaned, staring up at the sky.

'I need something really . . . vulgar.'

We were pretty well done in. Before we got to the Vatican, we'd already marched around the Colosseum, the Forum, the Capitoline Hill, il Vittoriano and the Trevi Fountain, via churches and piazzas. We ended our day at Palestrina's old church, Santa Maria Maggiore, where he'd sung in the choir as a boy. It was large, and ornate. We wandered around its hushed marble interior – Owen limping heavily and with his head still askew. I imagined poor toddler Pierluigi, miles from home, straining for top Cs under the raised whip of the evil choirmaster, and grimaced in sympathy. I stood, philosophically, at the vast ornate altar, and took a photograph of where I thought the choir might have stood. The Passion of Christ was played out in frescoes high along the walls. Owen shuffled respectfully over to look at them.

'Is it time to get pissed?'

'Yes.'

Opposite the church was a bar called Druids Rock; its logo was a neon picture of Getafix, the druid from the Asterix cartoons, holding an electric guitar.

'This place looks extremely cool,' said Owen.

We entered Druids Rock. We were not to emerge for some time.

Monday Night's All Right for Fighting

To be honest, I've never really been one for violence. I've been beaten up a few times, when I was younger, but I've never been all that fussed about fighting back. Tonight was a different kettle of fish. It started when Owen somehow managed to topple a giant iron bin, which then began to slowly roll down the broad avenue we were staggering up. I ran down the hill, managed to overtake and threw my entire weight behind it. The bin stopped rolling as it thudded into my torso. I heaved, trying to right the thing, but it was way too heavy; the best I could do was roll it to the side of the road and wedge it into the gutter. I sat on the kerb breathing heavily, faintly aware of a dull thudding sound coming from further up the hill. There was a huge clang, and here was another giant iron bin rolling down the middle of the road.

'For fuck's sake!' I chased the bin, overtook it, lay down

and took the impact. 'Stop rolling the bins!' I couldn't see him, but I knew he was up there somewhere. I heaved the bin to the kerb and puffed up the hill to find Owen thankfully beaten by his third bin. He was lying next to it, swearing, trying to light a cigarette.

'Leave the bins alone!'

He kicked at the bin half-heartedly.

'Stop that!'

But he couldn't really speak. He glared at me, cross-eyed, and the cigarette fell out of his mouth. Then he sprang to his feet and pelted off unsteadily towards the station. I ran after him, shouting. The problem was that we'd been on double Jack Daniel's chasers all night. Owen had suffered a major neural power-cut twenty minutes before we were requested to leave Druids Rock. We were bundled out of the door mumbling and pointing angrily at the bar staff. My own personal off switch wasn't far away either, but I was sufficiently together to know that my main responsibility lay in stopping Owen hurting himself or getting arrested.

At the back of Roma Termini station are a couple of acres of gardens – scrubland really – populated by millions of sparrows flapping around a load of scrawny trees. I trailed Owen into the park but lost him straight away; the only light was from a fine thread of murky streetlights lining a dirt path through the middle; it was dark and silent, and smelled of ammonia and dried grass. I shouted, 'Owen!' No reply. I walked further in. 'Owen! Where are you? Owen! You bastard!' Nothing. Some birds skittered in the branches above. I squinted out into the blackness. There was a slight scuffing sound to my left; I turned my head and then *blam*, I was on the ground. He had been hiding behind a tree. I lay on the grass, winded, as he ran off again.

I gave chase but he soon disappeared. I stood, slowly

circling, the ground began to shake and I span to my right and there he was, pounding towards me like a rabid, leather-clad elephant. Impact was inevitable.

'Raaaaaaaaaaargh!' he bellowed as he took me down again. I was completely laid out, and now quite riled, so this time, as he struggled back to his feet, I caught hold of his back pocket and pulled him back on top of me. We rolled around like this for a few minutes.

I'll take a short break here just to remind everyone of the dangers of alcohol abuse and the even greater perils of mixing your drinks while binge drinking. It's not big to drink as much as we did, and, as you can see, not very clever either. Just have a couple of pints, then go home, OK? Leave this kind of behaviour to the professionals.

I made it to my feet and started to kick Owen in the ribs, as hard as I possibly could. And then his head. I kicked him about twenty times. I was doing really well until he slowly rolled away, got to his feet and ran off again. I stood there breathing heavily, watching his jacket balloon behind him. What now? I decided that I didn't really want to be ambushed again, so I staggered off in the other direction, back towards the hotel. Ten minutes later I was lying on my bed in our room, staring uncomprehendingly at the mud all over my trousers. Two minutes after that, I was asleep.

I was awoken by my mobile phone, several hours later. In fact, judging by the traffic noise and the bright sunlight pouring in through the shutters, many many hours later.

'Hello?'

'Thank God you've answered.'

'Owen?' I looked at his bed. It was empty.

'I don't know where I am.'

'Where are you?'

'I don't know. I came to, standing on a train in rush hour,

79

surrounded by commuters, and now I'm somewhere else, and I don't know where the hotel is. Or what it's called. Or where I am. I've been phoning you for hours.' He sounded like he'd been run over.

'Jesus. What time is it?' I asked.

'About ten.'

'What were you doing on a train?'

'I don't know.'

'Are you still in Rome?'

'I don't know.' There was a long pause. 'Maybe yes, maybe no.'

'Tell me what you remember.'

'Nothing. I woke up standing opposite a beautiful Italian business woman, and now here I am, wherever this is. It's a nice day, though. Do you know why I'm covered in mud?'

'Don't you remember attacking me?'

'Someone *attacked* you?'

'Yes, you did. Several times.'

'I don't think it was me.'

'It was definitely you.'

'Ah. Well, I apologize.'

'It's fine. I'm sorry I didn't answer my phone sooner.'

'Don't worry about it.'

I told him the name of the hotel and how to get here, and an hour or so later he rolled in and collapsed on to the bed. He was completely covered in dried mud.

'Are you OK?' I asked.

'Yes and no.'

'It's the opera tonight.'

He grunted and passed out.

A few hours later, I awoke with a start, rushed to the bathroom and vomited into the lavatory bowl. I'd been dreaming of opera. I crawled back into bed and lay on my

This expression often signals 'trouble ahead'.

back, hurting all over – my soul especially. Owen rustled a bit and rolled around to face me.

'Better out than in,' he murmured.

We lay in difficult silence for an hour.

Breakfast consisted of pizza and eight cans of Coca-Cola. In between shaky mouthfuls of *quattro stagione* I had to rush to the loo again. Owen calmly watched me depart and rejoin the table while reading *The Economist*.

'Better out than in,' he said each time.

'But I don't want it out any more. I want it to stay in.'

'Fair enough.'

Today was supposed to have been our 'listening to Palestrina' day. I hadn't actually heard any Palestrina yet. But it was five o'clock already, and we were due at the opera for eight, and I couldn't stop vomiting.

'They won't like that sort of behaviour at the opera house,' said Owen, who, by the way, doesn't get hangovers.

'Oh man, you're right. I can't vomit all through the opera. That would be terrible.'

'Opera frowns upon that sort of thing.'

By seven-thirty I'd pretty much stopped vomiting. We trundled through the warm evening, following the map until we arrived at the Teatro dell'Opera di Roma. The tickets were pretty cheap, and we went to sit and wait in the bar. I clung to a glass of Coca-Cola while Owen tormented my fragile equilibrium by sipping at a glass of dry white wine.

'Delicious!' he said, waving it around.

It was obvious that the rest of the milling opera fans thought we'd made a mistake and come to the wrong place. Everyone was wearing thick overcoats and hats, with suits and silk ties and stuff underneath. We weren't. Their hair had oil in it. So did ours actually. They stared at us sweetly: poor confused English people! Well, yes, in a way. We finished our drinks and headed towards the auditorium. Owen tried to buy a programme, but the dolled-up, over-perfumed woman on the desk *wouldn't let him buy one*. Whoah, now this was getting personal!

Jacopo Peri Invents Opera. Claudio Monteverdi Popularizes It. Why? How? Whither Yonder Warble?

'Anything that is too stupid to be spoken is sung.' Voltaire.

Venice, 1607

'Oh, Claudio!' cried Mrs Monteverdi from her second-floor window as, down in the street below, her husband scuttled through the pouring rain.

'Please, Claudio, do not do this!'

'Leave me alone, accursed bitch!'

'Claudio, please!'

Monteverdi ignored her, striding onward towards the piazza.

'Think of ze children!' screamed Mrs Monteverdi, hysterically.

Claudio strode on. Rolled up under his arm was the first draft of his first opera, *Orfeo*. He ought to have listened to his wife. OK, *Orfeo* was performed – in front of his boss, Duke Vincenzo, who thought it was all right – but Mrs

Claudio Monteverdi. Surprisingly thin.

Monteverdi died just months later. Am I the first classical historian to perhaps suggest that, plagued with guilt and rage at her husband's ghastly new style of music, she committed suicide rather than have to listen to a single note of *Orfeo* ever again?

Greek classical literature became incredibly popular during

the Renaissance; its free-thinking philosophy was seized upon by artists and thinkers, helping sweep away the dogmatic iron fist of the church. Musicians wanted a piece of this too; though, yeah, they had all these harmonies, it was still impossible to hear what twenty or thirty people all singing at the same time were actually saying. Composers wanted everyone to know that they liked the Greeks too, so in 1593 Jacopo Peri decided to fuse some spoken lines of Greek tragedy to music. Instead of the choral blast of your polyphonic Mass, it was just one bloke, pumping out sad stories, sweating. He was backed by choirs, but gently. You could, at last, actually hear the words of the song. At first, this was just a semi-musical form of speech, but it didn't take long before they began to act the stuff out while they were singing it; and this soon blossomed into *full-blown opera*.

Whoah motherfucker!

Peri's operas were small potatoes. Monteverdi, who'd previously contented himself with writing madrigals, picked up opera's baby baton and ran, ending up with the famous *Orfeo*, based on the myth of Orpheus. Tonight, Owen and I were here to enjoy perhaps more of a connoisseur's choice: the significantly less classic *Il Combattimento di Tancredi e Clorinda*, which might also be based on the myth of Orpheus, but in a more roundabout sort of way.

We took our places in the red velvet auditorium, with the whole of the rest of the audience goggling at us openly. We sank low into our seats to try and deflect the attention, but instead a middle-aged, grey-bearded man in the seat in front swivelled around and glared at us with horror. He kept glaring for about two minutes, until his wife tugged him back around. I turned to Owen, who was hiding behind the programme that somebody had, at last, deigned to sell him.

'Have I got vomit down my face?' I whispered.

He kindly studied my washed-out visage. 'Not any more. But I don't understand a word of the programme. It's all in Italian.'

'Oh man, is it really?'

'Typical Italians.'

'Hey, you know what? I've just realized. This is my first-ever classical music concert.'

'Well, good luck. I hope you enjoy it. When I was a kid, my parents used to take me to the opera all the time. I always fell asleep. I've never, not once, been to the opera and not fallen asleep.'

'So it's potent stuff.'

'Extremely. Can't you feel the atmosphere already?'

'No. What is it?'

'Flaccid.'

He was right.

More stylish punters swept in. Some attractive young women, too. Refined ones. It had been a long time since I'd seen any of those. Nobody forgot to stare at us. I looked ahead at the stage; it was wide and darkened; I could vaguely make out some scenery – maybe some cardboard trees. The house lights went down and a line of duck-tailed musicians threaded along the front of the stage, to applause. The stench of expensive cologne and cigar smoke was overpowering. As well as violins, etc., there was a drumkit, a synthesizer, and an electric bass guitar; their presence gave me comfort.

Then the conductor came out, his route lit by a giant spotlight. The clapping got louder. He bowed, smirking, and the hall fell silent. Here we go. Opera. Live.

Live Opera

Act One, Scene One. A man dressed as a soldier comes out on to the stage. He starts shouting loudly in Italian. We sit and listen politely to his yammer.

5 minutes later: he's still shouting; pacing the stage and occasionally waving a sword. No music yet – just shouting.

10 minutes: he's still shouting. Owen asks me for a mint.

15 minutes: the shouting continues. And it's proper shouting, too, not just exclamation. The audience seem to like it; they murmur approvingly; I get the impression he's shouting something quite patriotic. Maybe *Viva Italy!* or *Italy is victorious!*

20 minutes: I'm not kidding – he's still shouting.

25 minutes: yep, still going. I get a bit panicky that maybe we have come to the wrong place after all. Also a bit headachy.

28 minutes: he stops. Another soldier comes out with a guitar and sings a sad song. I, however, am happy. The shouting soldier stands and watches the guitar soldier's song. He's deeply moved by it. He removes his helmet to reveal himself as the slightly fatter, thick-looking bald one from Right Said Fred. The soldiers depart. The audience applauds wildly.

My thoughts on the first act: I didn't understand it.

Act Two, Scene One. Everyone comes out. There's two people painted silver, dressed as statues, who may or may not be king and queen; two knights dressed in psychedelic suits of armour; the Devil (I think), wearing a fancy white suit with frilly plus-fours, a pointy moustache and beard, holding a large scroll; and a pair of glittery pantomime horses on rollers. The scenery is forest-like. Everyone settles down.

Act Two, Scene Two. The psychedelic knights have a shit prancing fight, while the Devil wanders about, singing from his scroll.

Act Two, Scene Three. The statues start to sing, with very high voices, and the psychedelic knights freeze mid-fight, to listen. Stagehands move the pantomime horses around.

Act Two, Scene Four. The psychedelic knights are almost dead from their unconvincing battle, and take off their helmets to say goodbye to each other. One's a man and one's a woman. Oh no! They were lovers but they didn't recognize one another with the helmets on! The Devil is sympathetic. The male knight gives the female knight a rose. She smells it and then dies. The End.

The curtain doesn't come down right.

My thoughts on the second act: exciting but sad.

Out in the lobby in the interval, Owen and I studied the show's poster. It was huge – it covered almost the whole of the wall. He asked what I thought so far. I told him that I thought it was completely brilliant.

'You're kidding.'

'No, it's madness. I didn't have the faintest bloody idea what the hell was going on at any point whatsoever, but it was amazing! Sheer entertainment. Bonkers! Bananas! Ridiculous!'

'What about the music?'

'Oh, just opera music. I don't know. I liked it. I had no idea what they were singing about either. But it sounded fantastic. All that stuff they do with their voices. The high singing and shit. All brilliant.'

'You're an opera fan already, then?'

'Damn right I am – it's my favourite!'

Maybe he thought I was lying, or showing off – both things I've been known to do in the past – but I wasn't. It had, truly, been love at first, erm, fright. I could barely wait to go back in and be confused anew by the rest of it.

'Come on. Let's opera!'

'Yes, let's opera.'

So we did. Any thoughts of vomiting had temporarily disappeared.

The second half was actually a completely different opera altogether. The music wasn't by Monteverdi any more; it was by Igor Stravinsky – i.e. quite modern. The theme was still war, but we'd jumped forward several centuries. The plot for this second half was way more freakish than the first – in a nutshell, the main soldier was called 'Theatre of War'; I know this because it was written on his jacket. Then there were three 'hip-hop' soldiers, who repeatedly came on and did some humorous call-and-response operatic rapping and formation-moonwalked. This time the Devil was wearing lots of clever disguises, so it was hard to keep track of which one he was. There was a separate, one-legged soldier, who spoke French standing in a cloud of dry ice. Then, suddenly, the hip-hop soldiers carried on a chaise-longue with an Egyptian woman lying on it with her eyes closed. She had 'Bach' written on her dress. Theatre of War then drank tequila with the Devil and made him crawl across the floor on his belly. Theatre of War and Bach made friends, and Bach opened her eyes and did a funny dance. A soldier crawled through some barbed wire, while Theatre of War and Bach watched, smiling.

The audience went nuts! Owen and I did too. As we walked slowly back to the hotel, thoroughly bamboozled, we haltingly attempted to dissect the performance.

'I think there might have been rather a lot of symbolism in that,' said Owen.

'Really, a lot of symbolism, yes.'

'You know, with war . . .'

'Bach . . .'

'And further deep symbolism.'

We continued to discuss the complicated symbolism until we reached home.

'Is opera still your favourite?' asked Owen at lights out.

'Yes. I love it. I want to go again, right away.'

'I'm so pleased. Goodnight then.'

'Goodnight.'

We flew back to London the next morning. Owen did fall asleep during the show, by the way. During the bit where the Devil was dressed up as a haberdasher, trying to fool Theatre of War into buying a violin.

*

Guillaume Dufay and the rest of the Early Renaissance guys score:

Sex: 2. Not very sexy – virtually chaste.

Drugs: 2. Not very druggy. Like smoking dried banana skins: seems like a good idea at the time, but ultimately pointless.

Rock 'n' roll: 3. They score points solely for their pious egomania.

Giovanni Pierluigi da Palestrina scores:

Sex: 7. He was fired from the Sistine Chapel for shagging around, remember?

Drugs: 8. Listening to Palestrina is like listening to Spiritualized on absinthe: a blissed-out zero-gravity headspin.

Rock 'n' roll: 8. He saved harmony for Chrissakes!

Claudio Monteverdi scores:

Sex: 3. Dry.

Drugs: 9. *Mental.*
Rock 'n' roll: 7. Turbulent

Seb suggests:

Desprez: *Messe Ave Maris Stella* by A Sei Voci (Astree)
🚐🚐🚐

(In HMV they had about fifty different Desprez CDs; I had no idea which one to buy, so Faye picked the one with the prettiest cover. It's OK – the best of all the Early Renaissance crap I bought. The cover is quite nice.)

Palestrina: *Masses and Motets Vol. 2* by Soloists of the Cappella Musicale di S. Petronio di Bologna (Naxos)
🚐🚐🚐🚐🚐

(This is, frankly, awesome. Palestrina's music is unlike anything I've ever heard before. *There's no dissonance.* In other words, there's no rough surfaces for any friction or gravity for the music to get caught up on. It's perpetual motion music; there's nothing to haul it back to earth; it planes on into space and beyond. This music can untangle hair, solve Rubik's cubes, heal wounds, settle wars – it's a magic potion for the ears; mathematical ecstasy; infinite white light. Yeah, baby!)

Monteverdi: *Vespers* by the Arnold Schoenberg Choir (Teldec Classics) 🚐🚐🚐🚐
(A civilized dip of the toe into the origins of opera. The tunes are great, the dynamics keep you awake, and it's amusing to turn it up loud and sing along really badly.)

Lassus: *Lagrime di San Pietro* by Ars Nova (Naxos) 🚐🚐🚐
(Lassus was a mate of Palestrina's. It's the same sort of thing only slightly bouncier, and only cost £4.99.)

4.

I emailed Fiona to tell her about our adventures in Italy. She was concerned that I had passed over Monteverdi so fast.

'In the meantime, you should get to grips with *Orfeo*,' she thundered. 'It was the first opera worth taking serious note of.'

'OK then,' I glumly emailed back.

But before we head back to Italy, it's time – at last – to declare . . .

Let There Be Instruments

I had been wondering when we were going to arrive at these. Despairing at times. Who'd have thought it would have taken so long to get to them? Although rudimentary instruments had been around for hundreds of years, it took ages for Western Art Music (classical music's correct definition) to get round to using them. Because of the highly religious nature of Medieval music, any instrumentation was regarded as vulgar and ungodly; unfit, certainly, to accompany the heights being attained by composers. In short, musical instruments were *sinful*; they were distracting you from, erm – what was it again? But, as the church's grip on music slipped, so did the instrumental animosity, and into music's growing complexity and emotionalism came – at long, long last – instrumental classical music as we know and love it today!

First to use instruments – and who have been playing them throughout our tale so far – were, of course, minstrels. Although classical music per se hadn't yet got around to using them, there was already a comprehensive mish-mash of contraptions being plucked, blown, fingered, bowed, keyed, thwacked, walloped and mastered by inspirational peasants all over the Western world.

There were two different kinds of minstrels: battle minstrels and house minstrels. Battle minstrels were deployed on the battlefield to sound charges, plump up morale, intimidate the enemy and melodiously imply their own army's effectiveness. It's not recorded how much of an impact they actually had on morale, or proceedings, but battle minstrels would have played along to every major skirmish that took place in Europe throughout the first 500 or so years of the second millennium; inspiring soldiers with the medieval equivalent of 'Eye of the Tiger' or 'The Final Countdown'. Sometimes they even headed up the charge; the poor guys on the trumpets were often the first to be hacked to bits (though they did manage to destroy the walls of Jericho all by themselves – a proud day for the trumpeting profession). When not in the thick of things, battle minstrels would accompany their master on his travels, heralding his arrival and departure at castles and pageants. You could, therefore, instantly gauge a nobleman's significance by casting an eye over the size of his merry men; they were the medieval equivalent of the hip-hop posse – a crew that went everywhere you went, bigging you up the whole time, really noisily. For example, when King Philip the Good's wife Isabel arrived in Bruges in 1429, she was accompanied by a tooth-rattlingly awesome barrage of *196* silver trumpets; though her response to this fanfare was unfortunately completely incomprehensible.

House minstrels had it easier; they just tootled away in the corners of courts and bars; chamber music lounge lizards singing songs of love, booze and death lifted from the hand-me-down repertoire of minstrel standards – like Nick Cave, only more varied. House minstrels serenaded meals, banquets, fêtes, jousts, public hangings and meditative strolls in the garden; one Belgian king even employed his minstrels to play discreetly in his bedchamber on his wedding night. Often they played music for dancing, which was already shamefully rampant by the mid-fifteenth century.

Though often crudely constructed, minstrels' instruments were prototypes for the more fully realized, complex and better-known models that succeeded them. Some of the most common contraptions were as follows:

Lute: like a short guitar
Sackbut: exactly like a trombone
Portative organetto: like an amazing miniature organ
Bagpipes: same as bagpipes
Bladder pipe: like a recorder but with an inflated bladder in the middle for some reason
Hurdy-gurdy: like a bagpipe crossed with a violin crossed with an amazing miniature organ
Psaltery: like a zither (which is a harp in a box)
Shawm: like a big recorder
Double shawm: super-size that (see picture below)
Lizard: like a long bent recorder
Crumhorn: like a really long bent recorder
Harp: small harp
Drums: drums

With all these going at once, you'd have quite a racket on your hands; certainly enough to unnerve anyone trying to

Geezers ripping it up on double shawms.

attack you. I was excited. What I craved now was to see some minstrels in action. But how to go about getting hold of live medieval minstrels here in the twenty-first century? First I considered contacting one of those battle re-enactment societies; maybe I could stand and watch battle minstrels serenading a bunch of twat civil servants clutching pikes and theatrically not killing one another in chain mail made out of coat hangers on Sunday mornings in Bucking-hamshire. But would they make me dress up? I didn't want to risk it. Next I tried some gig guides, which was stupid, but a good excuse for having a peek inside *NME*. The internet came up trumps straight away. Noise of Minstrels are a feisty troupe of contemporary minstrels from Harro-gate in Yorkshire, led by the reclusive minstrel visionary Mike Sargeant. Noise play at weddings, birthdays, business conferences, etc.; their repertoire includes a variety of min-strelsy through the ages, featuring tunes from the medieval era to the Victorian; all knocked out while kitted out in authentic period costume.

I couldn't wait to hear Noise of Minstrels shake their stuff. I emailed multi-instrumentalist Mike (bagpipes, lute, recorder, harp, percussion, rote, pipe drum, string drum) to ask where they were playing next, and if I could even maybe sit in on a gig with them (discreetly, at the back, on a small harp), but he sadly informed me that their season had finished and that Noise were on ice now until the spring. However, Mike informed me, they did have an album available, if I was interested in that? Yes, I was interested, and I hurriedly sent him a cheque for £12.

Mike's reticent about the run of bad luck that has plagued Noise's LPs. Their first (and best) album, *Pass the Hat*, had its master tapes mysteriously stolen, so is no longer available except on ultra-rare limited edition vinyl. Instead, Noise fans are forced to make do with the inferior *Noise of Minstrels: Medieval Music*, which, fortunately, remains widely available. Though I was sad to be missing out on Noise's own semi-lost, *Smile*-esque masterpiece, I was still pleased with what I got on the *Noise of Minstrels: Medieval Music* CD. The guys (Mike, Ray, Richard, David, John, James, two Peters and Penelope) hurtle through the album with commendable gusto. They tackle a wide range of interesting subjects on the album. The instrumentation is potent and thrusting. Penelope sings nicely. David shines on the hurdy-gurdy, as does John on the slatternly gittern. The production is effective. The recorders harry. The lutes cut through with psyched savvy. The percussion is foot-tappingly accomplished. I am satisfied with the album.

'I am satisfied with the album,' I email Mike. I then put some further questions to him, in the form of an email interview.

Seb: In a world of *Pop Idol*, *Fame Academy*, *Animal Hospital* and *I'm a Celebrity, Get Me Out of Here!*, is there still a place in the scheme of things for minstrels?

Mike: Yes.

Seb: Rock 'n' roll music can sometimes be 'sexually exciting'. Can minstrel music?

Mike: No, but that's not to say it couldn't be.

Seb: Would you like to have lived in the medieval era? If so, when?

Mike: No.

Seb: Have you ever played at battle re-enactments (as battle minstrels)? If so, did you ever get 'killed'?

Mike: We've played at events where battles have taken place, but we weren't actually in them.

Seb: Would you like to see young children taught more about minstrelsy at school?

Mike: Yes. They are the performers and audiences of the future. Medieval music being a building block of classical music can also help with the understanding and appreciation of later forms.

Seb: And how about older children?

Mike: Educational projects are an important part of my and the group's work.

Seb: What would you say is the hardest minstrel instrument to master?

Mike: All instruments have their difficulties. I am essentially a wind player, specializing in flutes, recorders, bagpipes and sundry reed instruments. Yes, I do play more than eight instruments, but it's best to think of it as *types* of instrument.

Seb: Do you make your own instruments or do you buy them?

Mike: We mostly buy them. Sometimes, however, we make them.

Seb: Period costume: yes or no?

Mike: Yes, if it is appropriate to the presentation.

Seb: Could you ever sanction a cynical 'disco remix' of a minstrel song, designed purely for chart success?

Mike: I see no harm in making use of Medieval music.

Seb: Have you ever been tempted to play any modern songs on your medieval instruments?

Mike: When playing to the back of people's heads at a banquet or reception, the odd phrase of a known pop classic helps to check if they're listening.

Seb: Where next for minstrels?

Mike: More concert-style performances would be nice. In addition, I am writing a show which combines music, song, mime, dance and narration. It takes the interpretation of Medieval music that little bit further.

It was clear that far from being a pointless relic of the Dark Ages, contemporary minstrelsy is alive and well and reacting to the challenges the present (+ future) places upon it with passion and intelligence. In my guts, though, remained the urge to hear live minstrels. CD wasn't enough – not even Mike's forthcoming minstrel concept album. I wanted to be hey-nonny-nonny-knocked off my feet by some sack-clothed motherfuckers, preferably within a sweaty, heaving auditorium full of whisky-sodden, E-popping dipso-maniacs. Fairport Convention chose not to return my calls.

I struck lucky. Whilst hungrily surfing the web for more minstrels, I unearthed a group called the Dufay Collective, who, to my delight, were due to play a show billed as 'The Art of Minstrelsy' at the University of Kent in just a few days' time. I snatched up the telephone and huskily booked a pair of tickets, praying that it hadn't sold out. I was told to relax: there were plenty of tickets still available. Then, less than a week later, I drove down to Canterbury, engorged with excitement and anticipation.

There's Snow Business Like Show Business

This was my first-ever visit to this city famous for its cathedral and cutting-edge archbishops. As I drove downhill through its dreary outskirts, I spied, lit up in the valley below, the clawhammer cathedral spires rising high over an otherwise low-level cityscape. It was late afternoon; cold and overcast; and I was in a bad mood, since the drive from London had taken about three times longer than I'd expected, and my intended companion for this jaunt – my dashing friend Pauly – had phoned when I was half-way down the motorway saying that he wasn't going to be able to make it after all. This was particularly annoying, as Pauly had been invited specifically because he'd gone to Kent University himself; I'd planned to amusingly splice his dreary student recollections into my description of the evening. Now my plans had been thoroughly scuppered. Not only that, but as I wandered alone around Canterbury city centre, I began to regard the place with treacherous hostility.

Canterbury is like Winchester, only much, much worse. Sure, it looks great; all its heritage fittings and fixtures are in place: lots of tottering pottery shops, winding cobbled lanes and – oh man – even a Winnie the Pooh store; but the place has as much charm as a House of Lords urinal. It reeks of the piss of contempt. Much though I tried, I couldn't get a single glimpse of the cathedral itself from anywhere in town. To get near it, you have to hand over £4; and this lets you into the 'cathedral precincts' – the old part of the city – the bit you might like to see. I couldn't even stand at one of the highly manned gatehouses to try and sneak a look, as a man with a bowler hat and shiny shoes lurched menacingly towards me. I refused to pay the £4 out of principle, and so enjoyed an embittered stroll around the high-walled perimeter, frothing with disgust at all the nauseously cavorting, dolled-up schoolboys who got in my way. I went and sat in a deserted coffee shop, obstructing a waitress Sellotaping badly cut-out red cardboard hearts to the windows for Valentine's Day.

As I didn't want to waste my spare ticket and was scared of going to see the minstrels by myself, I decided to phone Owen, and ask if he fancied hopping on a train and being a last-minute replacement for Pauly. He said yes, OK, but only if I reimbursed him the money for the train ticket. A few hours later, as I sat in my car in the station carpark, waiting in the cold dusk for his arrival, he sent me a text message asking how bad the snow was in Canterbury, as London had been completely blanketed. Eh? I replied that I had no idea what he was talking about, and could he please hurry up. But then at that exact moment, the heavens dumped snow all over the place; a loony blizzard; from nought to winter wonderland in 180 seconds.

<oh THAT snow> I texted Owen, <it was rather sudden. could you please hurry up?>

He eventually arrived and threw a snowball that hit me in the mouth, and we duly set off up the hill towards the Kent University campus and its Gulbenkian Theatre, where the Dufay Collective were due on stage at 7.45 p.m. precisely; an hour or so from now. We'd have plenty of time for a nice cup of tea, as the campus was only two minutes' drive up the road. Ten seconds later – five yards beyond the station exit – we were beached. It wasn't my fault – it was the car coming the other way that suddenly skidded in my direction, so I stomped on the accelerator only to wheel-spin sideways into the kerb and then, slowly, a hedge.

Snow is confusing.

'Shitting bollocks.'

'Wahey!' said Owen.

We ground and slithered back on to the road, and then out into the middle of the opposite lane and then, just in time, back into our lane again, before, with a soft crack of snowy bumpers, settling into our place in the haphazard queue of traffic. The snow was coming down even more heavily than before; I could hardly see anything; just a hazy blur of tail-lights through the spazzing windscreen-wipers. Owen said that he was starving hungry and was I going to buy him his dinner? I wheel-span gently to my right, ending up at a right-angle to the kerb. Somebody honked, and I gently span round further.

'Maybe we can stop at a Little Chef later,' I said

'I love the delicious Little Chef.'

Twenty minutes later we hadn't moved; we were still on the outskirts of Canterbury in heavy snow pointing in slightly the wrong direction. Another twenty minutes after that, we realized that we were at the bottom of a long, steep hill, and the reason for our lack of progress was that no cars could get up it. They'd wheel-spin for two minutes, then give up and head back into town. Our turn was approaching. We watched a transit van pirouette backwards down a cul-de-sac. I checked the clock – it was ten minutes till showtime.

'Why don't we just go straight to the Little Chef,' said Owen. 'We're not going to make it up this hill, and I'm starving hungry. Sod the minstrels, come on, I'm famished.'

I wanted to see the bloody minstrels, though. I looked at him, handsomely. 'We can make it.'

'But I didn't come all the way down here to suddenly be denied my Little Chef!' The bastardized logic was impressive.

'No. It's minstrels or nothing – and I don't mean the chocolates.'

Owen laughed hysterically at my brilliant joke; then it was suddenly our turn to try and crawl up the hill. The car splayed forward slightly, and then a young, working-class blonde woman approached us from the pavement. Owen unzipped his top and wound down his window.

'Don't be facking stupid,' she said as I haltingly regained control of the vehicle.

'Oh,' said Owen. He turned to me. 'I thought she wanted to talk to me.'

'You'll never facking make it,' she continued, then scuffed down to the car behind to say something hopefully more polite.

'Tasty, though,' said Owen, peering into the wing mirror.

By now it was 7.40 p.m. I reckoned that if we just ditched

the car here, it would still take twenty minutes to walk; we'd still miss a good chunk of minstrelsy. But it's not often that I get a chance to be heroic; at least not outside daydreams and minor – though significant – family tasks on Christmas Day. I took a deep breath, let out the clutch and we shimmied slightly then glided faintly upwards.

'Wahey!' said Owen.

My heart was pumping like crazy. If we lost traction, we'd slide back down the hill and smack right into the cars waiting behind or, worse, pedestrians. Maybe both. Pets. The hill was steep. First gear, 80 per cent wheelspin, just about holding a straight line. The sweat poured off me. Whirling tyre rubber rutted the snowdrift. We're talking *inches*. Halfway up, Owen discovered a large packet of sherbet lemons in the glovebox. He held the bag up to my face and I slipped several acres.

'Sherbet lemon?'

God, what an annoying bastard. Anyway, we made it – just in time.

The Dufay Collective Live at the Gulbenkian Theatre

The Dufay Collective is:

Paul – trumpets, recorder, psaltery, percussion.
Giles – vielle, rebec, shawm, bagpipes.
William – flutes, shawm, bagpipes, simfony, percussion.
Clive – I'm here to check you're paying attention.
Susanna – vielle, percussion, contempt for the rest of the Collective.
Peter – harp, percussion, banter.

As Owen and I took our seats, it was plain that not many of tonight's audience had made it up the hill; though those travelling from higher ground appeared to have managed to slide down it. The small auditorium was about a third full, and our seats were excellent; halfway up and right in the middle. On stage were five chairs in a semicircle plus a sprinkling of outlandish contraptions. Here, obviously, were the fabled gitterns, shawms and hurdy-gurdies. It all looked home-made.

We regarded the rest of the audience with interest. It was squares and pensioners. Owen and I stood out like a sore thumb: me an unhygienic, preppy Gram Parsons and Owen like a 35-year-old member of East 17. Suddenly the house lights went down, the confused OAPs started to mumble and bump into one another, and the stage filled with yellow light. The minstrels were coming out!

They're dressed in clingy black. Mid-forties. No period costume, though. Shame.

Track 1: William stands at the front of the stage holding a gigantic, two-metre-long black trumpet. He takes a deep breath and blows: *arsequake*. Paul, to his right, grapples with black bagpipes. They blurt into raspy life as his elbow pumps hard at the bag. Giles, left, is beating the living daylights out of a soldier drum. It's way louder than I'd been expecting. Owen's eyes stray lazily up from his programme, and he fixes Susanna, centre stage, with an 'and how about you then?' quizzical glare. She stands with her hands in her pockets, in Lennon specs and a donkey jacket, head shaved, glowering back at him. This is a bit weird.

The minstrels desist their battery and sit down on the chairs. Peter (Chelsea defender John Terry in a grey pageboy wig) stands to reveal himself as tonight's master of cere-monies. He tells us that they're going to play a song that translates into something like 'We Don't Like Jealous People'. We all laugh, except Owen, who grunts. Peter's self-deprecating delivery is spot on. They play 'We Don't Like Jealous People' and it sounds *exactly* like 'Tomorrow Never Knows' by the Beatles. Just as I'm wondering when the backwards portative organ is going to kick in, Owen leans over and whispers that the time signature is outstanding, and begins to discreetly conduct with his hand.

The second song features Peter on a small harp. He plinks, pulls and wipes it like a reverse Rumpelstiltskin; it's heartbreakingly beautiful. Then Paul and William burst through with mammoth crumhorns, while Giles and Susanna (who finally takes her hands out of her pockets) accompany on rudimentary violins (called viols). Whispering, I ask Owen if he could play the crumhorn as well as William. He wrinkles his nose: 'Yes, of course.'

The third song is a lament. William plays the guitar while Peter pounds a set of bongos. Owen leans over. 'Sounds like Led Zeppelin,' he whispers, and plays some air guitar. I'm relieved it's not just me who thinks that lots of minstrel music sounds like the Zep. This song is the best so far.

The fourth song is a dull lullaby on flute and harp. It continues for a couple of minutes until Paul coaxes enough wind into his hurdy-gurdy for it to be able to start, and Peter and Susanna accompany on handclaps. A zither joins in.

'Extraordinary time signature,' says Owen.

I'm sufficiently inspired by this one to enter my first writerly passage into my notebook. I write: 'Light rain in the Highlands on a bright spring morning.'

'What are you writing?' whispers Owen.

'Nothing.'

'Write "John Bonham",' he says. I refuse, but then appear to have written it anyway.

Peter tells us that the fifth song is Danish, and about the weather, and takes the opportunity to make a few jokes about the snow – blaming it for the empty seats. He thanks us for turning up, and we give ourselves a bashful round of applause. The Danish song features everybody singing (Susanna grumpily). Owen is beginning to twitch and fidget. I faithfully transcribe all of Owen's fidgeting and twitching.

'What are you writing now?' he whispers.

'Nothing. Shut up.'

The next song sounds uncannily like 'In an English Country Garden'. I whisper to Owen, 'What do you do, when you really need a poo . . . ?' but he doesn't get it. Then it's the interval. As we push past pensioners on our way to the bar, I continue: 'Pull down your pants, and fertilize the ants . . . ?' But Owen shakes his head and walks towards the lavatory. '. . . in an English country garden!' I sing after him, hopefully.

He's probably just standing behind the door.

During the interval, we delicately lie to one another about how enjoyable the performance has been so far. Though it's been loud, and quite varied, and surprisingly musical, I can't help thinking they lack some kind of magical X-factor. Maybe I was just freaked out by Susanna's terrifying, Kafka-esque demeanour. How is anyone supposed to relax and enjoy sophisticated minstrelsy with this woman's body language screaming out that she'd rather be *anywhere in the world* other than sitting next to Peter holding a miniature portative organ? Pondering this, I recall that Giles looked pretty icy, too. Maybe they had a massive bust-up backstage – poised to clobber each other, sackbuts raised. Musicians are the same all over the world!

Alongside the foyer bar is a gym table littered with Dufay Collective merchandise. Owen and I stand and sift through their many CDs. My eye is drawn to one called *Johnny, Cock Thy Beaver*. I buy it and get given another free – it's nice to see minstrelsy keeping pace with contemporary marketing techniques. This now brings my minstrel record collection up to three. Then a bell rings, meaning that we and the pensioners have ten minutes to elbow our way back to our seats. The pensioners fight dirty.

The second half kicks off with a long rudimentary cello solo which gradually builds to a pumping handclap crescendo; Owen and I tap our feet and nod along with the driving beat. Looking around the auditorium, we appear to be the only two actively caught up in the rhythm, which is a shame. In fact some of the audience now appear to be asleep. Next is a loose-hanging, improvisatory minstrel jam: everyone plays a solo, even Susanna – reluctantly – on her viol. Giles smiles thinly. It's getting slightly boring now; even Peter's between-song banter feels like it's drying up a little. We still laugh along with him, though – well, all except Owen. I lean over and whisper, 'Why aren't you laughing at the jokes?'

'They're all here in the programme. Look.'

They were. Scripted funnies. What a lame-ass.

Before Peter sits back down again, he fastens a leather harness to his upper body, decorated with those small cymbal-like bells that you see on shirehorses. He proceeds then to actually play *himself* through the next number: the theme tune to television's 'Are You Being Served', accompanied by Giles and William on clapping. Owen fiddles, twitches and twists his mangled programme into tighter and tighter rolls. Even I have to admit that this one feels like it's going on for several days. I lean back into my comfy velvet seat and gradually let my focus slide . . .

I awake to Owen poking me in the ribs; and just in time

too, as we've almost reached the end of the show. For the Collective's final piece of the evening, they take up the car-wheel-sized tambourines again and bow down to an inevitable Big Beat finale, pumping out a medieval glam breakdown that rips off the Chemical Brothers big-style. I briefly desist from my zoned-out clubbing trance to sweatily scrawl into my notebook: 'music to charm fleets of giant snakes to!' . . . and then the stage is suddenly empty and the Collective have disappeared and the pensioners are back to milling about in coat-searching confusion. Owen and I run out to the car, which is stuck fast in the snow, and put *Johnny, Cock Thy Beaver* into the CD player. It's mild. The roads are a disaster. It takes five hours to get back to London. We slide past a Little Chef on the way, but Owen's asleep, and I choose not to wake him.

A few days later, having listened thoroughly to the Collective's *A L'Estampida: Medieval Dance Music* album, as well as to *Johnny, Cock Thy Beaver* a bit more, I realize that I have unwittingly become a bit of a minstrel expert. If you completely blindfolded me and put me in a room in front of a minstrel band, then I could, without a moment's hesitation, open my mouth and say, 'It's minstrels.'

Could you? No.

In order to achieve a personal sense of closure and perspective, I decided to email Peter the same questions I'd emailed Mike from Noise of Minstrels.

Seb: In a world of *Pop Idol*, *Fame Academy*, *Animal Hospital*, and *I'm a Celebrity, Get Me Out Of Here!*, is there still a place in the scheme of things for minstrels?

Peter: Rolf Harris and Channel 4 are currently considering my proposal for an idea I'm calling 'Celebrity Academy Medieval Minstrel Hospital Idol', in which various sick medieval musicians, incapable of making a living and dressed in original dickheadsian costumes, are trapped on an island with nothing but a rommelpot. The answer to your question will have to await the outcome of their deliberations.

The bastard had hijacked my irony and turned it back against me!

Seb: Rock 'n' roll music can sometimes be 'sexually exciting'. Can minstrel music?

Peter: That depends on the size of the codpiece and the fee.

Seb: I noticed that the Collective doesn't wear period costume. Why not?

Peter: There are two ways to market medieval music. 1) Dress up like a prat and become a sideshow, get paid badly and have the audience talk through the whole thing. The advantage is that you can get pissed and play badly. 2) Take it seriously, present it as the equal of any other musical repertoire, play in international festivals, get picked up at the airport and put in a good hotel, have large attentive audience, receive ten times the money and get to see the world. Wait till after the show to get pissed. Which would you go for?

Seb: Does the Collective make money?

The Dufay Collective: Peter poking the harp, Susanna far right: asleep.

Peter: Do we sound that bad?

Seb: Where next for minstrels?

Peter: Minstrels aren't going anywhere. They're all dead.

I have decided not to reproduce all Peter's answers, as in most cases, he was funnier than me.

John Dowland: Master of the Lute

By the middle of the sixteenth century, instruments were regularly taking the place of voices in polyphonic music, to the point where music originally written for multi-part singing was now being reproduced by the kind of instrumental armour wielded by the minstrels above. The biggest and loudest instrument was the full-on church organ; but the most widely played and versatile item was the lute – the grandfather of the guitar. Lutes were incredibly popular: Henry VIII had a special lute room, in which he stored his massive lute collection; in fact he wrote 'Greensleeves' on one, perhaps.

The guy really pushing the lute envelope – the Lutefather – was a man named John Dowland. Dowland was born in London in 1563, and as a young man converted to Catholicism. After this he hastily became a lute genius. Then, in 1592, he was summoned to the court of Elizabeth I to entertain the queen plus her crowd of fops and hangers-on. He went down well – everybody clapped feebly at his thrilling, Hendrix-esque performance, and he walked home that night convinced he was about to be installed at the royal court as its resident guy-on-the-lute. And this is where Dowland got *heavy*, because he wasn't – Elizabeth refused him this honour because of his unfashionable Catholicism.

'I've played so long with my fingers that I've used up all my good fortune,' complained Dowland. He then started to write some of the most depressing, godforsaken songs in the entire history of music. Miserable, self-pitying dirge after miserable, self-pitying dirge flowed from his bleak quill. He plucked at his worn, lozengey lute and moaned till the cows came home. Then he moaned about the fact that they were a bit late. And that he'd had to go and close the gate behind them. And they were a bit smelly. Oh, why can't they moo a bit more quietly? Musicologists describe Dowland's œuvre as 'profound and melancholic' and 'exquisitely sorrowful'. He wrote over a hundred pieces for solo lute and voice. See if you can spot the genuine Dowland songs from among my decoys:

a) 'Weep Ye No More, Sad Fountains'
b) 'Oh Woe'
c) 'Smile Ye No More'
d) 'Can She Excuse My Wrongs?'
e) 'Weep for Me, for I Am Tormented by Sadness'
f) 'Me, Me, and None but Me'
g) 'Welcome, Black Night'
h) 'Wily Wench, Did'st I Not Love Thee Properly?'
i) 'Fine Knacks for the Ladies'
j) 'Tears Are Falling'
k) 'Queen Elizabeth, You Smell Strangely of Ammonia'*

Deeply depressed by Elizabeth's rejection, Dowland fled to Denmark – whose own royal court paid more, actually, so *nyer* – chivalrously leaving his wife and child back in

---

* Answers: Dowland wrote a, d, f, g and i; I wrote b, c, e, h and k; j is by Kiss, the saddest of all.

London to fend for themselves. In Denmark, his depression worsened. He wrote a long, complex piece entitled 'Always Dowland, Always Doleful', but then got in a huff whenever a Danish fop asked him to perform it.

But in England, Dowland's star was back on the rise: in his absence he'd been getting some decent reviews. Poet Richard Barnfield wrote: 'Dowland's heavenly touch upon his lute doth ravage human senses!' Thomas Lodge, a notoriously tedious show-off, wrote: 'Musicke rauisheth the minde much more by melody, than either Bacchus by the taste of Wine, or Venus, by the itching pleasures of Lust. This makes me admire John Dowland, an ornament of Oxford, whose Musicall consent (by reason of the aeriall nature thereof) being put in motion, moueth the body, and by purified aire, inciteth the aeriall spirit of the soule, and motion of the body: by affect, it attempteth both the sence and soule together; by signification, it acteth on the minde: to conclude, by the very motion of the subtill aire, it pierceth vehemently and by contemplation sucketh swetly; by comfortable qualitie it infuseth a wondrous delight; by the nature thereof both spirituall and materiall, it rauisheth the whole unto it selfe, and maketh a man to be wholly Musiques, and for her cause onely his: Thus much in memory of his excellence!'

He probably then ejaculated into his britches.

Delighted at his newly restored reputation, Dowland sailed back to Blighty, where he finally secured himself a place at the Elizabethan court. Such a happy conclusion to his travails inspired him to compose a special celebratory song: 'Wilt Thou, Unkind, Thus Reave Me?' Queen Elizabeth's response to this dolorous ditty goes unrecorded, though we do know she did not commit suicide.

All this crap got my pulse a-racing. I wanted to play the

lute too – and have someone write about my prowess on it so excitably. I emailed Fiona again, shyly informing her that I wanted to purchase a lute of my own and, to my relief, she wrote back saying she was *very impressed*, like that, in italics.

Where do you buy a lute from, though? *Loot?*

Lute Wars

I've always been wary of eBay. Too competitive, too many variables, too much on trust, too damn capitalist. But I needed a cheap lute, right? And I couldn't face the agony of trying to buy one in some stuck-up musical instrument shop. ('Would sir care to have a strum on this exquisite piece, sir? A veritable snip, sir, at seven hundred pounds . . .') Instead I bit the bullet and stuck the word 'lute' into the eBay search box, and up popped a load of lutey bollocks: some lute oil paintings, an enamel lute brooch, lute sheet music, stuff like that. But there, right in the middle, was a genuine photograph of something that looked like a lute. 'Egyptian Lute' said the caption. Perfect. The asking price was £45, nobody else had bid, and there was only one day to go before the auction ended. I merrily offered my £45, leaned back in my chair and began to daydream about, well, me playing Dowland covers on my new lute. Next day, I checked again and it was still there; nobody else had made an offer. I rubbed my hands. This was easy! The onscreen timer said there was less than an hour left to bid. Whistling, I strolled down to the shops to buy myself some lunch. When I got back, it had gone for over £70. There had been a last-minute feeding frenzy of bid followed by counter-bid, none of which had involved me. Luters fight dirty then, huh?

Livid and slightly humiliated, I soon unearthed another lute auction, and this time blasted proceedings with – *blam* – a straight £70-fuck-you lute bid. OK, I was top man again, this was more like it. Two days to go. Just a few hours later, someone came in with £75. I countered with £80. That night at 11 p.m., some evil mofo came in at £90. I parried him with a swift noble ton, even though I'd promised Faye that I wouldn't go higher than £80.

'What do you want a lute for in the first place? This is just a stupid, faddish waste of money.'

'Wily wench, did'st I not love thee properly?'

She wasn't laughing. Nor was she the next evening, an hour before showdown, when I confessed that I was still hanging in there – bruised and bleeding but still clinging to the top of the pile on a scalding £140.

'You fuckwit,' she said.

I'd lost all sense of perspective so I decided to remain silent.

'*A hundred and forty quid* for a poxy lute that you'll never even play?'

I began to hum, and raised my eyebrows. It worked. She walked away.

Then some maniac came in with £150 – it might even have been me. I sat vigilantly at the computer all night until falling asleep in my chair at about one in the morning. When I awoke several hours later, the screen informed me that the accursed instrument had been sold to someone called 'colin_all_the_heroes'. Colin had paid £301.50.

This was getting ridiculous. But I was in too deep – it had become a obsessional matter of principle that, by hook or by crook, I had to acquire a lute from off this Satanic piece of shit-sucking website. The very next day, a new piece of kit appeared – this time the caption declared a 'single-stringed lute-type instrument'. *Single-stringed?* *Lute-type?* There was a photograph. It looked pathetic – like an elastic band tied to a chicken drumstick. What possible use could this travesty of an instrument be to anybody in the world? I took a deep breath and bid £4.99. Five days later, while I was away at the seaside for the day, it went to a man named Alan, for £55.

Devastated and with sand in my pants, I immediately bought an East German zither for £30 instead.

'A what?' sighed Faye.

'It's a zither.'

It arrived two days later. It was black, and nice. And challenging.

'It looks like a children's toy,' said Faye.

I placed it on my lap. 'No it's a zither.'

'Go on then – try and play it.'

It's time for the next section.

I've Got a Brand New English Madrigal, and I'll Give You the Key*

While the Italian madrigal was being florally nuanced by the likes of Monteverdi and Palestrina, the plucky English madrigal was coming on in leaps and bounds.

'Why don't we make it rhyme?' suggested ruddy John Bull one night down at the Fox and Hounds, in Somerset.

'Aye!' replied Tom Morley, wiping the foam from his whiskers. 'Rhyme!'

'Do it up proper fancy,' interjected Thommo Weelkes, passing wind loudly.

'You stinky goat!'

Parp, went Tommy Tallis.

'Oi! Not you an' all . . . !'

'Oi! Stop that, you!'

Parp.

'Oi!'

They knocked the table over.

The English Renaissance was less sophisticated than the continental one, though it did make an effort. English composers had become obsessed with the magic of the madrigal, and everything the Italians had achieved with it. You know what, though? Despite the fact we've been looking at madrigals for a little while already, I'm still not sure exactly what they are. I forgot to really pay attention earlier, and now, whenever Fiona blithely drops them into an email, or I read about them while trying not to fall asleep perusing a CD's sleeve notes, I twitch, guiltily, inside. My dictionary says that a madrigal is: 'a medium-hot curry, named after a port in

* Key, geddit?

South-east India'. No, it's the line below: 'a type of sixteenth- or seventeenth-century part song for unaccompanied voices, with an amatory or pastoral text'.

In other words: just an old-fashioned pop song. 'Anarchy in the UK', then, is just a nihilistic madrigal. You see, it's reversible.

English madrigals were salty: chock-full of bawdy verses, double entendres and general rowdiness. Their composers likewise.

Thommo Weelkes: choirmaster at Chichester Cathedral and a chronic alcoholic. These two aspects of Thommo's life didn't blend together so well, and he was fired after urinating on the dean from up in the organ loft. You might call him the Liam Gallagher of madrigalists.

John Bull: Bull's name has become synonymous with particular aspects of the English character: red-faced chauvinism, bulldog-owning and high-minded drunkenness. Bull's madrigals, though impeccably stately and stirring, can't get past the bulk of his reputation. He did, however, compose 'God Save the King', which occasionally changes to 'God Save the Queen'.

Tommy Tallis: composed his best-known madrigal as the result of a wager. The Duke of Norfolk (a Tallis fan) had bet a bunch of snooty Italian madrigalists that an Englishman could write a madrigal just as good as theirs. He phoned Tallis, who came up with seminal madrigal 'Spem in Alium' (or if you are naughty: 'Spam in Aspic'). When the Duke of Norfolk heard it, he was sufficiently moved to give Tallis the heavy gold chain he wore round his neck. The duke was then executed. Tallis went on to write a madrigal-writing handbook.

Tom Morley: bit of a swot, this one. Took it all a bit seriously. Not nearly bawdy enough, though his 'It Was a

Lover, and His Lover's Lass' does make a cameo appearance in Shakespeare's *As You Like It*.

Jim Bowen: you can't beat a bit of Bully.

Orlando Gibbons: better known by his saucy nickname, which was 'The Finger of the Age'. He died young, in Canterbury Cathedral, from an apoplectic fit. His madrigals had been rich and varied.

Bill Byrd: leader of this gang. In fact he was, arguably, the greatest British composer of all time *ever*. Really?

'He's the man,' wrote Fiona. 'The daddy. The Grand Master.'

Ever? But what about . . . erm . . .

'Unless you think Handel was English? Please discuss,' wrote Fiona.

No, I believe you.

Catholic-hunting at Heathrow Airport

One shouldn't underestimate the perils that came with being Catholic in England during the reign of Elizabeth I. We've already covered woebegone loser John Dowland's religio-political ups and down-down, deeper-and-downs; but William Byrd provided the queen with an even bigger dilemma, since being a genuine Renaissance man, as well as the greatest composer thrown up by these shores ever, you couldn't just ignore him, or hope he'd mope off to Denmark with a chip on his shoulder.

Bill/Billy/William/Guilielmo Byrd/Bird/Birde/Birdo was known to his contemporaries as the 'Father of British Music', or 'The Phoenix' (he preferred 'The Phoenix'). Born in Lincoln in 1537, Byrd began his career writing music for his local church, where he soon became chief chorister and principal organist. He dazzled the congregation with his chirpy wink-wink-nudge-nudge organ style, but his rampant technique soon wound up the local Protestant puritans, who banned him from using their organ, which led to Byrd storming off to London, where he was offered a prestigious place at London's Chapel Royal (the equivalent of the performing arts school in *Fame*).

This was weird, since Byrd was Catholic and oughtn't to have been allowed into such a virulent Proddy hellhole – but for the fact that he had a giant trump card up his elaborate cuffs: the queen fancied the absolute ass off him. Bill was an attractive man: portraits show he had beautiful hazel eyes and a soft, lustrous beard. And he wasn't fat. This plus the woozy charm of his music made mincemeat of Elizabeth's harsh ginger exterior. She forgave him his evil Catholicism; in fact she went even further: she gave Byrd the first-ever patent to print music in England, which was great news, until – to his dismay – music shops reported back sales figures of approximately zero. Byrd, rightly, smelled a rat.

This scent of failure might have been due to the fact that Byrd was surrounded by people who wanted him dead – specifically: everyone. Catholics weren't just frowned upon, they were bundled up, tortured and executed. So while Byrd quick-stepped through the royal court plucking at his zither, the enemy's lips were almost certainly being fervently wetted in anticipation of his imminent gruesome demise. But Liz maintained her protection, thus Byrd continued to write music. He composed services (Protestants refused to call them Masses), madrigals, keyboard music, consort music, songs, anthems, triumphs, fantasias, pavans and galliards (I don't know what most of these are, but they're written on the back of my Byrd CD case), writing for a panoply of instrumentation. In fact, the only instrument Byrd never composed for was the lute (and Dowland bitterly resented him for it). But, by 1557, Byrd had had enough. Fed up with London's endless whispering hostility, he moved out to the far western edge of the city – to Heathrow airport – for a bit of peace and quiet.

Heathrow was actually not an airport yet by the mid-1500s. It was, however, an unusually fertile piece of land. The heathland was also a notorious hunting ground for highwaymen and bandits; Dick Turpin was active hereabouts. The site's first known name was Hetherewe; in the late fifteenth century it became Hetherow; and by the time of Bill Byrd's arrival it went by the name of Hitherowe – even though Byrd actually settled in a place half a mile up the road called Harlington.

More Catholic-hunting at Heathrow Airport

Heathrow airport suburban wastelands, March 2004

I arrived in Harlington on a squally grey Monday afternoon. It was terrifyingly awful: a screaming sub-suburban through-road whose laughable concessions towards any lingering pedestrianism were either accelerated through or raged at with horns. 'INSURANCE' read a large illuminated shop sign. 'NEWS' read a newsagent's. 'TAKE AWAY' tempted the local eatery. HARLINGTON'S NO FRILLS AND A COUPLE OF HUNDRED YARDS LONG. DEAL WITH IT OR FUCK OFF. The 'fuck off' vibe was pungent in the air. There's a bus stop opposite a spike-gated lorry dealership – it's covered in broken glass and spit. 'NO THIRD RUNWAY' reads the xeroxed sign in virtually every shop window, concrete front garden and vandalized telephone box. It seems that the government's plans to expand Heathrow include building a new runway right through the middle of Harlington. Neighbouring Sipton, too (which is even worse). I think that's an excellent idea. These places are shit, come on! A runway would be far nicer – a quick exit, you know?

I sat in my car in a piss-stinking layby puddle, wobbling with the rush of passing traffic, listening to William Byrd, feeling . . . not much. Byrd's music encompasses many different tones, moods and characters: light, shade, encouraging, discouraging, sad, and a mode that brings to mind mummification. Byrd's tunes are dignified. Measured. Diligent. Sober. I'm listening dutifully to his admirably varied output, but have yet to discover a soul. Palestrina's soul comes roaring out of the blocks from the off, but Byrd's? I think it's trapped beneath the measured and diligent sobriety. 'Byrd is naturally disposed to Gravitie and Piete' diagnosed a contemporary. Though he does let his hair down occasionally – my fave Byrd tune is 'John Come Kiss Me Now', which sounds like Austin Powers playing 'Bread of Heaven' on an electric harpsichord. Mostly, though, it's straitjacketed, suffocating viol instrumentals and a prim trilling soprano; her frail hand clutching a handkerchief to her trembling breast. *Get on with it, this is Harlington.* The greatest-ever British composer? Can't see it, sorry (not that I've heard any of the others). But he did write your big choral stuff, too. I've listened to it, and I cannot remember.

Having moved out to Heathrow, Byrd's ecclesiastical risk-taking increased. Forced deep underground, Catholic communities gathered in secluded country houses to perform Catholic Mass in secret. If they were caught – bosh – head chopped off. I drove around Heathrow's perimeter fencing listening to 'Fantasia No. 2', 'Fantasia (4 viols)', 'Fantasia

No. 3 (6 viols)' and 'In Angel's Weed'. Just when I was about ready to give up on Byrd entirely, I spied a hoarding advertising the Heathrow Visitor Centre. This was clearly a sign. Then I saw a sign. The signs were stacking up. I followed directions and parked up next to a broad glass building and watched an aeroplane land on the other side of the fence. It was dramatic. Seven or eight middle-aged men with binoculars leaped out of cars to follow the final descent, standing in the rain with beetled brows and murmurs of approval. Planespotters.

The visitor centre was superb: a deep-carpeted 'airport experience' complete with various mock-ups. There's a check-in desk (complete with working luggage scales), a foreign exchange display board, 'archway metal detectors' (which you can walk through – but don't forget to put your keys in the tray!), a slightly incongrous steel cargo container and a pleasant 'customs area'. The centrepiece is the 'Airline Pilot Flight Simulator', in which you sit in a British Airways plane seat (plus genuine folding plastic table) and watch a flickering 'sky' on a jerky computer screen behind some darkened perspex, with a crackling, taped 'captain's commentary'. The captain says things like: 'We're coming into land now,' and 'Roger.' On the first floor is a viewing area and a café. It was full of planespotters. I sat discreetly at a table and watched them, listening to Byrd's 'Qui Passe (for my Lady Nevell)' through my headphones. They sat with binoculars round their necks, fat and in extra-large t-shirts, bifocals and combovers, eyeing me with panicked suspicion.

We were distracted from this mutual reverie by a gigantic jumbo jet coming in to land right down in front of us. Its physiological impact was considerable. It was also loud as hell. The planespotters jotted stuff down and made some quips. But then one shouted, 'Fire!' and pointed to the far right-hand side of the airfield, where we saw a stationary Bangladesh Airways jumbo jet sitting with smoke pouring out of its left engine.

'Fire! It's on fire!' Binoculars were raised. A fleet of dinky fire engines went tearing towards it. I turned my music off.

'Fire! Fire!' exclaimed a planespotter, hysterically.

'Nee-nar, nee-nar, nee-nar!' These guys were a bit freaky.

The fire was getting worse. Billowing clouds of smoke poured from the wing, surrounding the plane completely. Flames licked the engine casing as the smoke drifted slowly towards the runway. I was scared to death, but the planespotters continued to jump up and down with excitement.

'Too much curry on board!' one of them yelped.

'What it is, they want to stay another day in the country, that's what it is.'

'They'll let anyone into Britain these days. Won't they. Eh?'

'No one wants you, pakis!'

I was somewhat taken aback by this new line of banter. Further quicksilver repartee flowed from their blubbery lips, along with some slurring and spittle. In the meantime, the fire engines put out the fire.

'All your local hotel owners will be looking at that and going, "I don't want that lot in my hotel!"'

'Go on, get on another plane and bye bye!'

They stood, glued to the binoculars, wheezing heavily.

'They're towing it back to the stand.'

'Told you they just wanted to stay in the country longer.'

'That's typical pakis.'

As they watched, they shovelled down crisps and bottles of fizzy pop. Some of it went down the front of their t-shirts. Once the racial hatred had subsided a little, they settled down on the benches to watch me again. Their foreheads were slicked with sweat. I suspected the signs that had led me to this place had been misinterpreted. I cued up Byrd's 'Fair Britain Isle' and watched them back. Soon another plane came in.

'Iberian.'

'Iberian.'

'Iberian Airlines I think you'll find.'

A barely perceptible pause.

'Dagoes.'

And a muffled wet snort. Fair Britain Isle!

William Byrd died in 1623. Elizabeth protected him right up until her death – and the Protestants never caught up with him.

Winston Churchill announced plans for an airport at Heathrow in 1944. It was finished in 1946: 'London Airport – Heath Row'.

Other facts like these are available from the Heathrow Visitor Centre, Newall Rd, Heathrow Airport, Middlesex UB3 5AP.*

*

Minstrels (Noise of Minstrels / The Dufay Collective) score:

Sex: 1. Minstrels aren't known for their looks.

Drugs: 7. Stoners, all. Susanna was probably in a k-hole.

Rock 'n' roll: 10. The only way the Dufay Collective could possibly have been more rock 'n' roll would have been to trash their instruments at the end of the show and dive off the stage. And to wear capes. Maybe some discreet pyro. OK, let's knock 'em down to a **9.**

John Dowland scores:

Sex: 2. He clearly never got any.

* Admission is free.

Drugs: 6. Bad shit. Crystal meth.
Rock 'n' roll: 9. Simply the Kurt Cobain of the lute.

William Byrd scores:

Sex: 7. Smouldering sex god.
Drugs: 1. Just say nay.
Rock 'n' roll: 8. Like Che Guevara meets Baader-Meinhof meets the KLF meets Magnum PI – playing a secret organ in wigs.

Seb suggests:

Pass the Hat by Noise of Minstrels (Noise of Minstrels Records)

(The great lost minstrel masterpiece. I've never heard it. Fetch your wallet and fire up eBay; but keep away from the lutes, y'hear?)

Johnny, Cock Thy Beaver by the Dufay Collective (Chandos)

(Catches the Dufays at the top of their game. Feisty minstrel workouts abound on this smart collection.)

Dowland: *Lute Songs* by Steven Rickards and Dorothy Linell (Naxos) 💣💣💣💣

(A fine, budget-priced collection of woe – also features a banging 'Greensleeves' improv lute solo.)

Playing Elizabeth's Tune – The Tallis Scholars sing William Byrd (BBC/Gimell DVD) 💣

(I challenge anybody to be able to sit and watch this all the way through. Ten minutes in I had to punch myself in the face to stay awake.)

5. Orchestral Manoeuvres in the Dark

One of the most unexpected results of my endeavours so far has been the discovery of the fact that people tend to lie when it comes to classical music. They lie a lot. And they don't expect you to challenge them – nobody usually does. Probably no one ever has. It's older people who are the liars. It always happens after I explain what I'm writing about. The older person replies – weightily, sniffily, authoritatively – that they have a deep and passionate love and appreciation of classical music. This is put across in a tone so grimly superior that any further delving into the nature of this love and appreciation is expressly forbidden; indeed, you insult them if you dare attempt to pierce this profound, rapturous sheen with any more of your impertinent vulgarity. But that's where the fun starts. One must doff one's metaphorical cap and respectfully reply: 'What do you like?'

You get a thick wad of stern, disapproving silence, and then a withering: 'Beethoven.'

Silence. Suitably 'awed', you must continue: 'And what is it that you love about Beethoven so?'

But, shit, you've already gone too far. They know sod all about Beethoven. So you try and lighten the mood by talking about what you like, and why; and going into detail, to show that you're not taking the piss or anything. And be humble. While you are saying all this, their solemn, blank expression betrays that they have no idea what you're talking about and really wish you'd shut up. Soon – completely ignoring everything you've just said – they close their eyes and rapturously say 'Beethoven' again, the same as before. And it's right there that you suddenly realize, with shock and a little anger, that this older person is just making it up. He doesn't care about music at all. He's just saying he likes classical because it's his generational duty to do so. All he really wants to say is that he despises popular music and all of its cultural trappings and, by association, you with it, actually. And you can suddenly see this, and feel rather foolish and cruel for having squeezed it out of them in this squalid way. You'd be astonished though – really – it happens all the time.

I, too, have a bit of a guilty secret: I've been listening to pop music again since the beginning of chapter three. I should've admitted this sooner, I know, it's just that the right moment never presented itself. I meant to 'fess up – really I did – but I kept forgetting to put it in. I capitulated because I was starting to get depressed. For a while everything was OK; I adjusted to the super-ethereal, linear challenge of perpetual plainchant relatively well; Faye came home from work and suggested putting some music on; my heart sank slightly, but I gritted my teeth and on went *Feather on the Breath of God*, and we smiled thinly through its duration. One of us would occasionally say: 'Yes. I like this. I'm getting used to hearing it *all the time* . . .' quite bitterly; but the novelty didn't take long to wear off; the bleak, grey, one-dimensional nature of early music started to flip me out; lay me low; suck all the life out. There was no colour coming in through my ears. It was like sitting in a bath with no water in it. Weekends were the worst. I became bitter. Lashed out. Cried a few times. In the end, much like my early attempts to give up smoking, Faye had to practically beg me to stop.

'Well, OK,' I replied, strangely smug and triumphant.

'But I'll only listen to pop at weekends. Weekdays stay the same: classical only.'

'Just . . . whatever. Anything except this.'

'But I thought you said you liked it . . .'

'*Stop messing with my head.*'

You see, it was getting to her too.

I'm much happier with the new regime. It's not cheating, so much as a subtle realignment of policy. Had I attempted to maintain a classical-only diet, then by now, I'm sure, I'd be openly hostile to pretty much everything I listened to and this would all be unfettered, unrelenting bad language. Well, even worse. Instead, my disposition is unwaveringly sunny and positive. Sometimes it is.

So, doing as Fiona tells me, I'm back to Monteverdi's *Orfeo* – the most important and significant early opera of all. It's based on a Greek myth, and I have been working out the story. It is:

Orpheus was an excellent musician. He played the harp and sang, and everyone liked his shit – even trees and rocks, it says here. Sadly, one day his wife, Eurydice, was bitten by a rattlesnake, and died. Fortunately though, Orpheus' music was popular in hell too, so the gods of the Underworld did a deal with Orpheus, whereby he could have his wife back if he promised not to look back over his shoulder while he took her out. However, just as Orpheus and his zombie spouse were approaching hell's exit, Orpheus looked back to check, and kapow! She fell, screaming, back to hell for ever. Orpheus became depressed and, out singing one day, was attacked by some women and torn to pieces. His severed head floated down the river and came to rest on the island of Lesbos, apparently still singing.

I was saddened by this. As I listened to Monteverdi's passionate and stirring score, I began to softly weep, as I am sensitive. But I tell you, Fiona's instruction to 'get to grips with' *Orfeo* isn't as easy as it sounds. How many times do you have to listen to something before you've officially 'got to grips with' it? Ten times? A hundred? I'm on two and a half and struggling.

But two incredible, planet-shifting things happened during *Orfeo*. Without realizing it, you and I have just been privy to the beginning of the Baroque period (don't ask – you just have), and the *birth of the orchestra*. To provide the necessary moods and dramatic accompaniment overlays to the sung story, something more than the usual gaggle of intellectual composer-musicians was now required. Instantaneous, multi-textural tonal shifts were now vital in order to create the desired widescreen effect, and the only way to guarantee those was to get a huge bunch of different players all sitting in one place at the same time – in a big semicircle – waiting for their cues. In other words, the invention of opera suddenly expanded the common musical palate twentyfold. Each bit of the story needed a different illustrative sound. So all the musicians had to turn up at the same time.

The orchestra had landed.

Woolly Lully

The next thing the orchestra required was, of course, a conductor. Step forward excruciating Frenchman Jean-Baptiste Lully. Lully straddled the seventeenth century in France almost singlehandedly. He spent his life kissing Louis XIV's arse, with the consequence that he was handed an exclusive licence to write and perform opera during the king's lifetime; so that, if any Frenchman wrote one, and wanted to stage it anywhere in the country, he had to ask

Lully's permission first. Unsurprisingly, Lully has emerged as the predominant French composer of the seventeenth century. His dead-eyed, prancing prattle sounds like a musical interpretation of:

'After you, my lord . . .'

'No sir! After you.'

'I beseech thee. You first.'

'Pray no. Please. After you.'

'I could not possibly go before you, my lord. I beg thee – continue.'

'You honour me with your . . .'

'No, after you . . .'

Fannying about. Fondant fancies. A mountain of blancmange superglued to the table. I am heartened when Fiona calls him 'incredibly dull'. It's terrible, soul-destroying stuff. Towards the end of Lully's *Atys*, my CD started to skip. The skipping was way cooler. I listened to it for ten minutes and went for a walk in the rain, hoping to be run over by a child.

Despite the gagging obsequiousness of his œuvre, Lully goes down in the history books as the first man ever to stroll around to the front and actively conduct his orchestra. Sadly, it was to be the death of him. One day, while fiercely conducting somewhere within the walls of the Palace of Versailles, Lully lost control of his baton and it flew up into the air. The orchestra screeched to a halt, the baton fell, pierced his left velvet bootie and went right through his foot. The wound became gangrenous, he pompously refused his doctor's suggestions of amputation and he died. Batons quickly became blunter.

Baroque 'n' Roll Over

Baroque really just means 'excessive ornamentation' or 'irregularly shaped'. All it means in regard to classical music is that everything was getting way more complicated. If Renaissance polyphony vertically reached for the sky, Baroque was all about settling down and spreading out; exploring new intricacies; forget exultation – think expansion; filling in the gaps the Renaissance – in its mad dash for the heavens – left behind.

But to many people – even me now – say the word Baroque and just one man springs to mind.

'Mozart?' I emailed Fiona.

'No,' she generously replied. 'Bach.'

Bach in Black

Leipzig, Germany, May 2004

Phrases commonly espoused when referring to Johann Sebastian Bach include:

'The Father of Western Music',

'Mathematical Genius',

'Organ Virtuoso'.

And so on. However, prepare for a shock, because over the course of my research I have also controversially uncovered the following just-as-valid descriptions: 'sex maniac', 'cash-crazed capitalist', 'violent thug', 'grump' and 'wanker'.

I was so horrified by these revelations, I instantly flew to Leipzig in old East Germany to investigate further. I took along my friend Andrew, who looks like Jesus, except he's slightly fatter, and Scottish.

Whoah — the Daddy. Holding some music, to prove it's him.

'Jesus was Scottish too!' foamed Andrew on the aeroplane, red-haired, red-faced, red-bearded and wearing an electric blue corduroy jacket.

'Says who?'

'Says a book I read!'

'Please keep your voice down,' said the stewardess.

At Leipzig airport, which is a two-hour drive from Leipzig and actually just a field in the middle of nowhere, we loaded our bags into the boot of the hire car Andrew had arranged for us. I'd asked if he could get a Trabant, for the vibes, he was coldly informed over the telephone that they only had Peugeots. I'd brought with me a huge pile of Bach CDs – some bought, some borrowed – and while Andrew cursed and jerked us out of the car park, I tried to stuff them all into the tiny glove compartment, as a low-flying Stasi chopper buzzed overhead.

'Right,' I said self-importantly. 'What Bach shall we start with? I've got cellos, violins, a Mass, a passion, a fugue, concertos, cantatas and some organs.'

'A fug?'

'You want the fug?'

'You don't pronounce it "fug", you pronounce it "few-g".'

'I see. So that's different to a normal fug?'

'Aye, it's . . .' He paused. 'But let's stick to violins for now.' We rolled through a stop sign, then suddenly stopped. My forehead hit the windscreen.

'Seat belts!' cried Andrew.

We sped through rolling, yellow rape-stinking country-side, under heavy warm skies, listening to plunging violins shimmer and shake.

'Slow down!' I said.

'Pish.'

Andrew breaks the mould of my travelling companions so far because he's the first person to claim that he really loves classical music. Even though, in all the years I've known him, I've never hear him utter a single word about classical music, I believe him, since he went to Oxford University and is stoically unflappable in all situations. Which is fortunate, as ten minutes after entering the black-ened Leipzig city suburbs, we were pulled over by a police car. We sat tight as two green-clad cops swaggered towards us in the rear-view mirror. Andrew was ordered to get out of the car; or at least that's what we thought they were ordering, as our German isn't so great. Andrew stood on the Leipzig cobbles and got yelled at.

'Bark, bark! Bark, bark-bark!' went the policeman. Andrew sensibly raised his hands in surrender, but this wound the policeman up even more and he angrily pushed Andrew against a wall to began a frisk. In the meantime, the policeman's female colleague and I exchanged grins.

'Please may I look inside the back of the car?' she asked, and I gave her a lovely smile. She sifted through our bags while Andrew continued to be shouted at against the wall.

'What did we do?' I asked the policewoman, who looked like Angela Rippon, but less orange.

'You didn't indicate when you turned left.'

'I had no idea we'd turned left!'

'We were following you for some time.' Her eyes were green, and cold.

Meanwhile the policeman glared at Andrew's driving licence. Andrew attempted to say something but the policeman shouted: 'Silence!'

'Why are you here in Leipzig?' the policewoman asked me.

'We're Bach fans. I've got CDs to prove it.'

'You are musicians?'

'I am, he isn't,' and I pointed angrily at Andrew. The policeman kicked Andrew's feet wider open and brutally perused his driving licence some more. His black-gloved right hand came to rest on the top of his leather holster; he toyed the catch with his thumb. I thought I saw some urine trickle out from the hem of Andrew's jeans, but in fact it had just started to rain. Eventually they let us go, after a pointy warning that next time we must indicate or else. Andrew sat morosely in the driver's seat. The rain fell harder. I petted his hand. He sniffled.

'Next time indicate, you twat,' I said softly.

'But he shouted at me,' whimpered Andrew, tears all in his beard. 'And I didn't understand anything he was shouting . . .'

We had to sit there for about ten minutes. Eventually we

arrived at our hotel, where we were sharing a twin room, and we could get on with it.

Leipzig's had it hard: we bombed it to shit, and it got stuck behind the Iron Curtain. These days, all things considered, it's looking remarkably chipper. You can hardly tell. OK, so there's a bit too much of a flat, grey municipal vibe going down in the city centre, some *Metropolis*-style flying walkways and mosaic exhortations towards higher standards of citizenship, but for the most part it's a lively, self-confident modern European city. There are trams. Buskers. Sunshine. Tourist information. A Bach statue.

Phew. But two hours later we were stuffed – standing in the courtyard of Leipzig's creaky old Bach Museum, we

belatedly learned that Johann Sebastian wasn't actually from Leipzig at all; he was born in the small town of Eisenach, 350 miles to the west. Andrew said maybe we could drive there, but I mean, it was almost 6 p.m., and time for a beer and that. We could work around this, I felt sure. I asked the old lady at the information desk where Bach went after Eisenach. Maybe he came straight here? But no, *Scheisse*, he won some choir scholarship thing to get into a posh musical academy in Lüneburg, south of Hamburg (yonks away from Leipzig – believe it). Oh, man.

'What did he do in Lüneburg? Was he there long?' I asked the old lady.

'Ah. It was in Lüneburg that Johann Sebastian became himself an organ virtuoso, and an expert on all the things about the organs, as how to build them and like this.'

'Oh really.'

'*Und* singing, und playing the violin, and he was mastering all these instruments with this ease, you see? And now then, in 1702 his studies at the Ritterakademie were concluded.'

'Then he triumphantly got a horse and cart to Leipzig, where he lived happily ever after?' I subtly inferred.

'No, *nein*.'

'I think we should go and get the car,' said Andrew.

'No,' I firmly replied. I turned to the old woman again. 'Where the hell did he go next?'

'He was created chief organist at Arnstadt, a small town . . .'

'How far?'

'Maybe it is two hundred kilometres, or . . .'

'Forget it.'

But it was in Arnstadt that Johann Sebastian left his studies behind and began his subsequent lifelong quest for the readies. Since top-grade organists were in high demand,

Bach was able to negotiate an eye-popping salary plus luxurious accommodation; as well as an enviable position as head of the choir, whom he was also employed to train. He did this with exceedingly bad grace. In fact, one night, coming back from the pub pissed-up on booze, Bach stumbled upon a merry group of six of his own pupils, all of whom he hated because he thought they weren't as good as him. They all stood around drunkenly in the Arnstadt town centre, swaying with paralytic suspicion. Pointing to a troublesome young bassoonist named Geyersbach, Bach suddenly pronounced (and these are the exact words): 'You, sir, are a *nanny-goat*. A nanny-goat bassoonist!'

Geyersbach was outraged. 'Why you . . . !' he shouted back, 'you dirty dog!' Then, with his mates urging him on, he picked up a stick and waved it at Bach menacingly.

'Nanny-goat!' piped JSB, stepping backwards and drawing his sword. 'You're a nanny-goat!'

Sword beats stick, so Geyersbach and his mates ran away. The Arnstadt authorities, despairing at these sorts of antics, begged Bach to calm down. A pig-headed man, he refused. Instead, he walked over 400 miles north to Lübeck, to hear an exclusive live performance by his hero, the old Danish organist Buxtehude.

'Maybe we should follow in this famous walk's footsteps, in our car,' suggested Andrew.

'What's the matter with you? Do you get some cash bonus for extra mileage or something?'

'I just think we should try and . . .'

'Be quiet.' I was missing Owen's violent drunkenness already.

Inspired by old Buxtehude, Bach stayed in Lübeck much longer than he was supposed to, and when he eventually deigned to return, was summoned before a committee to explain this prolonged leave of absence. To make things even worse for himself, Bach then began to ape Buxtehude's florid, acrobatic organ riffs during his church services, much to the confusion and dismay of the hyper-conservative congregation. (If you're finding this bit strangely familiar, you're right – William Byrd did exactly the same thing.)

'Stop showing off like this!' he was warned. Sulking, Bach went to the opposite extreme, playing grumpy minimalist stabs instead. He was fired.

'So – to Leipzig!' I suggested to the now rather tired-looking old lady behind the counter at the Leipzig Bach Museum.

'I am wishing this was true, but it is not so,' she sighed. 'Johann Sebastian becomes organist in Mühlhausen. This is two hundred fifty kilometres south-west of Leipzig.' She paused. We both looked at Andrew. He raised his eyebrows. She took a deep breath and continued:

'Where he wrote many cantatas. But then, after one year only, he is becoming frustrated by the musical restraints of the elders of Mühlhausen and Johann Sebastian must move on once again. He now travelled some miles to the east, to the town of . . .'

We all held our breath.

'Weimar.'

'*Weimar?*'

'Oh yes. Here Johann Sebastian is becoming court composer to Duke Wilhelm Ernst of Saxe-Weimar. The duke was loving all of the musics, and now was loving all of Johann Sebastian's musics also, which were written a lot, here in this pleasing town of Weimar.'

During his residency in Weimar, Bach's brilliant reputation spread like wildfire; though more for performing than composing. Despite an almost pathological compulsion to write music, the relatively modest fame achieved within his own lifetime came primarily from his skills as a musician and improviser: he could improvise complex keyboard pieces for hours at a time, barely pausing for hard spirits. Listening to him play, passers-by would be heard to comment: 'That can only be the Devil or Bach himself!' And: 'Bach's feet flew over the (organ's) pedal-board as though they had wings, and powerful sounds roared like thunder through the church. This filled the crown prince with such astonishment and admiration that he drew from his finger a ring set with precious stones, and gave it to Bach as soon as the sound had died away. If the skill of his *feet alone* earned him such a gift, what might the prince had given him had he used his hands as well?'

What indeed? A cake? (And does this mean that Bach could play the organ *just with feet?*) When asked, in awe, how he was able to play with such breathtaking virtuosity, Bach would modestly reply: 'There's nothing to it. You only have to hit the right notes at the right time, and the instrument plays itself.'

Everybody admired his smugness.

Johann Sebastian was delighted to have stumbled upon this music-loving duke, who liked to invite Bach over to his *Schloss* and jam along on his flute. But the duke soon became jealous of Bach's relationship with his closest rival, his own nephew, who lived in the castle next door. The duke eventually got so jealous that he banned any of his court musicians from going next door at all, but Bach being Bach, he went out of his way to snub the duke by putting on an extravagant show for the nephew, ending with a special poem about how truly nephew-tastic he was. Bach's open defiance meant that, yep – like Lassie, the Littlest Hobo and Bruce Banner – it was time to move on once again; and he tossed off

Young Bach at the organ. Here to entertain yoooou.

another resignation letter and began to pack his bags. Completely outraged by this behaviour, the duke responded by throwing Bach in jail for a month. That wiped the smirk off his puffy face.

'But I can tell by the way you're looking at me over your glasses that he didn't leave prison and come straight to Leipzig, right?' I muttered to the old lady.

'This is correct.'

'But how old is he by now? He must be getting on a bit, right? I hope he doesn't die before he gets to Leipzig.'

'He arrived in the city of Coethen at thirty-two years of age,' said the old woman. She turned to Andrew. 'Coethen is only eighty kilometres. You can easily drive this for sure.'

'I've gone off that idea now. I just want a drink.'

'What happened in Coethen?' I asked. 'No, don't tell me. He wrote a whole lot of music and then fell out with everyone.'

'I would not say it was everyone.'

'I want a drink,' stammered Andrew like a Scottish robot.

'Wait!' exclaimed the old lady. 'I am telling the story. Soon we are to arrive in Leipzig, so listen, please!'

Andrew adjusted his glasses and looked at me pleadingly.

'I'm sorry. We must go,' I said to the old woman. 'Thank you for the information. It was interesting and useful. We shall return tomorrow to listen to the rest of the story.' This was a shameful lie. The old woman gestured impatiently towards the bank of merchandise spread out on the tables before her: thimbles, hankies, biros, coasters and teacups, all monogrammed with a jaunty Bach logo.

Bach booze – tempting!

'Beautiful gifts, for you especially,' she growled, brandishing a crest-heavy pair of commemorative spoons. We ran out into the street. Ran into a bar. Ran up a big tab. Talked about the Beatles.

Bachfest!

During a mildly hungover breakfast at our hotel the following morning, Andrew came back from the juice machine to inform me that he'd overheard somebody at a nearby table talking about Bach. We agreed that this was a pretty strange coincidence. Then, as Andrew mauled the top of his boiled egg, two professorial types shuffled past deep in conversation, snippets of which we were able to pick up. They said: 'serendipitous', 'counterpoint' or something, and then definitely 'Bach'. How strange! Maybe the citizens of Leipzig literally had nothing else to talk about except Bach? Poor Leipzigians!

It turned out that, purely by chance, we'd arrived the day before the start of Leipzig's annual Bachfest – a two-week-long festival celebrating the music of the city's most famous son (even though he seemed to take an awful long time to get here). This was a quite exceptional coincidence and a welcome stroke of luck. It also explained why everyone was talking about him everywhere – or at least these guys in the hotel dining room. Back in the city centre an hour later, Andrew and I excitedly perused the complicated programme of events. The fest was to kick off tonight with a *Wanderkonzert*. This was seven simultaneous concerts at seven different venues which you could wander around and drop in on at any point during the evening, free of charge. How delightfully civilized! Andrew and I sat in a bar and planned our strategy with cold efficiency; we estimated that we'd be able to take in up to five shows in all. We kicked off at 8 p.m. sharp, at the Musical Instrument Museum; climbing a steep flight of stairs to confront an animated hubbub of pensioners milling around at the end of a small carpeted corridor. Joining the kafuffle, we slipped into a small room with a harpsichord in the middle of it, ringed with three rows of plastic chairs. We sat at the back and were stared at. It was hot. Five minutes later, two young people came out of a side door, and we applauded them: a ginger-haired male with a frizzy ponytail, beard, glasses and ducktails; and a wan female in a little Laura Ashley dress. They nervously clutched acoustic guitars. No harpsichordist emerged. The children sat on stools and tuned up. They began to play.

My listening notes consist of just the following description: 'Nerds on axes'. Unfortunately, ten minutes in, an anonymous emergency services vehicle screamed by outside. There must have been heavy traffic since the piercing screech of the siren went on for over a minute, completely drowning out the adolescent guitarists. Everyone tutted. The combined effect of the acoustic guitars, the rhythmic tutting and the wailing siren meant that the piece suddenly sounded uncannily like Madonna's 'La Isla Bonita'. Soon things quietened down again, and the pensioners were able to go back to sleep, woken only by speckled applause between tracks. The charming youngsters stood and took a bow every time. I sneakily taped the half-hour performance on my dictaphone. Listening back in the hotel later on, we agree it doesn't sound that much like 'La Isla Bonita' after all; but whatever they were playing, it was good stuff – mazy counterpoints and cool overlapping runs. Complicated intertwining axemongery always goes down a treat with me; indeed, the nerds reminded me of Iron Maiden's classic twin guitar attack, except quieter and without Steve 'Bomber' Harris.

We exited with the pensioners, both feeling energized by such close proximity to musicianship.

'Where next?' asked Andrew, his flowing red mane

glowing brightly under the yellow Leipzig streetlights. As did his flowing red beard, and cheeks.

'Tell you what – let's just follow the crowd. They'll know better than we will where's the best place to "wander" to next.'

'Aye, good idea!'

We followed a striding group of about seven; snaking through the narrow cobbled streets of the old town in slanting light drizzle. But then a hundred yards later, the seven split into two and went in separate directions.

'Follow the four, the four!' hissed Andrew. We followed the four for ten minutes, until they walked into a pub. We stood outside.

'Do you think there's a *Wanderkonzert* in the pub?' asked Andrew.

'Well let's find out.'

There wasn't. Instead, there was beer.

A heated discussion over which *Wanderkonzert* to attend next now prevailed. This argument proved to be particularly pointless after we realized that neither of us had remembered to bring the map, so we had no idea where the rest of the venues were anyway. But we carried on arguing over – we agreed – one more quick beer. Then a quick – we agreed – plate of fried pork with asparagus. And then – we agreed – one more quick beer to tide us over. Then we stumbled into what was – we belatedly agreed – a jazz club. And it was only half an hour later that we were *absolutely certain* that the jazz wasn't a *Wanderkonzert*. We finished our drinks and dutifully moved on. Neither – to our immense frustration – was there a *Wanderkonzert* in the next bar we visited. We drank delicious cocktails slightly disconsolately. The late-night velveteen-clad bar after that one was just as useless on the *Wanderkonzert* front; Andrew staggered to the toilet, livid at the lack of Bach in this otherwise rather splendid place.

Andrew says 'Cheers!'

But unfortunately he couldn't work my camera properly.

'These *Wanderkonzerts* are useless,' slurred Andrew loudly on his return, sinking a large martini. Sober as a judge, or an airline pilot or doctor, I nodded.

'How many did we ... have we seen ... of these ... konzerts?' stumbled Andrew.

I counted them on my hand. 'One.'

'One!' he threw his arms into the air. '*One?*'

'Two if we're counting the jazz.'

'Two! How many were they . . . were we . . . going to be meant to see?'

'I think about seven. I've got the leaflet with the . . .' But I'd mislaid it.

'*Fffff*, useless!'

'I know, but . . .'

'*Fffff.*'

He was right of course.

Next morning we awoke to much *Wanderguilt*, which was slightly made up for by my bootleg recording of the teenage guitarists, which we listened to while drinking tapwater. The sirens compounded our headaches. Soon we felt well enough to head back into town and, in an attempt to atone for the previous night's failings, book tickets for two performances scheduled for that very evening: a performance of Bach's *Goldberg Variations* by a bloke called Jürgen Wolf on a harpsi-chord in a church and a thorough programme of selected classics in the city's giant concert hall – the Gewandhaus, Leipzig's equivalent of London's South Bank – the Bach-fest's architectural centrepiece. It's hexagonal and brown.

To clear our heads and get inspired for later, we decided to take to the countryside in our car, retracing the steps of Johann Sebastian's final journey from Coethen to Leipzig, playing Bach at top volume with all the windows open; a bit like the helicopter/*Ride of the Valkyries* scene in *Apocalypse Now*. We tore through deserted, boarded-up villages at 30 kph, politely turning the music down whenever we had to stop at traffic lights. The *St John Passion* was mighty and stirring, the *Art of Fugue* was subtle and romantic, some solo cello stuff was nails-down-blackboard annoying. As we meandered, a line of grumpy German cars began to form behind us in a long snaking countryside queue. We carried on like this for miles, with the cars all honking at us.

When Johann Sebastian fled Coethen for Leipzig in 1722, having fallen out with Prince Leopold over his new wife (she was jealous of Bach), his music (they considered Bach's stuff 'boring') and, as ever, cash (Bach could never get enough), it was to all intents and purposes a substantial demotion. In Coethen he'd been Kapellmeister (top dog), whereas in Leipzig he was just Cantor (medium dog). But Leipzig was a bigger, more influential place, and he'd been getting genuinely busy with his nether regions (and Frau Bach – lowest dog of all) and suddenly had a fleet of mini-Bachs to provide for. Leipzig paid a bit better, and he got a bigger house. Leipzig it was, then; and he remained there for the rest of his life. Thank the Lord.

Running extremely late from our afternoon nap, Andrew and I arrived at the Nikolaikirche under buckets of rain. Giant TV trucks hulked around the outside of the church; we stumbled over thick cabling and into production assistants clinging on to golf umbrellas through our worried splash around to the entrance. Inside the church there was a lot of excited chatter, and pensioners. There were no free pews, so after a couple of hectic circlings, we mounted a cabled stone staircase to the gallery and sat on a marble bench and dripped and waited. Very soon a hunched-up gentleman with a big black fringe strode out to the harpsichord waiting for him up on a dais by the altar. He bowed, and went to sit on his piano stool, or harpsichord stool, or whatever it's called, where he sat and composed himself for some minutes. He eventually raised two huge hands into the air, spread his fingers wide, paused enigmatically, and began to play: it was very, very quiet. No amps. No speakers or anything. Nothing was miked up. It was just the harpsichord. Way down there, miles away from where we sat. We had to strain really hard to hear it. And everyone kept coughing, and scraping their chairs, and taking their waterproofs off halfway through, and moving seats, and whispering, and *talking*, and coughing more, it *drove me mad*. And not only that, but Jürgen Wolf made loads of mistakes. Sure, the *Goldberg Variations* are pretty darn tricksy, but in a professional, paying, televised environment like this, you'd expect him to be able to get through it without screwing it up every two minutes.

Although.

It was absolutely amazingly stunningly brilliant! I dunno what it is, man, but these *Goldberg Variations* have got something about 'em. It's like the sound of clouds, if clouds were in, like, a straight line on a psychedelic railway track or something. This is the true 'Stairway to Heaven', right here, right now. And maybe because it was being played on the harpsichord – the instrument it was written for – rather than the modern and more-expressive-however-cheating piano, that I found it so affecting and transcendent, I don't know. But what I do know is that I didn't get bored. Not once, throughout the entire duration (a whole hour and a half). This was a miracle enough by itself, I thought, emerging from my trance after it was done, scowling at our neighbourly pensioners. Andrew made a big show of stretching and yawning.

'Were you bored?' I asked.

'No!'

'Nor me. How weird!'

'I mean, my mind wandered, but only to good places. It wasn't boredom.'

'Yeah me too!'

We filed out spiritually transformed. I felt cleansed; irrationally happy; excitable; topped-up somehow; lifted.

'That was an enema,' said Andrew.

'It was?'

'An enema for the soul.' And he was right. And an enema

for the palate, and the ears; for all these bits and pieces. And you only realize you need it after you've had it. This was an important moment on my journey so far: it was the first time that listening to classical music had made me feel *intelligent and superior.*

At last!

How Was Bach So Clever as to Be Able to Do This?

I had no idea, so I asked Fiona.

'It's to do with using all those existing forms, which in lesser hands can be merely mathematical or formulaic, with a completely new spiritual and emotional force and freedom (= genius); i.e. everyone else was writing cantatas, concertos, counterpoint, etc. at the time; they all sound like each other, but none sound like Bach. I don't think either you can ignore the scale of his output, the speed he wrote, to the glory of God, etc. Made him all the more miraculous really,' wrote Fiona. And she referred me to a quote from Bach's first biographer: 'He is the river to which all other composers are tributaries.' In other words, Bach was a big genius, and we should just deal with it. There doesn't seem to be any rhyme or reason when it comes to geniuses (or genii if you prefer). They just come along every now and again and rewrite the rules. I was pleased about this, as I way-preferred the new rules. Bach had lifted shit; upped the ante. *Taken it to the bridge.*

Despite the indelible musical facts of the matter, in his lifetime, Bach was no more successful than any of his contemporaries; in fact significantly less so. While Kapell-meister in Coethen, Bach heard that George Frederick Handel (a super-big cheese at the time) was visiting a town about 20 miles away. Bach hurriedly set off to try and meet him to have an important musical chat, but upon arrival Handel professed disdainful indifference at the prospect of a meeting, and wouldn't let him in. And too, for decades, one of Johann Sebastian's sons – Carl Philipp Emanuel – was much more famous than his own father, whose music was considered stuffy and conservative. Counterpoint, fugue and cantata were old hat – moving this shit forward was the new consensus. Johann Sebastian's music only got the recognition it deserved as late as the mid-nineteenth century, after necrophiliac composers Mendelssohn and Schumann belatedly exhumed his life's work, shining a light which has remained illuminated ever since. They also erected this statue in Leipzig:

Andrew and I left the Nikolaikirche still reeling from the *Goldberg Variations*. It was still raining (it's rained everywhere so far), but despite the weather, there was definitely an exhilarating vibe going down in the centre of Leipzig tonight – young and old bantered through storefront-steamed puddles as the ghost of electricity howled in the bones of everyone's face. Ahem. Off the main pedestrianized shopping street we discovered a concrete courtyard with a rickety stage and a young German powerpop band playing original material to hardly anyone. 'Zis next song is for ze kids!' shrieked the bass-playing frontman to three girls holding crimson slush puppies, and Andrew and me. The song was poor, we were getting soaked and the chicks were taken, so we shuffled uptown in the vague direction of the Gewandhaus for the second of tonight's Bachfest performances – the city appeared to be going mad for Bach already, and this was only the second night of the Fest! Glastonbury was rubbish compared to this!

Bach in Bachfest

This chapter is similar to Bach's music, in that it goes round and round and round, chasing its tail, eventually appearing to eat itself at the end, if there ever is an end, that is; which I'm beginning to doubt; this sentence included – it seems to go on for ever – Bach's working methods are obviously getting to me, and not for the first time in this chapter, which seems to be going round and round and round, chasing its tail, eventually appearing to eat itself at the end, if there ever is an end, that is, which I'm definitely beginning to doubt. Oh, no, hang on. It just ended. A proper fugue would carry on like that all night, and you'd be pleased.

The posh brown-carpeted Gewandhaus foyer was rammed with gentlemen in dinner jackets and women in proper dresses and jewellery and guiding hands on their backs, which served as a warning to Andrew's and my innocently wandering eyes. Our places were up in the gods, and as we took our seats I was able to feast my gaze upon a bona-fide concert hall space for the first time in my life. It was pine-coloured and brightly lit and speckled with music stands and stools and eight-wheeled pianos. There was a civilized hubbub of anticipatory muttering. I was sitting in a nice comfy chair, the view was terrific, we forgot to buy a programme so the music was to be a thrilling surprise, and my spiritual colon was newly bleached and shining. I felt primed and impressive.

Where on a G-string?

I wasn't expecting Wagner to be first on the bill at the Bachfest, but what the hell, here he was. I guessed the Wagner was a bit like a support band. Wagner is famous for being mega-German and hyper-bombastic, so I was pleasantly surprised when the piece turned out to be pretty and restrained and quite lovely. With my face I tried to express 'rapture'. Also surprising was the sheer physicality of the sight of a full orchestra in flailing action. At the opera in Rome, the tiny orchestra had been almost out of sight, down in the pit. Here they were on full display; in-yer-face; elbows like pistons, bows lunging at strings, heads bobbing furiously at pianos, the conductor's baton ripping through the air. I was somewhat shaken by this unexpected livewire physiology; in fact I'm embarrassed to admit it, but I went a bit goosebumpy. The energy levels were exactly the same as you'd find at a rock 'n' roll concert. This appeared to be the real thing. Not faking it. Kick out the jams, motherfuckers!

The Wagner finished, and we moved into some Mendelssohn, which meant nothing to me. *Delightful*, I leaned over and whispered to Andrew. But it wasn't as good; it was lots of super-speedy up and down scales, and Andrew became visibly angry.

'Pointless shite,' he muttered, but it was OK. The two pianists had a thrilling, ten-minute 'duel'. They took exhausted, sweat-soaked bows at the end. Next up – finally – was some JSB; and, as if hypnotized, I went into my customary 'Bach trance'. It is strange how this happens almost every time I listen to Bach now; it's as if time's stripped away and all that's left is hazy 'logic plane' – a rigorously metred, incarcerated musical dreamscape, a fascist phonic Narnia. As with Palestrina, there's some alchemical cosmic chicanery going down, and it's *amazing*. I don't know enough (let's be honest – I know next to nothing) about musical theory to be able to explain any of this, but what I do know – from reading boring books about it – are the structural concepts JSB built all this stuff around. These are:

Counterpoint – playing one line of melody, and then playing it again over the top. And again, a bit later. And then again, later still, so that you've now got a big complicated harmony which is actually the same thing, only being played over the top of itself. A classic example of counterpoint would be 'Row, Row Row Your Boat'. Although it is also a *canon*.

Fugue – an out-of-control counterpoint. Take your basic melody, or theme, known as the *exposition*. Then play this over itself at a different pitch, then build on new voices until there are about five all going at once. Then drop a few out, add a new melody – an *entry* – repeat again in a new pitch, and so on and so forth. If it's a particularly clever fugue (i.e. a Bach one) you can further bastardize your exposition by making it overlap with itself (*stretto*), playing it backwards (*retrograde*), playing it upside-down (*inversion*), doubling the length of the notes (*augmentation*), or cutting the length of the notes (*diminution*). It's music as science, to be honest. Only in the hands of a mystic genius such as Bach does it transcend what ought to sound like a geometry A-level, and magically transform itself into a big slab of heart-exploding poetry.

Cantata — enigmatic French footballer whose glory days coincided with Manchester United's dominance of domestic English football in the mid-1990s.

Suite — to keep it short, a suite means an *allemande*, followed by a *courante*, followed by a *sarabande*, ending up on a rousing *gigue*. (If you want, you're OK to add a *bourrée* between the *sarabande* and the *gigue*.)

Partita — after you've mastered the *suite*, the next obvious step is the *partita*. And good luck to you.

Concerto — just some *thing*, OK? Can we just pretend we understand this one please?

Back at the Bachfest, in the Gewandhaus, Andrew had to physically shake me back to my senses after the evening's performance had come to an end. That's how deep my trance had been; it wasn't sleep, it was just a really deep trance.

'A snoring trance?' scoffed Andrew, as we hopscotched rides under posh umbrellas. There was, I reminded him, no need for sarcasm, especially here in Germany. We returned to our hotel as if anaesthetized, and in bed my trance soon picked up from where it had left off.

By the end of 1729, Bach had fallen out with everyone he could find in Leipzig, and prepared himself to move towns once again.

'The authorities care little for my music,' he wrote huffily, to his few remaining friends. But he was an old man now; he had tons of kids; and since these days his music was considered 'turgid', 'pompous', 'obscure' and 'futile' (words taken from a single review – by rival luminary Johann Adolf Scheibe), there was a distinct lack of further offers from alternative institutions. Reluctantly, he eventually chose to stay put in Leipzig, where he worked feverishly at his fiendish keyboard masterpieces *The Well-tempered Klavier* and *The Art of Fugue*, before contracting an eye infection which, having caused much pain and discomfort, eventually killed him on 28 July 1750. A week later, the Leipzig authorities installed a new Cantor, Gottlob Harrer, and the troublesome name of Johann Sebastian Bach was cast into the dustbin of Baroque oblivion for ever.

Or so they thought.

*

Johann Sebastian Bach scores:

Sex: 10. He fathered twenty children. That's some pecker.

Drugs: 0. JSB was as straight as a titanium Roman autobahn.

Rock 'n' roll: 10. Bach's music is the classical equivalent of Krautrock: metronomic, relentless, unceasing, motorik transcendent beauty. The power of the perpetual.

Here's a special 'Bach Edition' of the Ambulance Ratings.

The Art of Fugue by Evgeni Koroliov (Tacet) 🚑🚑🚑🚑🚑

(Piano music. One of the last things Bach wrote before he died. This is the perfect soundtrack to lonesome post-dawn motorway driving with an inspirational hangover through squalls and sudden sunshine. An eerily head-spinning masterpiece that never sounds the same twice. That's the art of fugue, you see? I consider this to be one of the most beautiful and extraordinary things I've ever heard. If you don't like this, you're either stupid or mad.)

The Goldberg Variations by Glenn Gould (Sony Classical) 🚑🚑🚑🚑🚑

(Recorded in 1955 when he was just twenty-two years old, Gould's historic debut recording is exceedingly famous. This tumbling, idiosyncratic interpretation revolutionized the way Bach has subsequently been performed. (Gould had *imposed his personality* upon Bach's music – shock horror!) One minor bugbear is that you can hear Gould tunelessly mumbling to himself as he plays the piano. It's quite offputting, but he plays so excitingly you end up not really minding. Gould was a strange guy – the Bobby Fischer of the piano, you might say.)

The Well-tempered Klavier by Jenö Jandó (Naxos) 🚑🚑🚑🚑

(More piano music. This is like the *Art of Fugue* except slightly more melodic and sleeve-wearingly emotive; therefore not quite as good.)

Suites Nos. 2, 3, 4 & 5 for Solo Cello by Daniil Shafran (The Russian Revelation) 🚑🚑🚑

(You think you like cellos, right? Nick Drake? 'All Apologies'? 'Let's Go Away for a While'? This'll cure you.)

The St John Passion by the Monteverdi Choir (DG) 🚑🚑 🚑🚑

(I have a love/hate thing going with this. It's a bit like anal sex: go slowly; be careful; your enthusiasm disappears pretty quickly; it's lengthy and painful, but you get there in the end. Respect the oboe.)

Violin Sonatas for Solo Violin by Itzhak Perlman (EMI Classics) 🚑🚑🚑🚑

(Sorrowful but moving. Pretty excellent.)

Mass in B Minor by Argenta/Denley/Tucker/Varcoe/Collegium Musicum 90/Hickox (Chandos) 🚑🚑🚑🚑🚑

(At first I thought this was just a Mass in B Minor. But it isn't. It has a depth and resonance lacking elsewhere in Bach's metred, aching world. Forget every other Mass you've read about so far: in fact if you only buy one Mass in B minor this year, make sure it's Bach's one.)

Bach Organ Music Generally by Various Organists (Various Labels) 🚑

(As Bach himself was such an organ virtuoso, this all sounded like it was going to be better than it was. Really boring and one-dimensional. Avoid, unless you're a Goth.)

Brandenberg Concertos by the English Concert (DG) If you're in a good mood this gets: 🚑🚑🚑🚑, but if you're in a bad mood, only: 🚑🚑

(Go and sniff some flowers instead. It's the same kind of vibe.)

The St Matthew Passion by Various Musicians and Singers (Various Labels) 🚑🚑🚑🚑🚑

('Don't forget the St Matthew Passion!' – Fiona.)

The Complete Hanssler Bach Edition (MDC) 💣💣💣💣💣

(This is a 171-CD set of the complete works of Bach. At just £99, that works out at less that 58p per CD, which is almost as cheap as blank CDRs. Why not buy this, and record over it when you get bored? Whatever you choose to do with your *Complete Hanssler Bach Edition* – perhaps even listen to it – it's magnificat value for money.)

6.

Bach was awesome; amazing; dazzlingly diggedy-dawg. I love him, and suspect this love might last for ever (it feels almost like a blood-group thing; genetic disorder; molecular destiny). But – unfortunately for me and my new-found Bach obsession – no one else around at the time sounded anything like it. I'd assumed that the rest of the Baroque would feature further holy elevated mathematics; but it didn't. Instead, your average Baroque consists of swash-buckling purple velvets, deep-sea diving banks of violins, and big sugar-rich melodies – all delivered with prissy, smug instrumental pomposity.

This is George Frederick Handel and Antonio 'Nigel Kennedy' Vivaldi.

Music for Fireworks?

Bach died in 1750, and was buried in St John's cemetery in Leipzig. The funeral was attended by his widow, an old man, his dog and some chickens. Nine years later, in London's Westminster Abbey, Handel's 'private' funeral took place, attended by over 3,000 mourners plus the King and Queen of England.

Would Bach have been bitter?

Yes.

In fact we don't even need to speculate – we know he was bitter. And it wasn't just because Handel had refused to meet with Bach in Germany that time. Bach's priceless gifts to music ultimately resulted in a catastrophic career slump, stress, insults, humiliation and a painful death, whereas Handel revelled in spectacular fame and success; eventually becoming the template for Britain's oft-handy 'assimilation' of talented foreigners. They might not know it, but Lennox Lewis, Zola Budd, even the nation's favourite Greg Rusedski all owe their careers to the trail-blazing naturalization of Georg(e) Friedrich (Frederick) Handel and his timely and opportunistic decision to walk among us.

It certainly worked for George Frederick. Check out these before and after portraits:

Handel in Germany –
humble, meek, bald.

Handel in England – wahey!

Georg was born in the north German town of Halle in 1685 and, like most of these composers, showed an automatic propensity towards music. Georg's father, Georg – a surgeon – was pissed off by this, banning toddler Georg from approaching any further musical instruments (he wanted him to be a lawyer). Little Georg naughtily disobeyed his father by somehow sneaking an *entire clavichord* up to his bedroom in the attic, but he was soon rumbled. Big Georg sat in the pub with his pals and asked for advice on how to deal with his frustratingly euphonious offspring.

'How can I keep my son from getting at harpsichords?' he's quoted to have despaired.

'Cut his fingers off,' was one suggestion.

The table murmured its approval, though Big Georg soon twigged that this might interfere with his law studies.

The situation came to a head at church one Sunday, when the two Georgs were 'accidentally' surrounded by a gang of musical clerics all gabbling at once, tactically befuddling Big Georg into allowing Little Georg to take music lessons alongside his schoolwork. But then one day Big Georg suddenly died. Mourning Little Georg threw together a commemorative poem:

Ah! Heart's sorrow! My dearest father's heart!
Is wrenched from me by cruel death.
Ah! Bitter grief! Ah! Cruel anguish!
Seizes me now that I'm an orphan.

Next day he packed his satchel and hopped on to a horse heading for Berlin to study music full-time. You win some and you lose some, I suppose.

In Berlin, Handel dazzled.

In Hamburg, he shone.

In Florence, he flummoxed. (The world's leading violin player at the time – fellow, yet minor, Baroque composer Arcangelo Corelli – struggled with the complexity of young Georg's overtures. Handel, annoyed, wrenched the violin from Corelli and played the part himself. Corelli still couldn't do it. Handel yelled at him in front of the rest of the guys. Corelli was besmirched.)

In Rome, he enchanted. (The world's leading harpsichord player at the time – fellow, yet minor, composer Domenico Scarlatti – challenged Handel to a public harpsichord 'duel'. It was a draw, so they had an organ duel as a decider. Scarlatti was heavily besmirched.)

In Naples, he was triumphant.

In Venice, he was warmly received and then floated about being seasick.

In Hanover, he was fêted and fawned upon. Noblemen literally collapsed at his feet. Plague was rife.

He landed on the muddy banks of the river Thames halfway through the bitter winter of 1710. A ruffian gobbed on his frock coat.

Handel's Triumphant Arrival in London

Handel had picked up a whole bunch of interesting stuff over the course of his European tour of duty. The German Style, the French Style, the Italian Style (especially the Italian Style) and here he was now, on the shores of the capital of Queen Anne's England, all set to quaff a bracing draught of the English Style.

Unfortunately, there wasn't one. The English Style, not for the first time, consisted of copying the French and Italian Styles (especially the Italian Style). Handel couldn't speak English, so he didn't realize this immediately. Instead, he teamed up with an infamous Swiss émigré opportunist frequently described as 'quite the most ugly man that was ever formed' (or as Henry Fielding dubbed him: 'Count Ugly'),

John Jacob 'Christ!' Heidegger, whose very countenance managed to sort of 'enrapture' Handel throughout his first couple of days in the country. I guess it took his mind off the peasants.

London had been in the musical doldrums since the death of Henry Purcell in 1695.

(Unfortunately I forgot Henry Purcell. Time for a flying factfile. *Name*: Henry Purcell. *Nationality*: English. *Died at*: thirty-six. *Hair*: white/wispy. *Eyes*: rheumy. *Complexion*: pasty/waxy. *Child prodigy/organist/court musician*? Yes/yeah/yup. *Principal work*: *Dido and Aeneas*. *Forgettable work*: *Love's Goddess Sure Was Blind*. *Interesting fact*: nothing. *Ambulance Rating*: 🚑🚑🚑. *Fiona says*: 'A genius'. *How much more room should a composer of Purcell's stature get in a book like this*? Loads, I apologize.)

Thus Handel's arrival threw everybody into a heightened state of excitement and expectation. London's dearth of classical inspiration meant that Italian opera was still the pinnacle of fashion; until Handel's arrival the capital's lords and ladies had been feeding off relative scraps: fourth-rate imported Italian hack musicians churning out shoddy, fourth-rate arias. Everyone was a bit sick of it. But here was the real deal – Handel was proper.

Before he'd even had a chance to unpack, George Frederick was commissioned to write a brand new (Italian Style) opera. Two weeks later he emerged from his room with the score to *Rinaldo*. London was dizzy with anticipation. Everybody filed into the Queen's Theatre (queen included) to watch it. Not only was it supremely splendid, but Handel also put in several headfucky touches; like releasing a flock of sparrows halfway through a scene, as well as a fire-spitting dragon and some 'convincing' thunder and lightning. Well. London rolled over like a wee sozzled puppy. (In fact it *was* sozzled – this was the middle of the gin craze.) From here, Handel could do no wrong on these shores. Treating 'em mean and keeping 'em keen, he sailed back to Hanover, where he was grouchy because he wasn't nearly as famous in Germany as he was in England. In the meantime, London sulked, pined, begged for him to come back.

Handel's Triumphant Return to London

Not only that, but he'd also learned to speak English in the meantime.

'Ja, I am lovink you also!' he waved to the heaving crowds who had gathered to welcome him 'home'. St Paul's Cathedral had just been completed, so he was driven past it especially.

'I am lovink that!'

They paraded him up and down Piccadilly.

'What a hexcellent roat! I am lovink all of these thinks!'

They stuck him in a palace, and he immediately founded the Royal Academy of Music, created expressly for 'Encouragement of Operas'. All right.

Bang! Out tumbled an opera in the Italian Style called *Teseo.*

Oof! Here's another one, name of *Silla.*

Wallop! This one's a cracker: *Amadigi.*

The operas hardly had any plot, but the packed English concert halls didn't care – their appetite for the stuff was insatiable. Next came *Radamisto, Floridante, Ottone, Tamerlano, Serse, Dwayne.* In fact, usually the audience wasn't paying much attention to the performers' laughable attempts at acting anyway; they came to see their favourite celebrity singers (imported especially – at huge cost – from Italy) and sometimes wandered about, chatted and played cards while they waited for him/her to appear. The singers themselves were as unprofessional. They rarely made any attempts to stay in character and gossiped to each other between their parts, sometimes even shouting greetings to friends in the audience. These star performers could get away with almost anything they liked; their behaviour was frequently up there in the J-Lo/Mariah Carey troposphere of chaotic power-delusion. The women were puffed up, iron-lunged hags, hissy fits perhaps to be expected, but the men had better excuses for their brat-like egomania – they'd all had their testicles cut off.

Wave of Mutilation

It was like when bluesman Robert Johnson did that deal with the Devil at the crossroads: you're a young Italian boy with a voice like Aled Jones; your voice moves adults to tears; it's as pure and clean as Tony Blair's conscience. But puberty is approaching. Your balls are ready to drop and your voice about to deepen. You have two options: 1) shrug and accept it. That's life. Move on to something else instead. Aled did all right – he presents *Songs of Praise*; 2) have your testicles cut off.

The consolations of becoming a castrato were numerous: fame, riches (their salaries dwarfed even Handel's), a Premiership footballer's lifestyle, and a voice whose pitch never dipped lower than glass-shattering. The flipside was that you talked like a baby, looked like a weird, barrel-chested, often hairless overgrown baby and threw toys out of prams with baby-esque consistency. You were, in other words, Jimmy Krankie, except real.

The word castrato comes from the Sanskrit word for knife – *sastram* – and the process is first referred to in the Bible – in Deuteronomy, Chapter 23, Verse 1: 'he who hath his privy member cut off shall not enter into the congregation of the Lord' (though it doesn't mention why this might have occurred in the first place). Castration continued into the medieval era as a form of punitive contraception for rapists and thieves (it was also believed to cure hernias and leprosy – whoops, ach well, it was going to happen anyway), later mutating into a form of sexual control – domesticated slavery – the physical results of which were soon harnessed to a brutal though musically astonishing phenomenon that continued for over 200 years. The church began to recognize the potential in eunuchs' voices as early as the twelfth century, the beginning of their musical rise to the heights of the Roman Catholic liturgy. Eventually they became embraced, encouraged and celebrated by music lovers everywhere, except for Belgium, where they all looked like that in the first place, and still do.

The optimum age for this procedure would usually be eight or nine, and your odds of surviving the operation lay between 10 and 80 per cent, which doesn't really narrow it down enough. Despite its popularity throughout the Baroque period, castration of your offspring remained officially punishable by death, so parents were forced to make up elaborate stories explaining how their sons had lost their nuts. The most popular excuses were getting kicked by a horse, or bitten by a dog or a wild boar or whatever might be ferocious in the vicinity. In reality you got your nads cut off on the quiet, in a barber's shop, or occasionally at the dentist's – a swift incision to the groin followed by a slice through the spermatic cord and severance of the testicles. Afterwards, your wound would be soothed by dunking the damage in a bowl of milk. If you hadn't bled to death yet, your body was about to be transformed; the physical symptoms of castrati included a total lack of facial and bodily hair, no Adam's apple, a small and underdeveloped penis, breast growth and a tendency to be unnaturally tall and obese. There was, thank God, a *yin* to all this *yang* – their voices were now unique, halfway between a child's and a woman's, and because of their large, rounded chests, this enabled additional blitzkrieg lungpower and bloodcurdling sustain. A proper seventeenth- or eighteenth-century castrato would have made Aled's legendary rendition of 'The Snowman' sound like Lemmy with laryngitis; the sound that came out of their mouths was breathtakingly sublime: *Never Mind the Bollocks*, you're damn right.

By the early nineteenth century, castrati were in terminal decline, although the practice wasn't actually banned until 1870 – by which time the public's appetite for the procedure had waned considerably. Castrati had become demonized; their neither/nor sexual activities were getting the blame for all kinds of physical and moral degeneracy; and they soon found themselves extinct but for a few remaining specimens in the Sistine Chapel choir. And, since their subsequent demise (the world's last ever castrato, Alessandro Moreschi, died in 1922), the only people alive today to have experienced a sound anything like it are fans of Rush, and Yes. Only a few ghostly recordings of genuine castrati remain, preserved on old faded phonograms. These voices are eerie – desperately sad – they seem to be wailing away at us from beyond the grave, reminding us of old castrato Parini's pained and rueful stanzas:

> I despise to see on stage
> An elephantine singer
> Who barely drags himself about
> On fleshy swollen legs
> Emitting from his big wide mouth
> A thin, and tiny voice.

Moreover:

> Ah, may he perish,
> That father who, first,
> Armed with his knife,
> Attempted the loathsome
> Cruel deed that crippled
> His suffering son.

Throughout Handel's pan-European reign of the mid-eighteenth century, the castrati were at the height of their powers, the stars of the show; and pragmatic Handel, now straining to put bums on seats for his never-ending flood of Italian Style operas, stuffed his new compositions with their disembodied presence. His favourite was Senesino – a celebrated pig-faced castrato from Italy who could hold a note for over a minute (he'd have a 'breath competition' with a flautist or oboe player and always win), and was regularly voted 'the greatest man who ever lived' by excitable London concert-goers. It wasn't too long, then, until Senesino began to believe his own hype; and his salary demands and primadonna behaviour got progressively worse until he was inevitably fired from the production or it closed prematurely. After this, stroppy Handel and self-obsessed Senesino (plus the just-as-bad celebrity sopranos) had to tediously renegotiate their contracts for the next one. Handel's opera company stumbled along like this for months, losing money with each performance. But when Senesino's arch rival castrato Farinelli (the most famous castrato of all time; there was even a film about him in 1994 – *Farinelli* – only I watched it the other day, and it's rubbish) arrived in town – hired by a new, rival theatre company with the Prince of Wales as its patron – things began to get out of hand. Audiences, now spoilt for choice, started to mock Handel from the stalls. Farinelli, it was said, could hold a note for over *two* minutes. He twittered just like a real bird! Compared to all this new foreign talent, Handel was old hat, churning out the same old slop opera (forty so far, including lots of self-plagiarizing); he'd run out of ideas. Things soon got so bad that he found himself teetering on the very brink of bankruptcy. It was, he decided, time to ditch the castrati. In fact, sod it, it was time to ditch opera altogether – if zees insultink Londoners are zo hunimpressed, let zem stew in zer own mizerable juices! Achtung!

Handel waddled miserably back to his modest abode in Brook Street, and began to plot his revenge.

Inside Handel House

London, England, August 2004

Handel's house at 25 Brook Street is next door to the house where Jimi Hendrix lived a few years later. How amazing, I thought, as I stood squinting at the pair of blue plaques on a roasting summer afternoon, that both musical visionaries should have lived in adjoining houses like this, as well as sharing an uncannily similar taste in jackets. Handel bought the property as part of a brand new townhouse development in 1723, and these days the upper floors are a small museum dedicated to the composer's life and work. Handel House's entrance is in a yuppified courtyard around the back; one ducks inside to be confronted by a chrome box-like area with a hi-tech admissions desk and banks of TV screens and unintelligible electronic security measures. This futuristic Fort Knox was sufficient disincentive for any thoughts I'd previously harboured of desecrating the maestro's gaff. I handed over my £4.50, glumly pocketed my security-encoded admissions ticket and was ushered into an impregnable steel lift. As well as taking no risks with his legacy *whatsoever*, Handel's trustees had also been watching way too much *Crystal Maze*.

Up on the top floor, I was shown into a small anteroom with two elderly ladies and a plasma screen looping an MTV-style overview of George's apparently terrifying cultural influence. You realize they're trying a bit too hard with this when one of the clips shows some classical musicians playing Handel in a heaving club full of ravers. 'An amazing night!' says somebody meant to look fashionable. 'The clubbers were totally mad for it!' Then it cuts to prolonged slo-mo shots of David Beckham, because television's Champions League music is actually Handel's coronation anthem 'Zadok the Priest', except they changed the words to the entente-idiotique: 'We are the champions / wir sind die Besten (*tr*.: 'we are the champions' in German) / nous sommes les meilleurs (*tr*.: 'we are the champions' in French) / the champions!' (or, as I'd always misheard it, 'lasagne!'). The two elderly American ladies sitting watching with me weren't impressed with this at all.

'Isn't this soccer?'

'*Soccer?*'

'Why would they be showing soccer, I mean I don't know . . .'

'*Soccer?*'

I turned to smile in sympathy but they were grimacing at Becks' looped goal celebrations with squinty sour faces. They rose and hobbled through to the next room. I sat quietly for a moment and then followed them. This was Handel's old dressing chamber.

'Handel's servant would have dressed him in here every morning,' offered a grey-haired man with a clipboard and name badge. It seemed that each room had its own separate tour guide.

'Every morning?' asked one of the American ladies.

'Yes.'

'In this room here?'

'Yes.'

The next room was Handel's old bedroom. It was small and box-like, like all the rooms. The bedroom tour guide hovered with his clipboard.

'Is that his actual bed?' asked an American lady.

'No, it's a reconstruction as to how his bed might have looked.'

We looked at the bed.

'Would you like any more information about Handel's bedroom?'

'No thank you.'

The three of us descended to the floor below. This room – Handel's living room – was slightly bigger, and there was a harpsichord in it, being played by a young man with short black hair and an ironed white shirt. A lady in a flowery dress stood beside him, singing along enthusiastically. When they had finished, one of the American ladies asked: 'Excuse me. Is that Handel you're playing?'

'No,' the man replied. 'It's my own composition.' It had, however, sounded suspiciously Handel-like, though maybe

I was fooled because we were in his house. The living-room tour guide said, 'The Handel House Trust proudly maintains this building as a working music centre. We encourage people to come and rehearse here – to keep the music alive.' He paused. 'Handel would have wanted it that way.'

We nodded sombrely.

'Is that Handel's actual harpsichord?' asked one of the ladies.

'No, but it would have looked very similar.'

We smiled at the musicians, and they began a new song. We stood and listened, slightly embarrassed. The American ladies left almost straight away, but I sat on a window sill and contemplated some things, like I thought would be respectful. Portraits of various castrati and Count Ugly lined the pale grey, wood-panelled walls. I took out my notebook and jotted down some profundities. The room guide sidled over and mock-whispered: 'I hope you're not giving them a bad review!'

'Er, no, it's a good review!' I whispered back.

The guide nodded and smiled and tried to look. I had written 'BAROQUE BREEZE' at the top of the page in capital letters. I decided to leave the room also.

As soon as I entered the next room I knew something was up: cosmic waves burst through the ether like a psychedelic tsunami, knocking me on to my back like an impatient whore. Because, you see, I was now in the room in which Handel wrote one of the most famous pieces of music of all time, ever, in the whole history of the world. It's the music with which Handel wreaked his unholy revenge upon the fickle flocks of feeble-minded folk who'd written him off as that sad, fat old operatic has-been obsessed with chaps who'd had their spermatozoa disconnected:

Messiah

Legend has it that during *Messiah*'s fevered, 24-day-long composition, Handel was so overtaken by emotion that he forgot to eat, drink, sleep or even go to the toilet. He was so caught up in sonic/religious fervour that he wept over the score as he scribbled. Even today, if you visit the British Museum, you can still see his inky tear-smudges on the faded manuscript. The story goes that, when he'd finished, he flung open his door and cried out to his manservant: 'I think I did see all heaven before me, and the great God himself!'

'Mug of cider, Mr Handel, sir?'

'Get out of my way! I'm off to St Paul's, or somewhere, at once!' replied Handel, forgetting to add his comedy German accent.

Messiah wasn't an opera, it was an *oratorio*, which is similar to opera, only it's unplugged. There's no acting, or plot as such (*Messiah* was a vague celebration of the story of Jesus – and written in English so everyone could understand the words at last); the singers all stand on stage and sing their lines or choruses as and when necessary. So you had all the power and range of operatic music, except it was shaped and compressed and honed into something way more ebullient and intense; plus there was no fannying about with over-elaborate sets, or singers unable to act, or actors who couldn't sing. The music was all there right in front of you – for maximum gut-wobbling effect. And don't forget religious effect too.

Messiah premièred in London in 1743 – in front of the King of England himself. It was an unprecedented triumph. George II, rapt throughout, was so overcome by the concluding 'Hallelujah Chorus' that he rose to his feet in spellbound awe. Royal protocol demanded that everybody present follow suit, so the rest of the audience in the hall stood with him – a tradition that survives today. *Messiah*'s success reversed Handel's fortunes; not only did it save him from bankruptcy and early retirement, it also cemented his popularity on London stages until his death in 1759. He went on to conduct his masterpiece over thirty times, much of its vast revenue going to the many charities he supported, including London's foundling hospital. Indeed, as one of his many biographers once noted, 'Perhaps the works of no other composer have so largely contributed to the relief of human suffering.' Thus the spiritual *and* material consequence of Handel's greatest work has been enough to propel it close to the absolute pinnacle of all the Great Works. I have, of course, listened to *Messiah* many times myself now, and I like it a lot. It's very, sort of, widescreen technicolor cinemascopey. But it does go on a bit – over two whole discs – and a lot of it's rather samey. Like the Beatles' *White Album*, I reckon it would be more effective edited down into a single album's worth of songs. *The Very Best of Messiah*, or something like that, would be perfect.

Many consider Handel to be one of if not the greatest composers of all. He certainly mastered – defined really – the spirit of the Baroque: all gorgeous emotion-soaked melodies and elegant operatic flair. I still prefer Bach, though: his music's lean as a butcher's dog, whereas Handel's podgy mutt's swallowed a tray too many of *Terry's All Gold*. Beethoven said about George Frederick, simply: 'Handel is the greatest composer that ever lived ... I would uncover my head and kneel down upon his tomb.'

So here's a photo of the tomb (which is in Westminster

Abbey), in case you want to kneel down before it yourself. Don't forget to uncover your head and bring a few cushions.

This is probably enough pictures of tombs for the time being.

The Red Priest

Antonio Vivaldi (Italian; red hair; a priest) is probably the composer whose music we hear more than any other over the course of our day-to-day lives: whenever we're on hold. This tooth-grating ubiquity is down to two things: The *Four Seasons* and Nigel 'The Ghost of Jimi Hendrix' Kennedy.

The *Four Seasons* is a violin concerto that history's spun disproportionately out of its orbit. Over the course of his life, Vivaldi wrote over 500 of these concertos (it's often said that he wrote the same one 500 times), and none of them really had much of a tune. They were all these über-Baroque, scudding, thudding sewing-machine music things that never went anywhere except vivaciously towards the horizon. We could merrily toss Antonio Vivaldi (from

Venice; sickly; taught music at a girls' school) on to the scrapheap of history were it not for the *Four Seasons*, which is astonishing within the context of the rest of Vivaldi's œuvre in that it a) has a tune, b) then has another tune, and c) keeps on having more and more tunes until the end, by which time you're feeling rather peeved, since you only phoned to check their opening hours and now you've been sitting listening to this for twenty sodding minutes.

It's more than likely that the smokin' violin you're listening to down the telephone line is being stoked by sizzlin' Nigel Kennedy, as he's recorded the *Four Seasons* more times than any other violinist.* In fact, Nigel Kennedy's 1989 recording of the piece remains the biggest-selling classical music album in the UK, ever. Kennedy, a child prodigy from Sussex, was taught by the incomparable Yehudi Menuhin (who also paid young Nigel's tuition fees) before graduating to New York's famous Juilliard Music School, soon whereafter he became a famous cool punk violin maestro and went out with Brix Smith from the Fall. Apart from playing the violin well, Nigel's career has been based around upsetting the establishment applecart: dissing duffers and trying to make classical music 'cool'. Nigel attempted to do this by speaking in a cockney accent, having spiky hair, swearing and saying that he liked football. Amazingly, it worked, and maverick Nigel – *enraging* classical purists – became classical music's first 'pop star'. For a while, until everyone realized that it was a stupid idea. But by then he was famous anyway, so ha ha ha.

Sadly, Nigel is too busy touring and stuff to contribute to this book. I must have sent about twenty ungracious, begging, pleading emails to his manager for just a brief audience,

* Possibly.

but the reply was always the same: Nige is busy. Leave us alone. And even if Nige isn't busy, leave us alone. So instead of an illuminative personal tryst with the great man, I have trawled through a pile of old interviews and distilled the key points from each. Nigel's basic tenets are as follows:

'Wicked! I'm just a fiddler, yeah? Vivaldi, mental mother-fucker! Don't talk to me about Hendrix – fuckin' mental, wicked! I love the Villa. I'm just a geezer, awright? Knees up Mother Brown. Shut yer face, you old git, I like Hendrix, not your old bollocks! Fackin' 'ell, you fackin' cant, fack off. Nah, not really, wicked geezer. Take me seriously. Oi.'

Then we had Vanessa Mae, whose management I also badgered, whose management and PR ignored my badgering. Vanessa's the same as Nigel, except she plays an electric violin and has a wind machine blow up the hem of her skimpy dress in her videos.

Instead of hanging with Nige, I thought an interesting experiment might be to go out on to the pavements of London to take the pulse of the man and woman in the street by playing them some Nigel Kennedy playing Vivaldi's *Four Seasons* on a ghetto blaster. Do we still call them ghetto blasters? Owen agreed to come and help out.

Dancing in the Street

We positioned ourselves outside John Lewis department store on London's Oxford Street. It was grey and damp. I held a clipboard self-importantly, while Owen got to grips with the ghetto blaster's complicated control panel ('play', 'rewind' and 'stop', the great dullard). The plan was to stop people at random and play them some *Four Seasons* (specifically, the beginning of 'Spring'), then ask if they recognized the piece, the composer, the performer, whether they liked it or not, and, finally, whether or not they considered it 'cool'. Getting people to stop initially proved quite difficult. 'Excuse me, madam, do you mind if we play you some classical music and then ask you a few questions about it afterwards?' didn't work. It was too much of a mouthful – I only managed to get out 'Excuse me' and a sickly smile before being shouldered into a plate glass window. After some experimentation, the best pitch proved to be: 'Music survey, thirty seconds!' and then a manic grin while standing directly in front of them as Owen pressed play.

The first person to stop was a middle-aged lady wearing a red coat. Owen boxed her in, pressed play and eventually some music came out. Very loudly.

'Oooh,' said the lady in red, irritably.

'Turn it down, for God's sake,' I said to Owen. He turned it up, and then off, and then fiddled around while the lady wriggled out of our grasp.

'Oh, well done.'

'Sorry, it's fiddly. I can't quite get . . .'

The next person to stop was a young lady called Vivienne. She listened to the music with a blissful smile on her face. Owen pressed stop.

'Do you know what that was?' I asked her.

'No, but I know the composer. Mozart.'

'No, it's Vivaldi. Can you guess who's playing it?'

'No.' Still she smiled, waiting for the punchline. It never came.

'It's Nigel Kennedy. Do you like it?'

'No.'

'*No?*'

She continued to smile.

'So you don't think it's cool?'

'Cool?'

We decided to let Vivienne go. Next were an old couple – John and Beryl – they were very friendly. 'Vivaldi's *Four Seasons*,' they chorused together.

'Right! Performer?'

'Probably Nigel Kennedy.'

'Correct. Is it cool?'

'Oh yes!'

That was very jolly. Altogether, over the course of about two hours, we stopped fifty people. On the nose. The scores broke down like this: 44 per cent knew the name of the piece, or guessed the name of the piece. 34 per cent knew the composer (12 per cent said Mozart; 8 per cent said Beethoven; 6 per cent said Bach; 2 per cent said Oasis, though we weren't sure he was listening properly); 16 per cent knew the performer; 72 per cent said they liked it – 72 per cent!

Other comments upon being asked whether they liked it or not included:

Sue: 'I absolutely love all classical music.'

Alistair: 'I am indifferent to what it is you just played.'

Fatima: 'I like music, that is all.'

Roy: 'I don't know, I am not from around here.'

Roger: 'Can't you play some garage?'

Middle-aged lady with toy dog: 'I don't know anything. I'm pissed.'

Mark: 'I'm a music consultant and I'd never use it.' Which was enigmatic, whatever it means.

14 per cent said they thought it was cool (and John and Beryl account for 4 per cent of those).

The moral of the story is that people do like Vivaldi's *Four Seasons*, but they don't think it's very cool. Nor do they think Nigel is very cool either.

Some weeks later, I went to see Kennedy's 'Vivaldi Experience' show at London's Barbican. Overall, I thought he was excellent, except he talked too much between the tracks, and kept thumping his chest to show how 'down' with the audience he was, an audience that was no different to any other classical music audience, so far as I could tell, although there might have been a few more young people there than usual – nicely brought-up young people, not the usual kind. Nigel laughed loudly at his own jokes, of which there were many.

'This one's a right motherfucker!' he exclaimed before going into a Bach piece. 'Oops, they told me not to swear. Oh bugger! Oops, oh, no, I've done it again!' And so on. I must say, though, when he keeps his mouth shut and plays the violin, it's like nothing I've heard before. This amazing, flaming sound comes out and sucks away all the oxygen from the room. It was awe-inspiring – Nige certainly kicks out them jams, mmm-hmm; I was rapt and sweaty throughout. Except during the encore of Jimi Hendrix's 'Purple Haze', where he wandered through the audience for ten minutes, giving people high-fives and thumping his chest again while he played. I think this was to show what a man of the people he was. Which he is, I suppose, in a way. He's a cheeky one. Cheeky hair!

The office of Vanessa Mae remain tight-lipped about everything.

*

George Frederick Handel scores:

Sex: a cheeky 7. Raw lust appears not to have been a part of George's life at all. So why the high score? I've deduced that Handel was gay, and got plenty from those castrati.

Drugs: 6. Not only was he a chronic boozer, but Handel's 'trance' throughout the composition of *Messiah* was quite possibly narcotic-fuelled.

Rock 'n' roll: 7. All that ego, the desperation for public love, all those wigs – Handel was an obvious prototype for Elton John. They look pretty similar too.

Antonio Vivaldi scores:

Sex: 7. The Red Priest, eh? In a girls' school?

Drugs: 3. His music sounds particularly good while *on* drugs.

Rock 'n' roll: 7. It's just so speedy.

Nigel Kennedy scores:

Sex: 2. Personally I don't find him particularly attractive.

Drugs: 7. Though I am aware of this country's quite strict libel laws.

Rock 'n' roll: 7. I suppose you have to give him this. Reluctantly.

Seb suggests:

Handel: *Messiah* by the Choir of King's College, Cambridge and Sir David Willcocks (HMV Classics) 🚚🚚🚚

(The full monty over two mega-discs. Definitive yet tiresome.)

Handel: *Messiah: Arias and Choruses* by the London Symphony Orchestra and Sir Adrian Boult (Decca) 🚚🚚🚚 🚚🚚

(This is more like it. All the good bits – all killer, no filler. Cheap too! Buy it or deny it.)

Handel: *The World of Handel* by Various Artists (Decca) 🚚🚚🚚🚚

(I picked this up in a charity shop in Winchester for 25p. It's got all the pre-*Messiah* classics: 'Arrival of the

Queen of Sheba', 'Water Music', 'Zadok the Priest' and a hidden bonus track: 'He Gave Them Hailstones'. This album is generally kicking.)

Vivaldi: *Vivaldi* by Nigel Kennedy and the Berlin Philharmoniker (EMI Classics) 🚐🚐🚐🚐

(This is Nige's latest – 2003 – recording of the *Four Seasons* plus some other shit to make the CD better value for money. Cool or uncool – I think his *Four Seasons* is wicked, geezer, and I like big Nige too, I just can't help it. Oi.)

Purcell: *Essential Purcell* by The King's Consort and Robert King (Hyperion) 🚐🚐🚐

(Guilty conscience.)

7. Tiddly Om Pom PROM

Fiona emailed, casually asking whether or not I'd sorted out my season ticket for the Proms yet. I replied that not only had I not done this, no, but that I also didn't even know what the Proms were, except that there was a Last Night of them. The idea that there might have been Previous Nights filled me with dread and horror.

'If you want to get to the bottom of classical music, you'll definitely need to go to some Proms,' Fiona wrote back. 'They're incredibly important.'

'How many, do you think?' I was holding out for maybe one – or two at a push.

'Well, if you can't afford a season ticket, then I should say ten, at the very least.'

Was this a fucking joke or what?

London, England, the whole bloody summer, 2004

What's the very worst thing you can do at the Proms? Eat crisps? Browse your ringtones? Bray like a donkey? (Last Night only, sorry.) Heckle? Throw up?

All bad, but none are right. I've lifted the following from a genuine post on the BBC Proms internet messageboard (and this is just one of many):

I'm disgusted by the behaviour of far too many people in the hall. We've had the talkers, the eaters and drinkers, the fidgeters, the mobile phone users, the camera flashers (thank the Lord they didn't flash anything else), the coughers (who should be put out of their misery),* and then, to add insult to injury, we've also had the inevitable *clapping between the movements*.

Clapping between the movements is far and away the worst thing you can possibly do at a Prom. And I nearly did it. Fear plus pack instinct pulled me back the split-second before my palms came together. Clapping between the movements isn't only irritating, it's also *stupid, childish, irresponsible, discourteous* and further adjectives familiar from the letters page of the *Daily Telegraph*. This year, unruly clappers have become such a problem that there's been some serious lobbying of the BBC to include a banning order in next year's Proms Guide. There have been pleading articles in newspapers, letters and telephone calls to magazines and radio stations, even face-to-face begging during the interval – but still the dirty applause continues. The most popular solution is to install a set of 'traffic lights' in the auditorium: red light means don't clap, green light means OK, go on – now it's time to clap. I'm not making this up.

Apparently one ought not to clap between the movements because it upsets the musicians (it must be devastating), detracts from the momentum of the piece, and interrupts one's reverie. It's easy to do, though: the music stops; the musicians briefly down their instruments; there's a tangible release of tension. There's coughing. Shuffles. Wind is broken. I liked it – I want to clap! Can I? *No*. If you do, somebody will post a message about it on the Proms website. They'll have your seat number and everything. It's possible that someone might then post dog poo through your letterbox.

* Yes, the author appears to be advocating *killing* those who cough.

This year (2004) was the Proms' 110th. Featuring seventy-four concerts; one every night (actually, sometimes two), it ran from 16 July until 11 September: this is the biggest, longest and most civilized music festival in the world. The original idea was the brainchild of two men: Robert Newman, manager of London's Queen's Hall, and Henry Wood, conductor, organist, energetic polymath. These two men got together in the spring of 1894, sharing a philanthropic desire to foist classical music on to the ignorant lower classes. Their masterplan was to wean us on the more easily digestible standards first, gradually upping the ante to include more complicated and obscure works, eventually arriving at something utterly terrifying – say, John Dowland's lute outtakes, or Anton Bruckner.

'Mr Robert Newman's Promenade Concerts' opened in the summer of the following year; the shows lasted upwards of three hours and tickets cost 5p. They played Wagner on Mondays and Beethoven on Fridays. So long as you stood, you could eat, drink, smoke, spit, fight, do whatever you wanted (even clap) – except, strangely though expressly, strike matches during the singing bits. They were an immediate success. Commoners flocked to the Queen's Hall and took their medicine with humble tugs of the forelock and buckets of grog. These Promenade Concerts continued uninterrupted for forty-six years; even the First World War didn't get in the way (though German music went unrepresented for the duration – *ah!* fallow years). Halfway through their forty-seventh season, however, the Proms were dealt a serious blow in the shape of a large bomb dropped from a German Stuka, obliterating the Queen's Hall. So everything was taken a few hundred yards up the road to the bottom of Kensington Gardens and London's famous Royal Albert Hall, where the festival has remained ever since (except that now there's a Prom in the Park too; and occasionally some small ones in the Victoria and Albert Museum; oh and one in Birmingham too, I think). And Radio 3 broadcasts *every single one*, live. Now that's what I call public service broadcasting. Or cruelty. Or something.

Henry Wood died in 1944, and ever since, his bust has sat in the Royal Albert Hall on a wee pillar above the orchestra; his avuncular, lightly bearded presence has overlooked every Prom that's been performed here. When I showed up for my first Prom I was unaware of this; I thought the conductor had put it there as a kind of good luck charm. It was only when I noticed it on my second Prom, then my third, fourth, fifth and onward towards infinity that I plucked up the courage to ask somebody who this stately bronze head was supposed to represent. The sweat-stinking man with a shock of receding hair, thick glasses and a yellowing t-shirt looked at me like I was insane.

'That's Henry Wood!'

'Right.' I wrote it down.

'The incomparable Henry Wood!'

I had heard him the first time. He stood staring at me with wide eyes, so I walked away. But then came back again because I didn't want to lose my place in the queue.

Ah, the Proms queue! Oh, the Proms queue in the balmy summer of 2004 – the rainiest summer in Britain for more than fifty years! What memories!

Why queue? Because if you queue you can get in for £4. No matter who's playing, no matter how big and famous, no matter how sold-out the expensive boxes, balconies and seats might be, if you're prepared to go and stand in line and wait, you'll get into the arena – the large open space with the fountain (why?) in the middle of the hall – where you can either stand up, sit cross-legged on the floor, or even lie down like a weirdo (I have accidentally stepped on a number of these people; they have all been extremely forgiving – at least after they've been shushed for yelping), and all for under a fiver. It's a textbook slice of socialism as well as being firmly, fantastically British: of all the venerated lore and tradition involved in the festival, the most fiercely guarded thing of all is the holy sanctity of the Proms queue. Especially if it's absolutely pissing it down with rain. It's an extremely moving sight – and all for the dubious privilege of having to stand for up to three hours at a stretch. You think that sounds easy? Here's another tip from the BBC Proms messageboard:

I often stand at public events to maintain my Promming abilities. I like to stand when watching television, much to the annoyance of my family. I've taken to beginning my training for the Proms by standing in front of the television when I watch the tennis from Wimbledon. A five-set match is quite good preparation.

Hey, you can get a seat in the upper circle for under a tenner.

Everyone in the Proms queue is always either embarrassingly friendly or a weird social misfit with cagoule and rucksack, nose deep in the *Guardian* editorial. But enough about me. The friendly ones come bounding up behind you and always want to chat, and unfortunately one of the things they always want to chat about is tonight's concert.

Them: I'm *so* excited at the prospect of seeing Deborah Voight getting to grips with *Tristan and Isolde*, I can barely restrain myself . . . ! Aren't you?

Me: Oh yes!

Them: But do you really think the Royal Phil have enough intrinsic sonority for fundamental delicacies of the task at hand?

Me: I'd say, erm . . . yes!

Them: You *would*?

Me: Oh yes!

They can smell blood. Next they ask a clever 'tiebreaker', designed to get me to say something other than the Churchill Insurance dog's catchphrase, and then listen in contemptuous disgust to my pained, stuttering reply. They turn to the person queuing behind them, and are best friends within thirty seconds. We exchange no further words. I bury my nose back in the *Guardian* editorial, listening bitterly – shamefully – to their jovial and enlightened banter.

Four hours later, and the time is approaching for us to begin to contemplate actual entry to the world famous Royal Albert Hall. Two lines of people snake down either side of the steps that lead down from the hall to Prince Consort Road; on one side are the season ticket holders and on the other the day trippers – the (sometimes even) normal people. The season ticket holders are a malignant mixture of obsessives: either hardcore music obsessives or obsessive-compulsive freakoid nutjobs. You see, there's a small but dedicated band of these people who make it their religious duty to attend every single Prom of the season. (I hardly need mention that they do this every year – how could it be otherwise?) They stand in exactly the same spot; every night for the whole two months; come rain or come shine; come Shostakovich, Stockhausen or Sprechgesang.*

But even ideologically bleached terrain such as this comes with its own set of schisms, the most pressing being: must one attend the *Blue Peter* Prom to complete one's set? Every year now, there's a special children's Prom under the aegis of the classic kids' TV show: the hall is full of kids and the

* My own little in-joke for classical lovers there. I think.

show's presenters introduce music from the Harry Potter films and lark about, shouting. This a real dilemma for the obsessive-compulsive season ticket holders: *does this one count as a real Prom?* So if one day you happen to be slumped in front of your television watching *Blue Peter at the Proms* and you see – amid the thousands of kids loaded on tartrazine – a row or two of wild-haired, bespectacled adults standing doggedly in the front row, grimacing; they're really no danger to your offspring: they're just over-competitive Prommers going for their full house. I got talking to a few of them in passing, and some have been to every Prom (give or take the odd bout of pneumonia) since the late *sixties*.

For my own Proms debut, I ignored the queue's rich folklore and decided to pay a bit more to sit in a chair. I planned to ease myself in; didn't want to run before I could walk; needed to get my head around this place before I worked my way up to standing rigidly upright for three whole hours without eating a single crisp. I was with my friend Rodney, a proper classical music lover, whose attitude towards my project so far has been one of courteous but wary distrust. Rodney was wearing a blazer – he's a bit older than me, and posh. I'd been told I didn't need to dress up for tonight, so I was feeling a bit underdressed what with the blazer. We were here to see a bit of Janáček and some Mahler, and Rodney was particularly looking forward to the Mahler.

'I *love* Mahler,' he said as we stood in the bar before the show, sipping chilled glasses of champagne. The evening seemed to be going all right so far. His blazer had big shiny gold buttons.

'I don't know anything about Mahler. I only know up to Vivaldi.'

Rodney quaffed some more champers. 'Oh you'll *love* Mahler. He's divine.'

Our seats were in the choir, which is up behind the stage, and is a cool place to sit because you get a great view of the conductor's facial contortions. We sat facing out into the hall. The hall gazed back. Looking around the vast circular auditorium, suddenly I didn't feel so bad about the fact that I didn't have a blazer; most people were dressed down – many were in just jeans and t-shirts; holy cow, people appeared to have just showed up and paid to sit and listen to this! It felt like I'd learned a lesson already – that ordinary people came to the Proms *because they wanted to*. Madness!

The Janáček was zippy and pugnacious: a large choir accompanied the giant orchestra in rousing Czech. I gazed down at the long line of combed-over bald spots and absorbed their incantation, trying to ignore the diseased smatterings of applause between the movements. In the interval Rodney told me what his favourite Mahler symphonies were: the First, the Fifth, and the Ninth. We went back in and watched the Seventh. It was long and loud. I zoned in and out, cursing my still-meagre powers of concentration (though this has been improving recently).

'That was lovely; though not a patch on the Ninth,' said Rodney afterwards, as we strolled back down towards South Kensington tube station. 'But superior to the Second.'

'What about the Third?'

'Oh, the Third's marvellous.'

'How about the Sixth?'

'Ah, the *Sixth*.'

'Do you like the Eighth?'

'The *Eighth*.'

I found this line of questioning amusing – I don't know why. But it also illustrated a natural flaw in being a classical novice – no matter how many times I attended these things, everything was always going to be new. There'd be minimal recognition, no sparks of familiarity (unless I was lucky). And, though hearing great music for the very first time is always an enjoyable and profound experience, it saddened me that I wasn't going to be able to get emotionally deeper into the music than initial impressions and reactions.

So that was that. The end of the evening – my first Prom – my cherry had been popped. There'd been no great shakes, no sociological mysticism. It was kind of underwhelming, to be honest. It was just a concert. A good concert in a big gilded bowl full of people who prefer classical music to popular music. A difficult sentence for me to write and face up to, that one.

My second Prom was the same sort of trip; this time it was Bach's *Mass in B Minor*. It was really good, plus I knew it pretty well already. My third was Stravinsky: I can't deny – it was brilliant. Fourth: Dvořák, Schumann and Chopin. What can I say? I enjoyed myself thoroughly. And not once – during any of this – did anybody make me feel like an outsider; despite my long hair and unsavoury aroma, the Proms crowd appeared to be utterly inclusive. For my fifth Prom I was determined to try and provoke a reaction – push at the edges a little. Is the Proms crowd really a non-judgemental oasis of democratic musical aestheticism and niceness?

Dammit, yes. Even though I wore pigtails and a Black Sabbath t-shirt, nobody even raised an eyebrow. I couldn't believe it. I stood there, alone in the main downstairs bar, surrounded by middle-class classical music fans decked out in Hackett and St Michael, drinking a bottle of beer as thuggishly as I could manage, but nobody even gave me a second look. I was crestfallen. I tried to burp but hiccupped messily instead.

'Bless you,' said a passing concert-goer.

'. . . no, that was a burp . . . !'

But everyone was nice.

Prommers

Prommers are different. I think they should be banned. These are the fearsome spanners who head up every queue, every night. They act like the whole Proms circus exists purely to indulge their own ritualistic elitist japery; their own special party with their own special rules. Once they're inside and in place, in their own demarcated personal space right at the front of the standing arena (that you'd better not go anywhere near – don't even look over there; it might seem like just a Tupperware box sitting on the floor but it's my own Special Marker), they prepare themselves for their 'thing' – this heinous synchronized chanting which they – and a few other sad sacks – find so hilarious. For example: 'Arena to orchestra,' the prissy huddle collectively yawp right before the lights go down. Sadly, everyone hushes in cod-rapt anticipation. 'Bienvenue à la Royal Albert Hall pour votre premier Prom!' (It's a Swiss orchestra, geddit? They always 'greet' any visiting orchestra in their native tongue – even, tragically, Australians.) The orchestra has to, sort of, play along with this, and smile and say, yes, very good, yes, thanks for that, you *dickheads*. (I am speculating as to their exact thoughts.)

Or, as when some poor sod coughs: 'Arena to woman with cough,' they chorus. 'Please take it outside!'

Or, if you've committed the ultimate sin and clapped between a movement: 'Arena to man with clap. Keep it to yourself!'

While stagehands are busy moving stuff around before the show, the Prommers shout 'Heave-ho!' at the shifting of the piano. Brilliant. Some guy comes out holding a bassoon. One, two, three: 'Is that thing loaded?!' they cry. Perhaps their finest moment – the nightly comic pinnacle – is their ironic round of applause after the orchestra leader hits a single note on the piano for the rest of the musicians to tune to. They do all this every night. There really is no beginning to the astonishing heights of wit attained by these crazy Prommers!

Though it's presumably only meant to be light-hearted, this ritualistic intolerance is guaranteed to discourage any hungry or new music lovers from intimate close-up connection with the music or its players; it's the same old people in the same old places night after night, year after year. There's no room for inquisitors anywhere near the front – it's a closed shop. *This isn't for you, it's for us.* Which is a shame, because otherwise I reckon the Proms are fantastic. As I counted them off in my tatty, well-thumbed Proms guide, I got more relaxed and began to enjoy myself; this had gone beyond novelty – I was starting to look forward to my regular prescription. By my tenth Prom, I was waving a merry daily (or, you know, thereabouts) hello to my fellow umbrella-cowering, overbite-stricken queuees. Promming was in my blood now; I felt at home; every day was an education – something new to discover and delight and doze off to. But, as we moved into September and the days got perceptibly shorter, I felt a cool nip of melancholia seeping into the air; the party was rolling towards an end and it looked like we were all going to have to try and think of something else to do with our evenings. The Proms season does not, however, just roll to a stop and then pack up discreetly with a bit of hushed Brahms and some contemplative mulling. Oh no, no, no. Oh *no, no, no, no no.*

Land of Hope and Glory

If you were to do a nationwide straw poll asking the public everything they know about the Proms, it's likely 90 per cent of the population would only be able to think of single reply – the same as mine: there's a Last Night of them. Ask them to expound, and it's unlikely you'd get much further than 'toffs with flags'. And that's about the sum of it. Some might manage: 'young Conservatives'. Or 'old Conservatives', or 'fuck off'. Featuring hundreds of hysterical upper-class loons in dresses and dickie-bows, yanking giant Union Jacks like semaphore signallers with Tourette's, the Last Night of the Proms is *the* night of the year to put aside any post-colonial remorse, multi-cultural embrace or realistic perceptions of the United Kingdom's place in the general scheme of things, and lose yourself in an unending blissful eddy of nationalistic songs, hymns, racist polemic (just kidding) and the patriotic Hovis music written by Czech composer Antonin Dvořák.

Last Night custom demands 'notably unruly' behaviour from the Prommers (the fact it's televised doesn't help). They don't need to be asked twice: like walruses on Red Bull, they harrumph along to the likes of 'Rule Britannia', 'Pomp and Circumstance' (featuring 'Land of Hope and Glory') and 'Jerusalem'. The hits keep on a-coming, the faces get redder, and all over middle England, pensioners scramble to their feet before their television sets, hot tears pooling under their liver spots.

And why the hell not? Hey, it's their party. They don't seem to care how any of this comes across, so they're not going to need me to do it for them. This is tradition. I have to say, though, despite my proud new Prom veteran status, I wasn't able to stomach going along to the Last Night myself. The prospect of somebody somewhere seeing my face on television, lumping me in with all this horse-faced malarkey, was too horrifying. So, as a compromise, Owen and I found ourselves in a field outside Richmond-upon-Thames, in Surrey, for the Last Night of the Marble Hill Proms: a picnicking/jingoism/fireworks/musical extravaganza, in the grounds of an English Heritage site stately home. Like Knebworth, only Barbour.

Technically this wasn't just the Last Night of the Marble Hill Proms, it was also the Only Night. Marble Hall had already hosted 'Queen – A Symphonic Rock Spectacular' and something called 'Music to Watch Girls By' this summer, so the 'Last Night' tag was just a sly wink and a nod to the paying public, reminding them *not to forget your flags tonight, OK?* But if even if you had forgotten, this wouldn't be a problem, Owen and I discovered, as we were instantly accosted by a jovial, fluttering flag seller.

'Flags!' he boomed. 'Get your flags here!'

'Do you have any German ones?' asked Owen.

'Ha, ha!' replied the flag seller. 'Flags!'

'No really, do you? Or a French one?'

The flag seller took a step backwards.

'Or a *European Union* one?'

'Ha, ha!' the flag seller stuttered, backing away even further. A passing family glared at us with open hostility.

'You should be careful saying shit like that around here,' I muttered to Owen. 'You'll get punched by some granny.'

'I'm not scared of some granny,' he replied, looking at

the grannies with defiance. We were at the top of a huge lawn that sloped gently down to a half-moon stage at the bottom; the Thames ran silently behind through the trees. It was dusk. The site was rimmed with concessions stalls – everything from Ernest & Julio Gallo wines to Volkswagen 4x4s. Flag sellers wandered throughout – they outnumbered programme sellers two to one. Owen and I bought a cheap green blanket at a stall and shuffled through the thousand family picnic spreads down to the less-populated grass area directly in front of the stage, where we stretched out our legs and cracked open a bottle of Jack Daniel's.

'Have we got any mixer?'

'Oh please.'

We swigged at it like men. Youngsters were impressed.

Soon the Royal Philharmonic Orchestra and their conductor Anthony Inglis wandered onstage in white dinner jackets. Inglis raised his right arm, flicked imperceptibly at his ivory baton and the Royal Phil came roaring out of giant PA speakers like a convoy of off-white Volkswagen 4x4s going slightly too fast on the Bayswater Road. We sat on our rug with the bourbon and watched. The setlist was a shameless crowd-pleaser. Messiaen was conspicuous by his absence.* Here are my concert notes:

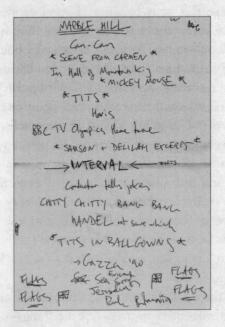

I think by tits I'm referring to the emergence of uncannily busty blonde Welsh mezzo soprano Katherine Jenkins. Every time she took the stage – in a variety of revealing dresses – small groups of middle-aged men scuttled down to the crash barriers with their digital cameras.

'Shall I?' said Owen.

'Oh, go on then.'

He took six or so.

* Another in-joke, you anti-classical losers.

197

Walk on the Mild Side

Ms Jenkins is a fast-emerging star of the classical world; her big break came in 2003, when as a guest on the *Max Boyce Down Under* show she was beamed into Welsh televisions right before the rugby. Aroused Welsh rugby fans immediately voted Katherine their official Rugby World Cup mascot; lo, she recorded the Official Welsh Rugby Team Song and it was plain sailing thereafter. (She does, of course, have her knockers.)* Her debut album, *Premiere*, went to number one on the classical music charts, as did its follow-up, *Second Nature*. These albums are chock-full of photographs of Katherine and lush classical ballads; she even has a twitter through 'You'll Never Walk Alone'. All very classy; and where there are beats, they're discreet and low in the mix. Her voice is high in the mix. This year she's off to Las Vegas to star in an 'opera spectacular' called *Diva Las Vegas*. Catch it if you can.

Also on the bill at Marble Hill were operatic crossover act (there will always be crossovers of everything – opportunists demand it) Amici Forever. They're two babes and three hunks. 'The voices sing opera, the looks scream pop!' goggled the *New York Times*.† There are loads of these dumb crossover groups, way more than you'd think. Purists get upset, but they're harmless; they attract thick people and help sell magazines and threaten a more 'glamorous' side to the world of classical. Like manufactured pop, these are comforting sounds for people who are scared and intimidated by music. They're not interfering with any of the

* Sorry.
† Yes, they sing 'Nessun Dorma'.

proper business, not stepping on anyone's tones except, perhaps, those of the Taste Police, who come knocking every time these malefactors step out. Here are some others:

Opera Babes: two babes who sing operatically (with occasional techno beats), especially at football matches for some reason.

The Celtic Tenors: three hunks, who are *celtic*, like the Corrs! If you like the Corrs or anyone like that, you'll love the Celtic Tenors.

Bond: four violin-playing babes with beats. Dismal bollocks.

G4: four hunks. They were on television's *The X Factor*. Their chart-busting debut album features 'Bohemian Rhapsody', 'Everybody Hurts', 'You'll Never Walk Alone' and 'Jerusalem'. Sometimes they even wear jeans.

Red Priest: four middle-aged weirdos. They play enthusiastic Early Music (one plays the recorder) and have strange costumes and high-tech visuals as a distraction to the recorder and themselves.

The 5 Browns: five American brothers and sisters who all play the piano. That's five pianos. There's something not quite right about these fun guys.

Nicola Benedetti: winner of the BBC's Young Musician of the Year 2004. Were Nicola unattractive, she'd probably be able to keep her head down and get on with her career, but she's not, so *uh-oh*.

Il Divo: four vain, pretentious hunks. Just looking at their photo you want to punch them.

That's enough crossing over; the place is beginning to reek of aftershave.

On the whole, what with the summery riverside ambience and the Jack Daniel's, Owen and I had quite a nice evening. But I have to admit, the final twenty minutes – the crescendo party mix – were difficult. It was like the crowd had been caged; as soon as the Anglo-jingles began – *doing* – everyone was up on their feet, waving flags in the air like they just didn't care. It was freakish and bizarre. As we sat uncomfortably on our green blanket surrounded by ankles and calves, I suddenly realized that the Last Night of the Proms, be it in the Royal Albert Hall, in a field or on television, doesn't actually need classical music. It's got nothing to do with it: classical music's just there out of default – it's an excuse.

'What's the matter with these people?' strained Owen above the zombie-esque singalong. 'What are they *doing*?'

Well, they were standing in a field getting the words wrong to 'Jerusalem' while waving Union Jacks.

'Yes but *why*?'

They'd call it tradition, or celebration of national identity, but it's fear.

Right, kids?

8. Classic Classical Classical Music

What happened was this: folks wanted less confusion in their tunes. Screw counterpoint; fugue can kiss my ass; cantata, your mom's a whore; concerto grosso can go to hell, boy. *Get out mah house, goddamn. What's wraang with keepin' music simple? Music ah can whistle? How mah s'posed to hum along to that bull-sheet?*

Fortunately for these late eighteenth-century post-Baroque rednecks, help was at hand in the form of Franz Joseph Haydn. Haydn was a lovely man; nobody had a bad word to say about him, not even his musicians (which was strange). Haydn was loyal, humble, witty, charming and utterly capable. He was pathologically nice. Sadly, this relentless cheeriness meant his music was incredibly bland – we're talking about the Cliff Richard of classical music. And his career lasted almost half a century – like Sir Cliff, the man just refused to die. Haydn just kept on writing the same old tunes and being happy and friendly and lovely. Deep in his Leipzig grave, Bach slowly rotated.

Chipper Maestro 'Papa' Haydn deduced that it was time for things to move on a little; punters were looking beyond prissy baroque masturbation, towards a more straightforward and artless style: *style galant*. The complex techniques so celebrated just a couple of years before were being supplanted by the simpler, more languid pleasures of pure, unadorned melody. Don't mess with it. It's easier. This simpler shit came to unhelpfully be known as Classical classical music. And it's where I'm finding classical music is beginning to take a turn for the worse: it's sounding duller; distinct sensations of suffocation are creeping in; everything sounds like a big golden cushion; and I feel like I'm stuck fast in some interminable goddamn quicksand. Morale is low. Motivation is hard to find: I want to break free.*

But, fortunately for everybody, at this exact same time, a wee wigged baby boy was born in the Austrian city of Salzburg whose psychotic, potty-mouthed antics would liven everything up considerably. Although not that much, to be honest.

I flew to Austria to investigate. And on my own, because I'm brave.

The Prodigy

The word 'Mozart' gets used a lot as a clichéd metaphor for alleged artistic greatness; someone's always being touted as the 'new Mozart' by lazy journalists. Brian Wilson gets it all the time; Aphex Twin used to get it back in the nineties. But the original boy genius was one Johannes Chrysostomus Wolfgangus Theophilus Mozart; born in Salzburg, Austria on 27 January 1756, of parents Leopold (the town's deputy Head of Music and a respected violinist) and Anna Maria (she had a big forehead). Leopold Mozart realized something slightly out of the ordinary was up when, at the age of three, young Wolfgangus mastered the art of the harpsichord.

* Let me just qualify: this does *not* mean I have any desire to listen to Queen. Things aren't that bad yet. I see no mushroom clouds on the horizon just at the minute.

At five, he began to compose his first minuets. Also 'Twinkle Twinkle, Little Star'.

At six, he'd learned to play the violin.

At seven, the organ.

His first symphony was composed at the ripe old age of eight (Symphony No. 1 in E-flat Major, K.16). Leopold's reaction to these startling developments was perhaps a premonition of the freakish power of contemporary celebrity – he put his own career on ice, stuck wee Wolfgangus in the back of a rickety old carriage and went off on a massive European tour.

The Mozarts were soon the toast of the continent; Leopold, Wolfgangus (I'm gonna drop that '-us' now, OK?) and older sister Nannerl played sold-out shows in aristo-courts throughout Italy, France, Germany, Switzerland, Holland –

Left: *Little Wolfgang in Vienna, aged six.* Right: *The Mozart family mid-performance. If Wolfgang played a wrong note, Leopold would whack him over the head with his violin bow, and everyone would laugh. Then they disgustingly gang-raped the poor lad.*

even London. As Leopold writes in a letter home to his wife, 'We took almost everyone by storm!' Not only did they sometimes play for up to three hours at a time, but their astonishing show also included tricks such as getting Wolfgang to play music from sight, and covering the harpsichord's keyboard with a handkerchief so he couldn't see what he was playing. And playing one-handed. Woo.

Despite Wolfgang's frequent stress-related illnesses, this infantile exploitation made the Mozarts rich, and, back in Salzburg three years later, they were welcomed as international superstars. By now – perhaps inevitably – they considered themselves way too important for that stinky old backwater, so Leopold hurriedly arranged another gigantic Euro-jaunt, during which, aged eleven, sickly Wolfgang composed his first oratorio, and then at twelve, his first opera, *La Finta Semplice* (*The Pretend Simpleton* 🔊), for the Emperor of Vienna. Sadly though, due to older musicians' jealousy and behind-the-scenes political shenanigans, the opera was never performed, and the family limped back to Salzburg to re-engage with provincialism and limited prospects. Three visits to Italy followed. And then one more to Vienna. Well phew. Mozart was still just seventeen, and he'd barely even started.

Rock My Ass Off, Amadeus

Vienna, Austria, November 2004

I hadn't been to Vienna before. The train into town from the airport dawdled through gasworks; a graveyard; grisly government housing. In the city centre, after a couple of hours of quasi-aimless wandering around in a chilling sub-zero gale that came howling in off the frozen Magyar steppes, I speedily deduced the following:

Viennese people like	. . . hence a lot of
Dogs	Faeces on the pavement
Sausages	Hot dog stands
Pretzels, loaves, cakes, buns and pastries	Bakery shops
Being polite	Dead-eyed courtesy
Falco	Plentiful double-CD Falco 'Greatest Hits' collections
Their imperial past	Palaces
A quiet life	Silence
Fascism	Most recently, Jorg Haider's far-right Freedom Party
Exploiting Mozart	Mozart marketing, e.g. the popular 'Mostly Mozart' retail chain

So, first things first.

'Ein *Pustakrainer* Wurst, bitte,' I muttered through numb lips.

'You want a hot dog?'

I always hate it how they can tell straight away you're not from round these parts.

'Yeah, or I mean *ja*.'

He tossed a floppy little finger-wurst into a finger-roll and handed it over.

'You're sure this is a *Pustakrainer*?'

'It's a hot dog. Four euros.'

I paid, hobbled into the public gardens and perched on an iron park bench. It was so cold my bottom instantly stuck to it. A raven flapped down and stood glaring at me from the bench's wrought arm. It pecked aggressively in the direction of my sagging ratwurst.

Even when the sausage selection is as heavily and helpfully illustrated as above, it's still difficult to understand what the difference is between them. My thinking is: you'll probably be all right so long as you avoid the white one. What part of a pig is white except for its brain?

'Shoo, go away.'

The raven hopped to the ground and pecked at the tumbling crumbs. I waved a foot in its direction. 'Get away, shoo, get off, no . . . *no!*' It tried to hop on to my knee. 'Piss off!'

In the end I had to run out of the park to try and escape it. The raven hopped along behind, giving chase.

This incident was symptomatic of my first day in Austria. Vienna had given me agoraphobia.

You know how sometimes, when you're alone in a new

place, and it's getting dark, and you're cold, and you're not sure exactly where you are, and your knee's hurting from walking, and your nose is running, and you haven't got a tissue, and your backpack's too heavy, and your shoes rub, and everyone looks weird and like they're laughing at you, and you're too scared to try and get on a bus or a tram or hail a taxi, and you're wondering what the hell you're doing here in the first place? I felt a bit like that.

Limping back towards St Stephen's Cathedral (all roads seem to lead back there; it has a cool multi-coloured roof; it's free to get in – *hear that, Canterbury?*), I realized that I was in too much of a frozen mess to do anything of any use whatsoever; in fact, the lack of bloodflow to my brain drew me into panicked photography of anything I saw that related to Mozart. Ignoring Vienna's astonishing classical architecture entirely, and with my fingers so numb I couldn't feel what I was doing, I methodically snapped all the 'Mostly Mozart' stores I could find within the old Viennese town walls (i.e. the ring road). This seemed to satisfy me for a while. (Typically for the Viennese, 'Mostly Mozart' is being way too modest with its moniker – their stores aren't 'mostly' Mozart at all, they're *entirely* Mozart.) But soon, fully destroyed by the city's overwhelming refrigeration, I finally embraced defeat and zigzagged blearily over the Danube canal (a weedy offshoot – the actual Danube is north-east of the city centre, and it's gun-metal grey, not blue) over towards my pre-booked hotel on Praterstrasse, up near the famous Ferris Wheel. Along the way I passed a grimy charity shop; it was dimly lit and stank of mildew and death – the complete opposite of our cheery UK ones. I know this because I had gone inside, as I have a fondness for charity shops. Except for this one. I realized straight away that Austrian charity shops are there exclusively for *really* poor people – i.e. not Austrians, i.e. disenfranchised immigrants. Paint peeled off the walls and the non-functional heating system was completely exposed; it teetered over the scarred shop floor like a pantomime robot. Three jolly Arab men stood vamping through a reeking rack of fur coats; I squeezed past them and was instantly mesmerized by three rows of old-fashioned Austrian National Dress – owners clearly deceased – covered in theatrical-looking dust. In my Arctic delirium I mistook these kitsch tweed monstrosities for Jarvis Cocker-esque statements of über-cool individuality. I pulled on a bunch of jackets, all of which were, sort of, quadruple-breasted, with lots of secret pockets for horns, etc. The Arab guys and mouse-like store assistant stopped what they were doing and stared. I turned to face them in blue lederwaistcoat with black felt trim and a thick coating of bereavement ash. We all just stood there for a few seconds. I wasn't sure what to do next. I listened to the wind howling outside and hummed 'Twinkle Twinkle, Little Star'.

Unfortunately my eye was now caught by some old-fashioned Austrian shirts – at least I think they were shirts; they might actually have been nighties – four of which I took into the changing cubicle, before realizing they were *Tyrolean* nighties, and *that's* how I'd got confused, so I sheepishly took them all back again. Luckily I then found quite a normal red jumper; it smelled less of death, maybe more of some sort of wasting disease, so I bought it, put it on over my shirt, and strode out into the street and then my hotel, where I took a lift up to the third floor, locked my door, lay out on my bed and watched CNN for two hours before I realized it was insidiously brainwashing me with intermulticorporate banality. Thus I threw myself out of my window and died from my injuries. I was pleased.

Fun in Salzburg

While I was being depressed in Vienna, Mozart was depressed in Salzburg. Both brilliant musicians, both frustrated by our current nowheresville circumstances, what could we do now? Well, I guessed *I* could see what it was like in Salzburg, and *Mozart* could take another shot at Vienna. After all, his legacy is claimed by the place – he spent the whole latter part of his life here. And one day in Salzburg for me was one day less in Vienna. It was probably worth a shot.

The following morning I climbed on to the Salzburg Express with a leaping heart and half a spring in my left leg. The sun was nearly shining, the rain wasn't too bad, and I detected a distinct thaw of almost half a degree. Today was going to be a success – I could feel it in my bones already – three blissful hours crossing the vast Austrian Plain with Alps rising out of marble skies to our left and thick misty forests enveloping the landscape to our right; how could this trip be anything less than superlative?

Fuckin' easily.

Salzburg is gorgeous but oh, doesn't it know it; the city's so good-looking it was designated a UNESCO World Heritage Site in 1997. The old city's warren of narrow pedestrianized streets nestles beneath the terrifyingly sheer rock face of the Monchsberg cliff and its fortress, visible for miles around; all watched over by the steely Capuchin mountain rising on the other side of the wide, winding Salzach river. It looks a bit like an Alpine-style Edinburgh, except it totally reeks of sausages, and everyone's a bastard. But in the meantime, my Salzburg pilgrimage led me to the house Mozart was born in: number 9, Getreidegasse. It's a small apartment in a narrow, slightly teetering house with a plunging, yellowing inner courtyard one wends one's way up and around until you arrive at the Mozarts' old rooms. Stepping across the family threshold is actually quite a sagacious experience – its historical significance wasn't lost on me as I timidly stepped into the third-floor family music room with its views out over a bustling market square below and stood peering at several incongruous illuminated information panels featuring massively blown-up portraits of the Mozart family. Their heads are two feet high. It was like being on mushrooms. Right in the centre of the low room hangs young Wolfgang's old violin, inside a reinforced glass box. *Mozart's old violin?* Wow! It's weeny – almost *Action Man* size. I looked at it. But it was in the next room, in the deep, crisp and even winter of 1756, that baby Wolfgang emerged triumphant from his mother's straining womb. I raised my camera and took a photograph of the floorboards the maestro was born unto.

These are the actual Mozart birth floorboards. Nowadays people walk about on them, willy-nilly.

'*Nein!* Stop!' I jumped out of my skin. 'No photographs!' A bloke in a green jumper rushed through and waved his arms in front of me.

'No photographs!'

'Oh, I'm sorry.'

'It is forbidden!'

'I heard you, I'm *sorry.*'

Everyone stared. It was so embarrassing. And as a consequence, this moustachioed man remained doggedly at my side for the whole of the rest of my tour. We read the information panels together, had a good look at Mozart's old harpsichord side-by-side and trotted down the steps to check out the old Mozart kitchen virtually arm-in-arm. It was like we were lovers – he wouldn't leave me alone in a room for even a second.

'Why are you following me? I'm not going to take any more pictures, I promise.' Although I was actually planning to, out of malicious principle.

'No photographs,' he repeated.

'I *know* that.'

'Photography is not allowed in the Mozart birth-house, it says this on your ticket.'

'Look, can't you just . . .' He shook his head and made a tutting sound. My minor transgression seemed to have made his day.

This guy was just the beginning. Like I said, everyone in Salzburg was unpleasant – nobody was friendly the whole time I was there (four hours), except the lady who served me coffee in the station as I waited to get the hell out of there. Check it out:

Mozart's birth-house custodian – rude and shouty and wouldn't let it lie.

Two women and one man in Mozart's *Wohnhaus* (the

large townhouse the family moved into after they made a bit of money from all that touring) – really rude (twice at the cash desk, once in the cinema bit, because I was 'taking too long').

I managed to sneak this photo. It's Mozart's old piano, which he used for concerts in Vienna; he'd have it hauled about the place especially. I risked my life taking this photograph, so please take a long, hard look.

Guy in t-shirt shop – incompetent as well as gormless.

Guy in other t-shirt shop – plain rude, even though I bought a 'SALZBURG – The Sound of Music – Alps & Fun' t-shirt.

Hot-dog stand woman – I asked for a Mexicanwurst, but they'd run out, and she *couldn't have given a shit.*

Hot-dog stand punters – unhelpful with napkin etiquette and starey.

Tourists who blocked the door to the hat shop for two minutes without saying sorry – thoughtless bastards.

Hat-shop woman who let the door slam in my face – bitch.

Hat-shop sales assistant – thought I was a shoplifter; hey, I tried.

Station toilet attendant who charged me fifty cents to have a piss – *wanker*.

People standing at the bus stop watching me behave oddly on the river footbridge when I didn't realize anyone was looking – cruel.

(These notes were made on the train back to Vienna with pen clenched tightly in fist.)

You know, I reckon this is what travel writing should be like – forget all those pretty adjectives and stupid descriptions of 'stunning vistas' and shit – tell it how it is: these people are *evil*. Jesus, I couldn't wait to leave. *Don't go to Salzburg. DON'T GO TO SALZBURG UNLESS YOU'RE A PENSIONER WHO DOESN'T NOTICE, OR CARE ABOUT THESE THINGS.*

Mozart Hated Salzburg Too

Mozart and I have so much in common. Really so much.

At twenty-one, deeply sick of his interminable life as house musician to the grouchy and unappreciative Archbishop of Salzburg, Mozart found himself going nowhere, way too fast. Though he still tossed off symphonies and concertos and sonatas in his sleep, and despite his highly regarded position within the community, his early taste for foreign soil meant ambition wriggled through his frock coat – he was desperate for a highly paid court composer job at one of the biggie royal European households, just like his mentor-from-afar held down – Sir Cliff 'Papa' Haydn. Thus, in 1777, Leopold sent Wolfgang away again – this time to Munich – to seek the family fortune one more time; and as he didn't trust him to go on his own, with his beloved mother in accompaniment. She would not return alive.

Exploring the Psyche of a Genius

The flipside of Mozart's symphonious mastery was that he was a bit of a tiresome cock (this is where my similarities to Mozart end, I'm afraid). As his multitude of letters home (and to friends) from his travels attest, he was abnormally obsessed with farting, poo, willies, wee-wee, double entendres, puns and especially anything and everything to do with the bottom. That was his favourite. The letters are top (though worrying) entertainment – you'd never guess the same mouthy gobshite was simultaneously responsible for penning some of the most exquisite music known to humankind. He wrote, as he put it, 'like pigs piss', i.e. free and easy, without giving the metaphorical loo seat a wipe down afterwards. Here are some examples. I'll lower you in gently.

To his sister: 'I kiss Mama's hand and my sister's face, nose, neck, and my wretched pen, and her rear end if it's clean. Ha ha!'

To his father: 'Today I did some rhyming in the presence of Cannabich, his wife and daughter, nothing too serious, in fact, nothing but crude stuff, such as muck, shitting and arse-licking – all of it in thoughts – but not in deeds!'

A poem to his mother:

> Of course, the people I see
> Have muck in their bellies, just like me,
> But they will let it out with a whine,
> Either before or after they dine.

There's a lot of farting during the night,
And the farts resound with thunderous might.
Yesterday, though, we heard the king of farts,
It smelled as sweet as honey tarts.

then,

The concerto I'll write in Paris, it's fitting,
For there, I can dash it off while I'm shitting.

and finally,

For I'll have the honour of kissing your hands,
Though before I see you, I'll shit in my pants.

I often write to my own mother with similar such poems.

To his (female) cousin: 'Oh my arse burns like fire! What's the meaning of this? Maybe *muck* wants to come out! Yes, yes, *muck*!' and: 'Wherever I go, it stinks – when I look out the window, the smell goes away, when I turn my head back into the room, the smell comes back – finally my mama says to me: *I bet you let one go?* I don't think so, Mama. *Yes yes, I'm quite certain.* I put it to the test, stick my finger in my arse, then put it to my nose, and – there is the proof! Mama was right!' and: 'Before I start writing to you, I have to go to the john ____ well, now that's over with! Well, it's true, after you've completely emptied yourself, life is twice as much fun!' and arguably the ultimate: 'I'll get muck in my face. Muck!-muck-oh muck!-oh sweet word!-muck!-chuck! That's good too!-muck, chuck!-muck-suck-oh charmante!-muck, suck!-love this stuff!-muck, chuck and suck!-chuck muck and suck muck!! Now let's talk about something else; have you had good fun at this year's carnival?'

So we know Mozart liked a beer, a shag and a number two. Scholars today claim Mozart was afflicted by a complex form of Tourette's syndrome, but I suspect they're desperate to take the responsibility for this sort of humour out of his hands – to blame it on a condition out of his control. I think it's fairer to try and understand it as the inevitable exhaust pipe for the skies he was scraping at the other end of his body (the quill at his fingertips; also, his brain) – as he was in tune with the heavenly cosmos, so he was too with his dirty old arse, and up yours if you can't take a joke. Mozart would've loved *Viz* magazine, and those top-shelf ones that come in opaque bags next to the granny porn that somebody once told me about.

Now Wash Your Hands

But everything changed after Mozart and his mother arrived in Paris, having been urged there by Leopold after they'd failed to score any tricks in Munich. Their perilous financial situation – due to Wolfgang's profligate and over-innocent, trusting nature (thus subsequent abuse thereof) – meant they were forced into a dark, grotty apartment, where Mozart's mother, especially, had a miserable time; so cowed was she by the swarming metropolis, she barely ever ventured out; just sat there, in the dark, laughing along with Wolfgang's fart gags. Or pretending to.

But soon she fell ill and died very suddenly, leaving Mozart traumatized and bereft and alone and horribly directionless, in a city that now threatened to engulf him completely. His only option was to throw himself into his work. He schlepped his way through the muddy Parisian streets looking for aristocratic commissions, but things didn't go well – Paris had loved him as a performing circus freak child, but now he could barely get himself arrested. 'If this were a place where people had ears to hear, hearts to feel and some measure of taste for music,' he writes, 'these troubles would make me laugh heartily; but as it is, I am surrounded by brute beasts.'

Poor geezer consoled himself by writing some venerable, ass-mulchin' tunes, like his beautiful Flute and Harp Concerto in C Major, K.299 🎸🎸🎸; and his swish 'Paris' Symphony No. 31 in D Major, K.297 🎸🎸🎸.

What's with these Ks? Is It a *Kerrang!* Thing?

No, they're the mysterious 'Koechel numbers', conceived by Ludwig von Koechel in 1862, in an attempt to numerically catalogue Mozart's music – over 600 works in all. It sounds pretty simple, doesn't it? Well yes – K.1 is the first thing Wolfgang wrote, aged five: it's a perky Minuet in G Major. Sadly, however, K.2 and K.3 are believed to have been written by someone else. (How did that happen? Jeez.) Further examples of foreign authorship are his Symphony No. 2, K.17, which was written by his father; and Symphony No. 3, K.18, which was composed by someone called Carl Friedrich Abel. However, sanity eventually prevails, and Mozart is believed to have written the majority of the subsequent 600 pieces himself – brilliant news for Mozart fans. (I'll ignore the symphonies whose numbers come in inverted commas, i.e. Symphony '55', K.45(b), which is actually much earlier; and Symphony '45', K.73(n), which gets assigned all over the bleeding shop. Don't ask me – it's hard enough typing them out.)

The Koechel numbers are very serious business. Proper classical music buffs like to learn them, and then refer to specific pieces by their number rather than their name (or their other number, i.e. Symphony No. 32 (erm, K.318)). Even better, they sometimes come with subclauses, i.e. K.299(b), or K.196(d); this is because for years after Koechel, people would come along and attempt to reclassify some of the music just to annoy and confuse everyone; then they did it *again*, e.g. K.124a(K.6). Soon it got stupid; even Albert Einstein – on his days off from physics and that – waded in with some new suggestions; but luckily everyone ignored him, and the Koechels were free to settle down and become perpetually memorized by people like David Mellor. As an experiment, I decided to test Fiona's knowledge of the Koechel numbers. I emailed her the Ks for five well-known pieces and asked her to name that work. Here are the results:

1) K.550 – 'I'll guess (Symphony) No. 40 because I think the 'Jupiter' is K.551 and I don't think you'd trick me so meanly with something unknown.' *Correct*.

2) K.525 – (A load of excuses followed by) 'I'm not sure.' *Incorrect*. Fiona ought to have got this one – it's 'Eine Kleine Nachtmusik', one of the most famous pieces of classical music ever.

3) K.488 – 'Pretty confident this is the piano concerto in A Major.' *Correct*.

4) K.3 – 'I definitely don't know this one, unless it's some prenatal work of genius or something very juvenile for jew's harp written by Leopold or as some sort of hoax.' *Spot on*.

5) K.385 – 'Not sure, though I'd guess it's one of the big symphonies, as the 300s don't tend to be known by K

numbers.' *A cunning way to get half a point.* It's the famous 'Haffner' Symphony in D Major.

Fiona scored 3½ out of 5. Not bad – I'm amazed she got any, to be honest. (She also wrote: 'What a GREAT GAME (ho ho).' Which was a bit harsh.)

Mozart wasn't alone in having strings of confusing capital letters trailing behind his compositions: all Bach's works have BWV (*Bach Werke Verzeichnis*) numbers, of which there are several editions and which are way more confusing than the Ks, trust me. Beethoven had Op. numbers – or opus numbers – which at least he had the foresight to actually number himself. Sadly, however, there remain a further 205 Beethoven works without opus numbers; these have WoO (*Werke ohne Opuszahl*) numbers, which sit alongside yet further numberless works that are catalogued by over 300 *Hess* numbers. Then there are the works of which there is doubt as to Beethoven's actual authorship – these come with *AnH* numbers, but fortunately we're not giving a sheep's arse about *AnH* numbers.

(Schubert had *D* numbers – now they really were interesting.)

All this arcane numerical apparatus provides yet more brambles for yer common man to negotiate his path through on his journey to classical enlightenment – more cultural smoke screens. Could you imagine if pop groups did the same? At the jukebox, instead of looking for 'Tomorrow Never Knows', you'd be keeping your eyes peeled for 'L&McC.211(d), Lp.7, Tr.14 in C Major'. Heaven help you if you're after a B-side. Or 'Maxwell's Silver Hammer'.

Mature Mozart and His
Mellifluous Melodies

Poor Wolfy never got a chance to wholly ripen, because he was dead before the age of thirty-six. After the Parisian débâcle he reluctantly retreated back to Salzburg and his father and the archbishop and a miserable pile of crap, and his previously ultra-sunny musical tone began to gradually darken. Once he got into his mid-to-late twenties, Mozart's music acquired a new mystical depth, whose bottomless fathoms are responsible for his critical sainthood today – nobody really cares about any of his musical output before this point (we're in the mid 300 Ks – about 1779); everything beyond here is what his gargantuan reputation rests upon; before this *depth*, he was nothing but a poop-mouthed prodigy with parping potential. Now, though, he was a god.

But no one realized.

Having left Salzburg for good – after a public screaming match with the archbishop – in the summer of 1781, Mozart came to Vienna, where he was to remain until he died. The quality of his musical output over this period is probably unsurpassed in human history (ignoring Chris de Burgh's astonishing seam of form in the mid-1980s); almost everything he wrote over this decade is now considered entirely untouchable – nowhere have I seen so many references to a body of work achieving 'perfection' except in reference to Mozart's late music. Critics don't even bother to argue about it – that's how straight-up solid gold this shit is. To all intents and purposes, this body of work is *beyond criticism*.

And although there were a fair few people around at the time who recognized Mozart's purifying genius (these people became his support network – they lent him money, commissioned his music, spread the word as best they could), Viennese society still preferred to hold him at arm's length, where he could do the least damage – either via his music, which Emperor Joseph II famously derided as having 'too many notes!' (Mozart's reply: 'there are exactly the right number, your Majesty'), or via his excessive lifestyle, which always seemed beyond his modest means – i.e. he constantly pissed his money down the drain.

In some ways his life in Vienna was conventional and workaday: Mozart married Constanze Weber, the sister of a woman he'd obsessed over a few years before; and though – as ever – this annoyed his father, the couple settled down to a life of relative stability in a pair of apartments in the centre of town (one's closed to the public and the other's shut for refurbishment, so I can't illustrate the floorboards). Mozart busied himself wheedling into advantageous positions, scoring commissions to write a couple of operas. These operas, mostly written down his local pub, are probably the most famous, and 'perfect' operas of all time:

The Marriage of Figaro (a saucy romp about lust, the class system, betrayal, and further lust) 🚌🚌🚌🚌

Don Giovanni (a passionate romp about lust, betrayal, revenge, death, wanton lust, and finally deathly revenge and blood) 🚌🚌🚌🚌

Cosi fan tutte (a comedy about infidelity, war and laughter) 🚌🚌🚌

and finally, the deeply strange:

The Magic Flute (which involves a deadly monster, Masons, a birdcatcher, a magic flute, some magic bells, mystic portals, a flying chicken, a priest, some slaves, a mysterious old woman, two more priests and a goat, a trial of fire, a trial of water, and isn't really about anything) 🚌🚌🚌🚌🚌

The Magic Flute is considered slightly less 'perfect' than the others, though it was easily the most successful during Mozart's lifetime; which just goes to show – plot, schmot, it's tunes we want, and *The Magic Flute*'s got 'em – it's easily the most listenable of the four.

Mozart's reputation as a true master of opera rests upon the lead-encased magnificence of the four works above. But one thing I hadn't realized until just recently was that when a composer writes an opera, they don't actually write the words that go with it, they just write the music. Sure, they'll probably have a general idea of what it is they want to do and how they're gonna go about it, but most of the composer's art is setting music to words that are already there. The lyrics (the *libretto*) are written by a completely different person, called a *librettist*, and Mozart's most famous librettist was a guy called Lorenzo da Ponte (whose auto-biography doesn't even mention Mozart). However I think that's enough opera for now, as I'm beginning to get con-fused again.

Not only was Mozart writing opera down there in the pub, he was also writing symphonies, concertos, quartets and other treats for you, me and our friends to enjoy. His failure to cement a bona-fide music-master's position at any eighteenth-century court meant that Mozart unwittingly became the world's first freelancer. Soon, of course, every-one would be freelance, but for now, in his spare time – when his woeful finances weren't forcing him into giving spoilt girls piano lessons – Mozart wrote symphonies, just for the hell of it. And although, as even I know, soon everyone and his uncle would be writing symphonies, until now they hadn't been. Mozart kind of invented them – he certainly invented their structure. This means it's time for . . .

Fiona's Sponge Cake Metaphor

A week or so before I left for Vienna, Fiona and I met for lunch. I was nervous. Though we'd exchanged plenty of good-natured emails, I was worried she'd be much more fierce in real life. I was right to have been worried, for as soon as we sat down at the table, she started to take the piss, as I was unconsciously overcompensating for my un-educated loutishness plus for having dragged her down to darkest Victoria one cold lunchtime for a cheap pizza. I began pointlessly listing obscure composers in the vague hope that she'd be impressed I'd memorized them.

'Stop this stupid namedropping,' she said. Fiona is petite and blonde, and kind of fizzes and is sly.

'I'm sorry.'

I told her how things were going. Then I started to say something about Mozart's compositional style but became muddled quarter-way through.

'You're trying to impress me,' she said. 'Stop that.'

'I'm sorry.'

'Tell me how it's really going.'

I told her that I was still finding it hard to concentrate, and that I was struggling with all the opera. And that I'd been finding most of Mozart's symphonies about as exciting as pylons (I'd bought a box-set).

'Oh God, don't bother with all those,' she said.

'Don't bother with Mozart's symphonies?' I was aghast, quite frankly – the box-set had cost over £30. What was she going to suggest instead? *Beefheart?* Under the table, I crossed my fingers.

She said any symphony post #30, any piano concertos post #20, the four operas above, the *Requiem Mass*, and some other stuff that I've forgotten.

'But then, anything Mozart wrote is going to be worthwhile, however you look at it.'

Aha! The Stalinist rulebook of Mozartian perfection – she couldn't help but toe the party line! I jiggled excitedly in my chair but she ordered me to stop. I was pleased though, because this meant my box-set might have been value for money after all. Fiona continued to take the piss some more and then she had to rush off to interview somebody for a newspaper.

'Good luck!' she cried over her shoulder.

While I'd been talking with my mouth full, Fiona had jotted down some of the intricate, mysterious mysteries of life on my notepad. First was the sponge cake metaphor, which involves looking at a symphony like it's a sponge cake. Mozart* baked it, shaped it, and left it out to cool. All anyone's done since Mozart is add jam filling, cream, icing, marzipan, candles – bulked it out; done it up fancy (the ultimate seven-tier pink Las Vegas wedding cake being Mahler). In fact, the foundations Mozart† laid for symphonic form are still firmly in place even today. You take any symphony, from 1781 to the present day, and sitting there proudly in the middle is Mozart's redoubtable sponge cake base. This is one of the reasons he's so highly regarded – his remarkable bakery foresight.

Fiona had also drawn me a diagram that basically unlocked the mystical secrets of symphony-writing. It was so plain, so simple, that after she'd gone I stared at it open-mouthed for about eight minutes. Was *this* what all the fuss was about?

* Or Haydn, if you're fussy.
† Or rather Haydn, if you're a stickler for *facts*.

Symphonic Secrets Laid Bare!

Symphonies are a sham, a ruse, a confidence trick. I'll show you. Take any symphony. Any one! There are millions of 'em – pick any!

First, all symphonies have four movements.

The *1st movement* is the most important, as it has to catch your attention. It goes:

A – big tune

B – development of tune

A – back to the big tune again

(This simple equation is called 'sonata form' – one of the holiest artistic concepts known to man. And it's an absolute piece of piss!)

The *2nd movement* is a *slow movement*. So long as it's slow, it's fine.

The *3rd movement* is a *minuet* (a dance vibe) and/or a *trio* (like a waltz); in other words, it's a bit jazz.

The *4th movement* is a *rondo*. This goes:

Theme – A

Theme – B

Theme – C

Theme – D

Which is almost the same as the first movement if you squint a little.

And that's it! Just write anything you want using the rules above and you've got a symphony. You don't need to beat yourself up about it – just tune, morphed tune, tune again, slow bit, jaunty bit, ending with tune, tune, tune, tune (redux). Do that and you're a composer. Bravo!

I believe being privy to this knowledge is so horrifically illicit, it's a bit like catching your parents having sex.

Mean Streets

Back in Vienna, I decided the very least I could do was drag myself along to a Mozart concert; I needed something to pep myself up; take my mind off my new clothes. On my way into town to pick up a gig guide, I happened to wander forlornly past something called the Klangmuseum – a space-age interactive museum of sound. Hungry for information and central heating, I went inside. Unfortunately so did a coachload of German schoolchildren, so I ducked down into a toilet to escape but ripped the back of my jacket on the corner of the hand-dryer. This trip was cursed, man, *cursed*.

The museum was weird – half multimedia futurism (whose hands-on exhibits didn't work right, as ever), half aimless chrome wander; and I could have learned a heck of a lot about the technology of sound had most of it not been in German. Twenty minutes of fascinating sine wave patterns and 3D graphs of frequency resonators later, I stumbled into a classical music room. There were violins in cases and music and photos and portraits; but over in the corner loomed a large pulsing blue computerized exhibit, which meant everyone just ignored the other stuff. A side panel explained that Mozart and Haydn (who'd been pals) used to compose little waltzes – for a laugh, down the pub – by rolling dice. Depending on what they threw, the notes would go up, down, around, up/down and around, or whatever. This exhibit enabled the common thicko punter to recreate these maestro dice games on a giant computer screen and with giant fibre-optic dice. I stood and waited patiently for the pensioners before me to finish, which took ages, as they didn't really get it, and then took my position

– ready to compose some classical music for the first time in my life. I rolled the dice. The computer screen went *tra-la-la*. Mmm, nice. I rolled again. It went *tra-la-la-la-la*. Tune. *Again. Tiddly-widdly-dee.* A few more times. *Blah.* My creative juices were bled dry now so I approached the man on the information desk and requested a printout of my composition.

'You know this is not free of charge,' he said, switching on the printer.

I didn't say, 'You can't put a price on genius, Fritz.' Instead I said, 'Here is my money, thank you very much.'

The attendant stared at my composition, then said: 'This is a masterpiece. How did you manage such a thing?'

Back in the old city centre, I was repeatedly struck by the cultural ubiquity of Wolfgang Amadeus Mozart and the fact that we're taught about his genius from childhood – our parents are depressingly keen for us to follow in his footsteps, so they force us into humiliating piano lessons from a cruel and tender age, just in case we might be geniuses too. If you didn't know who Mozart was (say you were an Eskimo or a yeti), you'd realize soon enough if you turned up in modern-day Vienna.

Aside from the inspirational retail opportunities presented by the city, there are almost as many musical ones too; Vienna hosts a bewildering array of concert halls, palaces, orchestras, chamber music thingies, whatnots and you-knows – all on the go, full-pelt, all-year round. The choice is vast, but I found it impossible to resist the mega-glitz charms of the Vienna Residence Orchestra at the Palais Auersperg – the very place that touring, six-year-old Mozart had leaped charmingly into the arms of the equally infant Marie-Antoinette, and asked the yet-to-be-beheaded future Queen of France to marry him. She told him to piss off and get back to playing the piano blindfolded, or I'll chop *your* wiggy head off, *Wunderkind*.

Eine Wiener Nachtmusik

The Vienna Residence Orchestra are a specialist chamber music ensemble, and the Palais Auersperg, built in 1710, is their home. First of all, I got them all to line up in a row so I could take their photograph.

They're sumptuous. And ravishing. And they'll play Mozart deliciously, I just know it.

For tonight's concert I'd put on a superior pair of cords; and a shirt with a full set of buttons down the front; and I'd brushed my teeth, washed my face, given my mucky shoes a wipe and tied my hair up in a bun; yikes I fairly gleamed as I stood shivering in the howling wind, lost again, holding my map upside-down in the light of the deserted metro station on another cold, cold Viennese night, all by myself, oh well, never mind, don't worry, I'll be OK, I'm enjoying this really. ☹

But then I spotted two coaches parked front-to-back, outside a palatial-looking building with light pouring out its glittering imperial doorway. Here it was – the Palais Auersperg – I'd found it. But *coaches*? *Did this mean . . . ?* Yes.

Inside the belly of the plush lobby, adorned with gold and silver and red velvet and smelling of complacent neglect, I saw tonight's audience was split violently down the middle: half were kitted out in black tie, posh frocks and monocles, and half was the double-coachload of Japanese tourists. The twain had met. And one half was taking a lot more photos than the other, who didn't appear to enjoy posing next to four grinning Japanese in hardy waterproofs. The palace ushers were dolled up too – smug, permagrinning and heavily gelled. Elegant female programme sellers swooned with compliant modesty as you flattered them by accepting the proffered small change from a ten euro note. Paul Burrell lookalikes breezed through the crowd with trays of bubbling champagne flutes which the posh Viennese held at demure arm's length and the Japanese stared at while murmuring rapt, wide-eyed approval. And it was then that I realized what this actually was. Tonight was a Madame bloody Tussauds of a classical music concert. This was the musical equivalent of the five-course set meal at those tourist trap restaurants you get on the Champs-Elysées or in St Mark's Square or wherever. I'd been sold a dud. Easy prey. I flapped through the aromatic programme – through the bow-ties and the *welcome*s and the original Biedermeier costumes – until I got to tonight's musical repertoire, where my suspicions were instantly confirmed. The set-list was not only printed (i.e. set in stone, never to be deviated from), but it came in German, 'American', French, Spanish, Italian and, of course, Japanese. Its simplicity was poetic: first half: Mozart; second half: J. Strauss (the waltz guy); finally: bugger off quick so we can count the cash and underpay the musicians.*

Just as I was mulling over going to ask for a refund, a

* I have learned this from bitter experience.

gong sounded (nice touch), and we were all ushered through into the oval Rosenkavaliersaal, the 'heart of the Palais Auersperg', where we took our seats; or rather some of us began a fun but complicated game of musical chairs that went on for approximately ten minutes, accompanied by multiple popping flashbulbs and ah-ing at the giant bay windows, ubiquitous gold leaf and massive chandeliers.

With this palace you are really spoiling us.

Soon the Residence Orchestra swished out – gents in black tie and gel, ladies in low-cut peach and cleavage. They resembled accountants. It was like sitting inside a giant yellow wedding cake. The lights dimmed, the Japanese hushed as best they could, and off we went.

Track one: the lady pianist bobs up and down as she plays. That's all.

Track two: two audience members suddenly start singing along. Oh no – nutters! But then they jump up and clamber on to the small stage to reveal themselves as proper operatic singers – it's part of the show. What a brilliant gimmick. We laugh and applaud and they soon leave, bowing. The Japanese particularly enjoyed this one.

Track three: a smiling violin solo.

Track four: a whole number full of smiling from everybody.

Track five: la-la-la-la-de-de-dum, dum, de-de-de-de dum. Ta-daaaa!

Track six: two dancers emerge from giant side doors and do some precarious leaping ballet. Their thudding footfalls almost drown out the seven musicians lined up behind them.

Track seven: Badda-bum, badda-bum, badda-daaaaaaaaa!

During the interval, the Japanese drank champagne and took photographs. The second half was the same as the first, only with more dancing, as the music was waltzes and polkas, which, judging by this, was all Johann Strauss ever wrote.* After this, we shouted *bravo*! And some stooges threw bunches of flowers on to the stage, and the lead violinist held them to her heaving peach chest and pretended to cry. They looked plastic. The Japanese leaped up and gave a standing ovation, then scuttled towards the exits. Bratislava by ten! Budapest for lunch!

Slumped in front of CNN back in my hotel room, I noticed that the back page of tonight's concert programme was speckled with strange quotes from various international publications:

One of the best orchestras that has ever visited Uruguay! – *El Pais*, Montevideo.

This orchestra will be famous all over the world one day. Many thanks to all musicians. – *Epikerotita*, Athens.

P. Moser was the star of the open-air concert before 100,000 people at the International Festival of Marrakech. – *Kronen Zeitung*, Vienna.

* Yup.

and finally the heartbreaking,

The audience was enthusiastic! – *Allgemeine Zeitung*, Hanover.

Death in Vienna

Mozart died in 1791, of a mystery illness he'd been struggling with for years. Some say it was rheumatic fever; a few claim it was progressive kidney failure; others demand it was a uraemic coma. Has nobody given credence to the notion of a broken heart? The film *Amadeus* claims Mozart was poisoned by his jealous rival, the Viennese court composer Antonio Salieri – who did actually confess to the murder in his old age, only he was completely deranged by then, so it doesn't count.

A few months before his agonizing death, Mozart was commissioned by an anonymous patron to compose a Requiem – a death Mass. It suited his frame of mind and the work soon began to take shape as a Mass for his own demise. Feverish Wolfgang laboured over its composition laid up in his bed by candlelight, but died before finishing it. This dark, tortured masterpiece was eventually completed by one of his pupils, Franz Xaver Sussmayr, though not performed at his funeral as, legend has it, Mozart's remains were tossed into an unmarked pauper's grave, the spot of which has been lost to history for ever.

By dying so young and never achieving the fame, success and riches he and his father so craved, it's easy to interpret Mozart's life as ultimately tragic. History, of course, has provided the mother of all valedictions, but there's no denying that it *is* a tragic story, yes.

*

This is as far as he got with Requiem. *This music – in Mozart's own hand – is the last thing he ever wrote.*

Johannes Chrysostomus Wolfgangus Theophilus Mozart scores:

Sex: 7. As a weedy shortarse, his sex score should maybe be lower; but he had two kids and enjoyed frolicking with whores, so I think this is fine.

Freemasonry: 10. Ask a Mason their favourite composer and they'll reply Mozart. Thus it figures that anyone who says their favourite composer is Mozart must be a Freemason. Beware of this in otherwise meaningless conversations with people who don't shake hands properly

Rock 'n' roll: 10. How could he score anything less?

Seb suggests:

Great Piano Concertos by Vladimir Ashkenazy (Decca) 🎹🎹🎹🎹

(I think I like Mozart's piano concertos most of all. They're just so . . . *of themselves*, I don't know how to explain it.)

Symphony No. 40, K550 by Sir Charles Mackerras and the Prague Chamber Orchestra (Telarc Digital) 🚙🚙🚙🚙

(Super-famous melody. Pushes all the right buttons. Tasteful and sunny as ever, but with shade and length, like good wine.)

Die Zauberflöte (Magic Flute – Highlights) by Karl Bohm and the Viennese Philharmonic (Decca) 🚙🚙🚙🚙

(I do like these plebeian 'highlights' CDs; it makes it so much easier to enjoy opera when half of it's missing.)

Requiem by Herbert von Karajan and the Berliner Philharmoniker (Eloquence) 🚙🚙🚙🚙🚙

(Out of all the music I've heard so far, this makes my spine tingle the most. You can *hear* the creeping death, *experience* the wounds of a soul stripped bare; here is all the evidence one could ever need that Mozart was an indescribable motherfucking genius. Even a boulder would be moved by this – it's absolutely *banging*.)

Falco: *Final Curtain: The Ultimate Best of Falco* (EMI) 🚙
(For any Austrian readers.)

Opus: *Live is Life!* (Euro Trend) 🚙
(Ditto.)

DJ Otzi: *Never Stop the Alpenpop* (EMI Liberty) 🚙🚙🚙🚙
(Thritto.)

9. Top Cat

We've been on a bit of a run: Bach followed by Handel followed by Vivaldi followed by Mozart – unimpeachable visionary genius following unimpeachable visionary genius; the stakes have climbed higher by the man; even though I feel I'm struggling slightly to keep up with all this over-whelming firepower (my ears are OK, but my brain labours to keep up with developments). And there's only been one composer, say experts, to have ever peaked higher than Mozart, and that's the clenched, grumpy, pock-marked little misery-guts who paid Wolfgang a visit one rainy afternoon in Vienna, and whose ugliness and huge bushy eyebrows are said to have put the Salzburg maestro right off his hair-of-the-dog Gewurztraminer. It was the only time they met: the ailing, distracted thirty-something buffoon and the early-teen prodigy with fingers like tree-trunks who wouldn't take no for an answer, not even after Mozart told him sorry, he couldn't give the kid piano lessons, he had enough on his plate as it was. Hearing this, the teenager flushed bright red and beat his hands up and down on the piano lid and demanded a retraction. Mozart stared at him, a bit freaked out, and said, *All right I'll teach you, I'll teach you, calm down, for Christ's sake.* The swarthy child grunted with pleasure, jumped down off the piano stool and left the room, slamming the door behind him.

'Well who the fuck was that?' muttered Mozart, scratching his wig.

'That was Ludwig van Beethoven,' replied someone.

Mozart and Beethoven never met again, because a few days later Beethoven was called back to Bonn, his home town, having received news of his mother's imminent death (Mozart was to die soon himself). For Beethoven, the 500-mile trip home was a wasted one, as he disliked his mother – she'd never understood his brooding silences and swarthiness – and some days later he arrived back in Bonn, and she died. Great. Now Beethoven was left with his embarrassing alcoholic father and shite younger brothers, none of whom respected or understood the young man's silent, brooding genius. Life, so far, was a complete pile of shit.

All this made Ludwig very depressed. All this and everything that had happened to him already (smallpox, parental rejection, humiliation at school, humiliation with the chicks, frequent brooding strops, buck teeth, getting rained on) made him very serious. Very very serious indeed. Also very brilliant. And brooding.

'You're pretty much at the pinnacle of all music,' wrote Fiona. I read her email feeling rather like Sir Edmund Hillary must've felt at the summit of Mount Everest in May 1953. I'd been looking forward to Beethoven for months; his passion and noisiness precede him, and I was ready for a whole new school of dynamic bluster – Mozart had been cool, but even he lacked that killer cutting edge that I'd been craving since all this began.

'There's a school of thought which says it's downhill all the way from here,' Fiona continued. In my mind I thrust my flag into the snow and gazed towards the distant horizon. *Thanks, Sherpa Fiona*, I croaked through metaphorically frostbitten lips. 'But it's not mine.'

Sherpa Fiona, you're pushing me too hard.

Symphony for the Devil

All the Beethoven quotes in this chapter are real

London, England, December 2004

The majority of Beethoven's fame stems from his string of nine symphonies. I decided that it would probably be a Very Enlightening Thing to get as close as I possibly could to these symphonies, to get to know them as well as I know the contours on my mother's sweet face. This, I considered, would probably take a week or two: some brooding solitude and a muddy river to passionately bestride. Fortunately I live two minutes from the Thames and it's often pretty muddy, especially now in winter. So one Saturday, following a petty argument with Faye over whether to listen to the football results now or wait until *Match of the Day*, I stormed out of the house, slammed the front door and strolled bitterly down through the traffic to Kew Bridge. Only then did I remember to clench my fists properly, like Beethoven, and put my woolly hat on. Brooding along nicely by now, I crossed the bridge, climbed down to the river's edge and, squinting into the fierce late afternoon sun, pressed play on my mp3 player and began to stride sullenly west. My bottom was ever-so-slightly itchy, but fuck it.

(After each symphony I'll include a small comment from Beethoven himself, which will I hope illuminate the personality of the man; as befits a genius of such stature, his psyche was terribly myriad and complex.)

Symphony No. 1 (by Herbert von Karajan and the Berlin Philharmoniker, recorded in 1985) 🚐 🚐
Beethoven wrote this after he'd moved to Vienna from Bonn

in 1799, and right away everything sounds different. Music's leaped forward, acquired a new, post-Mozart dimension – there's more texture and nuance: it's like when TV switched from black-and-white to colour. Beethoven was the first composer to treat the dynamic markings on the musical score (*fortissimo*, *allegro*, *staccato*, etc.) as importantly as the notes themselves. This is still dainty and delicate in places, like Mozart, but basically this is like a revolutionary guerrilla fighter has marched on to the scene in jackboots, covered in blood and silage, sobbing. The new regime isn't about melody any more, this is about *ache*. It's not totally sorted in Symphony No. 1; Beethoven was still learning and chock-full of egocentric rumination, but you can see where he's coming from; there's enough bump 'n' grind in this to distract you from zoning out, just about. Those in the know are usually quaintly patronizing about this symphony, but I have to say it sounds all right to me. It's a bit flimsy here and there, but then maybe I'm just saying that because everyone else says it. At its Viennese première in 1800, no one really liked it much at all. That'll be the shock of the new.

Beethoven says: 'In order to become a capable composer one must have already learned harmony and counterpoint at the age of from seven to eleven years, so that when the fancy and emotions awake one shall know what to do according to the rules.'

Symphony No. 2 (by Claudio Abbado and the Vienna Philharmoniker, recorded in 1988)
Beethoven was a hardcore nature-lover. Not for him the cupcakes and courtesy of the salon-dwelling establishment; instead Ludwig loved nothing more than to cock a snook to everybody and pound the banks of the Rhine, the towpaths of the Danube, forests, hills, meadows and dales, brow-a-

beetled, soaked from rain and covered in Romantic mud. Some days after my initial excursion, I set off down to the river, this time with his Second as my muse. During this particular circuit, something very strange took place: at some unremarkable point between the Isleworth ferry (arthritic ferryman in rowing boat) and Richmond Lock (sticky around the hems), I unwittingly began to *properly listen to the notes*. Instead of letting the music wash through my subconscious and taking note of its impression and effect like I've only been able to do so far, I found myself actively hanging on to every note and melody and harmony and nuance and progression – all for the very first time. This was a true awakening, listening without my mind somewhat elsewhere. I forgot where I was and what I was doing and stood wide-eyed at the plunging swoopy bits, rapt at the hushed niggly bits, gripped through the avalanche runs, following themes, movements, following the *whole symphony*. It was weird – it was wonderful! My listening skill had reached a new and mature elevation. I worried that it might disappear again, but it didn't; it seems to have stayed.

Beethoven's second symphony is *busy*.

Me by the snowy Thames: enraptured.

Beethoven says: 'How happy I am to be able to wander among bushes and herbs, under trees and over rocks; no man can love the country as I love it. Woods trees and rocks send back the echo that man desires!'

Symphony No. 3 'Eroica' (by George Szell and the Cleveland Orchestra, recorded in 1958) 🚌🚌🚌🚌🚌

As everyone knows, Beethoven went deaf. Schoolchildren ask their teacher how a great composer was supposed to compose music if he couldn't hear what he was doing, and the answer is that he had all the music inside his head, so all he had to do was write it down. Ah, that's so sad and unfair (and clever!), sigh the children. This way everyone remembers Beethoven because he's the deaf one, like Mozart was the infantile one and Bach's the coolest cos we both have the same first name (almost). But what they're not taught is that it was actually much worse than that: Beethoven's hearing problems began in his early twenties, and got steadily worse until, by the age of forty, his deafness was total. Thus, by the time he came to write his Symphony No. 3 at thirty-three, his condition had already been diagnosed as incurable; Ludwig could only hear his own piano-playing if he was completely spazzed out on wine and surrounded by the cool silence of his filthy Viennese apartments (he moved house about sixty times, and his personal hygiene was non-existent). This significantly increased his levels of swarthy and brooding single-mindedness and drunkenness.

The Third is a long, strange trip – this was the big leap forward. Three times the length of any symphony yet attempted (Mozart's only lasted about twenty minutes each), this monster was originally conceived by Beethoven as a tribute to Napoleon Bonaparte, whom he admired as a true man of the people, despite his recent annexing of the entire

Rhineland plus his own home city of Bonn. (Beethoven changed his mind about the dedication after Napoleon went on to crown himself Emperor – that was a *step too far*, thought Ludwig.) It's called the 'Eroica' (Heroic) Symphony; and this one's probably my favourite: there are no weak movements; it has a distinctly superior degree of weirdness and *welly*. It struts out with two blasting stiletto chords right out of James Bond, then clouds of hope drift past until back comes a violinquake, which dissipates before surging up to a vegetable-cutting knife and collapsing back into the mirrored sea. That's two minutes. The sea's calm for a while until the wind stomps through like a *bitch*, chopping more of them veggies before blowing itself out on some human rocks that begin to dance. The wind is defeated for a good thirty seconds until strings and wind have a McCartney-esque conversation before the wind demands revenge. Trumpets aid the storm but, phew, just in time are more dancing humans, who reveal themselves to be worried about this situation after all; tragedy smoulders through them; they stand aghast for a few minutes and then, holy fuck, from out of nowhere rings a chord that sounds like Philip Glass. It's 200 years too soon, so everyone flees, and the sea calms down. Next, the sea's showing off because it's huge and deep and significantly more triumphant that the wind could ever hope to be. A theme recurs here, but I was so busy typing I'm not sure which bit to link it to. The wind returns suddenly with its mates thunder and lightning, but it's still way in the distance, so we listen to the sea's love talk to its whales and fish. The whales do a beautiful slow muffled dance to prove they don't care about the thunder and lightning, and then it's that theme again, the waves have nicked it. Sharks circle for no good reason, it's a jungle under there; lurching slabs of waves jostle with buffing wind with spray flying everywhere, but here come the humans again, celebrating this dumb wind/sea battle! Now, as the camera pulls back, we get some perspective: how insignificant we are compared to the power of nature. We nod with the violins as white tips skim off the tops of the waves as it's apparent that the wind and the sea are back friends again. Our hearts are warm with flatulent brass, but you see those dark clouds on the horizon over there? *Watch out.* That's the second movement – you'll need an umbrella for it. For symphonic descriptions of movements two, three and four, send an SAE to Societal Re-adjustment, Hounslow Social Services, Middlesex TW1T TW00. Don't forget to include a crayon if you want a reply.*

Beethoven says: 'I must say that I live a wretched existence. For almost two years I have avoided all social gatherings because it is impossible for me to tell the people that I am deaf. If my vocation were anything else it might be more endurable, but under the circumstances the condition is terrible; besides, what would my enemies say – they are not few in number! To give you an idea of this singular deafness, let me tell you that in the theatre I must lean over close to the orchestra in order to understand the actor; if I am a little remote from them I do not hear the high tones of instruments and voices; it is remarkable that there are persons who have not observed it, but because I am generally absent-minded my conduct is ascribed to that.'

Symphony No. 4 (by Bela Drahos and the Nicolaus Esterhazy Sinfonia, recorded in 1995)
As Beethoven came from old-fashioned working stock and

---

* The second movement takes place in a spooky cave, dripping with dry ice and dinosaurs. This symphony really is the business.

was openly contemptuous of nobility, he didn't bother with wigs like everyone else. He was rugged, macho and didn't care what anyone thought. This makes him the first composer whose hair we see.

This portrait is excessively flattering.   *This one's plainly ridiculous.*

Maybe it was because of this unusual 'up yours, your lordship' attitude – the polar opposite to Mozart's – that the nobility loved him quite so much back in return. I mean they *really* loved him. But Beethoven was stubborn. Previous composers were well practised at bowing and scraping for a living, more concerned with hawking for commissions than sitting brooding in silence, ignoring the front door. Or not being able to hear it. Beethoven's answer to pretty much everything was:

'Ich bin *Beethoven*.'

'Tonight, Ludwig, you will be performing in front of Prince Lobkowitz, Prince Lichnowsky, a clutch of counts and a sell-out crowd. Please make sure you brush your hair and wear a clean shirt and that both shoes are the same colour.'

Beethoven would roll his eyes in livid annoyance: 'Ich bin *Beethoven.*'

Or: 'Ludwig, we all agree you're a genius, and that actual performance is beneath you, but we also know you've got no money, so we've arranged a sell-out concert with all the proceeds going into your own pocket. How about coming on at the end and playing one little song?'

'Ich bin *Beethoven.*'

'Or just a wave to the crowd at the end?'

Ludwig stormed off in the direction of the muddy forest.

The Fourth begins with some genuine tension and tingle, almost as if *Beethoven had written this in the forest*. It tiptoes warily through the woods until boulders crash down and turn the symphony into something more regular (as is inevitable with seventy violins). But it's still fab. My cynical defences are useless in the face of this stuff. Honest, I tried not to like this; I was ready to dismiss the Fourth, as I'd taken too long over the last couple; but it's absolutely lovely, and fascinating and innovative and entirely listenable. And yeah, so let's go 🚐🚐🚐🚐 and be done. One more thing to mention: it has some top clarinet/bassoon action going on that sounds like political chickens.*

Beethoven says: 'I have often cursed my existence; Plutarch taught me resignation. I shall, if possible, defy Fate, though there will be hours in my life when I shall be the most miserable of God's creatures. Resignation! What a wretched resort; yet it is the only one left to me!'

Symphony No. 5 (by Claudio Abbado and the Vienna Philharmoniker, recorded in 1988) 🚐🚐🚐

---

* Fiona says this symphony is 'very much for the connoisseur'.

Well, it's a relief to finally come to something we all recognize. I can lean on this and relax for a few minutes. Drink a glass of water. Crack my knuckles and pick my nose. Visit the little boys' room. The *Fifth* begins with what is unquestionably the most famous sequence of notes in all history – of pop, classical, jazz, folk, everything.

This might resemble Beethoven's fair hand,
but it is in fact my own; aided by a ruler.

Bom bom bom *BOMMMMM*
Bom bom bom *BOMMMMM*
Bom bom bom bom (bom bom bom bom) bom bom bom bom
Bom bom bom bom (bom bom bom bom) bom bom bom bom
Bombombombom (bombombombom)
Bombombombom (bombombombom)
Bombombom *BOM* BOM *BOMMM*

Then it flips up a key and does it all over again (but different). Beethoven's really flexing his muscles with this opening salvo; sweaty; punchy; sweet holy Jesus he's angry; Angry Anderson; jabbering Johnny Rotten; hollering Henry Rollins; *no*, he's GG Allin in a suicidal faeco-funk – look out! What comes after that opening bit, though. Does anybody know? Has anyone ever listened beyond that point and unlocked the secrets behind the symphony? Methinks not, but don't worry, I'll do it.

Altogether, in the first movement of the Fifth, the

'bom-bom-bom-*bom*' riff occurs 124 times (it doesn't technically have to be 'bom' – any syllable will do: ta-ta-ta-*ta*; la-la-la-*la*; cow-sheep-duck-*horse*). Technically it's just three quick Gs and a longer E-flat – Iggy and the Stooges couldn't have written it simpler – but what it does have is (raw) power. And I know Beethoven repeats it 124 times because I just listened and noted them all down. The number's even higher if you include the riff's appearance in the middle of runs, or when it makes up entire runs by itself. It's amazing how they all fit together; the movement's almost entirely built from that phrase alone. Beethoven called the sequence 'Fate knocking at the door'; and he was right there, dude, because with this single symphony (and a little help from his Ninth and the sonic debris of the earlier Third), he'd invented the Romantic era, all by himself; and if that's not fate then tell me what is. What he'd done was to cast aside the formality of traditional structure and express his raging inner nature. This was total punk rock. With the cow-sheep-duck-*horse*ing of the Fifth he'd smashed through the formal repression of classical music (which, hey, we've all felt, right?) and let loose his inner sensibilities – plain *feeling*. No longer did a composer have to hide how he felt inside within layer after layer of dullard 'suggestive' orchestration. You could express yourself however you wanted! No rules. Bom-blooming-*bom*.

The rest of the Fifth is quite rubbish; plus I only seem to be able to detect three movements. Where's the fourth, Ludwig? The *fourth*?

Beethoven says: 'Never did my own music produce such an effect on me; even now when I recall this work it still costs me a tear.'

Symphony No. 6 'Pastorale' (by Nikolaus Harnoncourt and the Chamber Orchestra of Europe, recorded in 1987) 🚚🚚🚚🚚

By this point in his life (thirty-eight), Beethoven was recognized throughout Europe as the most important, pre-eminent composer and pianist of his era, as good as, perhaps even better than, Mozart already (so why aren't there any *Basically Beethoven* shops in Vienna, hmm?). And Symphony No. 6 sounds like Ludwig decided to compose something in honour of his own true muse – not the ravishing temptress Countess Schmidt, nor that coquettish slut Archduchess Mönchengladbach, but Mother Nature herself, ever resplendent within Beethoven's ill-mannered yet ardent heart. This is the sound of the countryside come to life via glorious, stately orchestration: trees writhing in the cool breeze as flies shimmy drowsily through the fragrant summer haze, while the Danube sighs and burbles along its gentle, meandering course through the valleys and meadows of the sublime Austro-Hungarian countryside splattered with the blood and bones of the freshly mutilated soldiers of the Battle of Austerlitz. It's the closest Beethoven ever came to a chill-out record – there's a barely a single hot-under-the-collar violin or exclamation mark to be found. For this may the Lord make us truly thankful, Amen.

Beethoven debuted his Fifth and Sixth symphonies, plus his brand new Mass in C, Fourth Piano Concerto and the hastily thrown-together Choral Fantasia at Vienna's Theater an der Wien on 22 December 1808. Punters were sparse, since not only were Napoleon's armies bearing down hard upon the Viennese outskirts, but there was also a big official charity concert in town that night, which had nicked all the good musicians who hadn't already fled. Beethoven, therefore, was left with a bitterly cold half-empty theatre and a second division orchestra with which to get through over four hours' worth of brand new music. Oh, and the orchestra had only had one rehearsal. As the miserable trickle of overcoat-wrapped concert-goers filed into the icy auditorium, Beethoven glowered in the wings, downing glass after glass of cheap red wine, bellowing unnecessary obscenities at his pitiful orchestra. Tonight already looked like it was going to be brilliant!

The concert was a spectacular disaster. Beginning with the spanking new Sixth, the audience actually laughed out loud at parts (mostly where the flutes were trying to imitate cuckoos), as did the players themselves (perhaps during the cuckoo passages). Thrown, bemused and angry, Beethoven turned to the crowd at its finale and was greeted with complete silence – even the odd mocking cuckoo impression – which thankfully he couldn't hear anyway. Undeterred by the lack of applause, he moved on to the next piece, the reservist soprano of which fled the stage in tears before they'd even got to the end. Beethoven sat at his piano and shrugged. Women, eh?

During the interval, most people walked out. Beethoven glowered in the wings, swigging more booze. Friends came backstage with suggestions on how to make the evening a little more fun for everybody, but Ludwig told them all to get lost.

The second half was even worse. The orchestra refused to play any more with Beethoven conducting, so someone else was hurried to the podium. The new, revolutionary Fifth received predictably short shrift, and then during the piano concerto, Beethoven (on piano again) and the orchestra went off in separate directions, so that nobody left in the audience knew what the hell was going on. Enraged, Beethoven stopped playing, ran over to the orchestra and screamed, *You useless bastards, can't you read? Play it properly! I've never heard such a pile of shit in all my life!* Then the reservist conductor discreetly whispered into Beethoven's ear trumpet that *he* was the one who'd fucked up, not the orchestra. Beethoven stood there for a minute, went back to his piano and played five minutes' worth of improvisations in C Minor, hoping that would paper over the cracks a little. Then he knocked both his candlesticks over and had to stop to pick them up. Twice.

After this was all finished, the orchestra stood to receive a little well-earned sympathetic applause from the remaining frozen punters. When Beethoven stood for his own ovation, he was met once more with silence; even some boos. The moral of this story? Beethoven wasn't really a people person.

Beethoven says: 'Oh ye men, who think or declare me to be hostile, morose or misanthropical, what injustice ye do me! Ye know not the secret cause of what thus appears to you! My heart and mind were from childhood disposed for the tender feelings of benevolence; I was always wishing to accomplish great deeds!'

Yeah whatever, Beethoven.

Beethoven also said: 'Madame _____ is completely changed since I threw half a dozen books at her head. Perhaps something of their contents accidentally got into her head or her wicked heart!' (Could this be the legendary 'Immortal Beloved', the mystery woman to whom he actually once wrote something kind?)

Symphony No. 7 (by Roy Goodman and the Hanover Band, recorded in 1988) 🚐🚐🚐
As the Napoleonic wars thudded by, with Beethoven completely oblivious to their progress, various shell-shocked physicians attempted to cure Ludwig's deafness, with varying results. Below are a few genuine examples, along with his verbatim post-prognosis:

Almond oil poured down the lugholes.

Beethoven's response: 'Nothing happened. My hearing grew worse and worse, my bowels remained as they had been (arduous) and I was often in despair.'

Tree bark affixed to his lower arms (in an attempt to 'suck out' the impurities occupying his ears).

Beethoven: 'I am in constant agony and can barely move my arms to write my music! This situation is ridiculous!'

A cold bath (washing was unfashionable).

Beethoven: 'Get me out! The man is a medical ass!'

A lukewarm bath, with water from the Danube.

Beethoven: 'That worked wonders, my belly improved but my deafness remained and became even worse!'

Various herbs, forced down the ear canal by a priest.

Beethoven: 'My ears sing and buzz constantly, day and night!'

A hearty stroll through a muddy forest in the rain.

Beethoven: 'Zat ist much better!' (You might have noticed that Beethoven rarely said anything without a flaming exclamation mark at the end. Sadly, for all those who ever met him, this was very much the case.)

Only recently have contemporary doctors been able to diagnose Beethoven's deafness as some sort of mystery viral infection. It might have been something called labyrinthitis, or neurolabyrithitis, possibly even otospongiose. 'We will never know the state of his ossicles,' mourn doctors today, though they haven't entirely ruled out syphilis.*

At around this time, Beethoven's younger brother Caspar died. Beethoven didn't give a toss, though for reasons known only to the maestro himself, he decided it was his duty to attempt to raise his brother's surviving teenage nephew Karl by himself, ignoring the protestations of the

* Or Satan.

boy's own mother (indeed, suing the selfish bitch); this did not go very well: a few weeks into his co-habitation with cuddly Uncle Ludwig, young Karl decided to commit suicide. He shot himself in the head twice, but one bullet missed and one just made him bleed all over his uncle's music. Karl fled the apartment and joined the army, thus ending Beethoven's solitary attempts at parenthood.

Beethoven says: 'I am a king!'

Symphony No. 8 (by George Szell and the Cleveland Orchestra, recorded in 1958)

Can listening to classical music give you toxic shock syndrome? I fear I may be afflicted with something similar. It would seem that intensively force-feeding the human brain Beethoven symphonies can result in short-term mental health damage and depression. I have constant headaches, I'm grouchy, I find it hard to get up in the mornings, I've little or no energy, I have a big itchy red rash to the right side of my nose that I can't seem to get rid of. I'm like the guy out of *Super Size Me* – I've *foie gras*ed myself through Beethoven overexposure. Also, my feet ache from all the walking around the Thames. And, to my shame, I've even found myself beginning to sympathize with Beethoven's pathological misanthropy. I email Fiona to tell her I haven't got any stamina left for Symphonies 7 and 8, asking for advice. My tone is whiney.

'I wonder what sort of recordings you're listening to?' Fiona replies. 'The style of playing Beethoven has changed dramatically – especially the speeds, with the taste now being for far quicker tempi, and that doesn't half lighten things.'

Lighten? Arse, this was all the wrong way around – I wasn't finding it too light, I was finding it too oppressive. Which is the same as dark, isn't it? Either way, I was confused.

Which wasn't helped by Fiona's subsequent listening tip: 'I could suggest you go to see *The Mousetrap*, in which you hear an old gramophone recording, probably conducted by someone very famous like Furtwängler, of the slow movement of Symphony No. 7. I saw it about 150 years ago and I may be misremembering, but I think it was the best bit of the play.'

What useful information this was. Regarding Beethoven's Eighth, Fiona added: 'It tends not to be one of the most talked-about ones.'

Which means we're not obliged to talk about it, so let's not. We're going to take a 'symphonic day off'.

Beethoven says: 'Ah! It seemed impossible for me to leave the world until I had produced all that I felt called upon to produce; and so I prolonged that wretched existence.'

Symphony No. 9 'Choral' (by Herbert von Karajan and the Berliner Philharmoniker, recorded in 1977) 🚌🚌🚌🚌🚌
For some reason I've owned this CD since way before this whole thing began; I think I bought it in one of those brief, bogus flashes of inspiration you occasionally get in the record shop when you suddenly, blindly decide to go enlighten yourself in the classical zone. These moments are often accompanied by an hangover and involve a specific kind of half-arsed mope, trying and failing to look like you know what you're doing and where exactly you're going, until you belatedly realize you're standing bang in the middle of the opera box-set section, everything costs £100, and you're wedged between an irritated man with a beard and briefcase and David Mellor. You read something, somewhere, a few weeks ago about a piece of classical music that you quite liked the sound of but now you can't remember what the hell it was called, or indeed anything about it whatsoever, but you're damned if you're going to go and

ask one of those smug-looking counter staff if they read the same interview with whoever it was whenever that was where he talks about his love of thingy, you know, that harrowing haunting whatnot which made him feel like really amazing and, oh, come on, they must have it *somewhere*. Why isn't it in a special display? Which, I think, is how I came to acquire this CD of Beethoven's Ninth; I don't know, I can't remember. Or unless someone gave it to me as a present one time; or all my other Beethoven symphonies gathered themselves together and procreated and this came out.

The Ninth though. I love it, and urge you to get hold of a copy as soon as possible; it's a steaming, stomping apogee of all Beethoven's iconographic *Donner und Blitzen*, all wrapped up in one noisy, sweeping snowball of fire *und* ice *und* beauty, joy *und* angst. And even though the final movement does go on for an excruciating twenty-four minutes, it has 'Ode to Joy', the official European Union national anthem, at the end. Yes it's true. This was the high watermark against which every composer's subsequent symphonies had to measure up. Nine times out of ten they failed.

Beethoven cries: 'When I composed that, I was conscious of being inspired by God Almighty. Do you think I consider your puny little fiddle when He speaks to Me?'

Ludwig died in March 1827, after a long and grisly stomach illness. On the night of his death there was a violent thunderstorm, and legend has it that, following a bolt of lightning and terrifying clap of thunder, he thrust himself out of bed, clenched his fist at the heavens and roared a defiant challenge back at the skies, before falling back dead upon his pus-stinking pillow. Apocryphal or not, it's a very Beethoven way to go.

Classical classical music died with Papa Haydn. Beethoven

opened a door into a new world; the rainy-day world of the Romantics; whose numerous foppish advocates dominated the rest of the nineteenth century. The intrinsic emotionalism of Beethoven's music comes, I reckon, from the rumble and frisson of the tectonic plate-shift between the formal rigour of the old musical structures meeting the free-flowing Romantic lava beginning to flow against it. This struggle is what makes much of his music so poignant and affecting; this unique and explosive alloy of collision. And like Brian Wilson, Bob Dylan and other such visionaries, living any kind of 'normal' life just ain't possible when you're burdened by these kinds of weights. Bad for them, good for us, worst of all for their wives. Actually Beethoven was such an ungrateful, up-himself, grumpy old bastard that no woman could ever bear to marry him; instead, the stave was his wife, the notes his mistress, *the dynamic markings his whore*.

*

Ludwig van Beethoven scores:

Sex: 7. Beethoven was hideously ugly but undoubtedly wanked like crazy.

Drugs: 10. He was an alcoholic but nobody ever mentions it because they're scared to diss him even in the slightest.

Rock 'n' roll: 10. 'Roll over Beethoven' is about *Beethoven*.

Seb suggests:

Symphonies 3, 6 and 9 by the conductor with the craziest hair, worst temper and deadliest baton you can find, conducting the world's most almighty and sonorous orchestra in a giant Inca temple, completely spannered on schnapps and horse tranquillizer, recorded during a full-on multi-megaton atomic sunset (Naxos) 🚐🚐🚐🚐🚐

(The three times table.)

Piano Sonatas by Daniel Barenboim (EMI Classical) 🚐🚐
🚐🚐

(It wasn't all ensemble dynamite with Ludwig. His piano sonatas (for solo piano) are the polar opposite – delicate, honeyed, perspicacious in their twinkling delight. These include the famous 'Moonlight' sonata, which is one of those pieces they embed on galaxy-foraging satellites for aliens to listen to, and is impossible not to like (at least for the first 500-or-so listens); as well as some equally affecting alternative sonatas.)

The Late String Quartets by the Quartetto Italiano (Phillips) 🚐🚐🚐🚐

(These, too, can be mellow, but they're also fiery. They've definitely got a touch of the insane about 'em – twilight days, suicidal nephews, a cosy padded cell. They tend to split opinion: some say they're dry and inaccessible, others plain worship 'em. Fiona says: 'I rate the Late Quartets as just about the Top of All Music and can listen to them any time – but only if I'm not doing anything else, which in practice therefore means not very often.' Since she told me this, I've been listening to them a lot more, and have found myself becoming significantly more intelligent.)*

---

* A useful word of warning for any intrepid classical music bullshitters: true classical aficionados never bother talking about Bach, Mozart or Beethoven, as everyone likes these three already, and assumes everyone else does too. So, if you're trying to bluff your way through a classical conversation, avoid those guys – you'll only reveal yourself as a shallow dilettante. A good name to drop might be Bax; my stepfather owns at least thirty of his CDs, but I can barely find a mention of him anywhere. Bax, then. A sonorous mofo and no mistake.

10. Living in Ludwig's Shadow

And what a shadow it was. Although not much of an *actual* shadow – Beethoven was only five foot four; and Schubert was even shorter: just five feet, and fat. Franz Schubert wore little round glasses, had girly wet lips, pudding-red cheeks, a tight curly perm and was a smug, annoying little shit. As soon as I set eyes on some of his portraits, I knew right away that I wasn't going to get on with him or his pathetic, conceited music.

As was the case with the whole of Vienna in the first quarter of the nineteenth century, Schubert cowered in thrall to the all-consuming spell of Ludwig van Beethoven. There wasn't much point in being a musician around this time; Beethoven had the town sewn up, no one else was getting a look-in, so why not try and get a proper job, hmm? Schubert's arrogance denied him this insight, so he, plus his annoying gang of guffawing bohemians, sat in coffee shops and tried to write music to Goethe poems. It didn't go well – they were useless fops, what did they expect? But a couple of punters checked out tubby little Schubert's stuff and thought they saw a bit of potential; not much, but a bit. This fat kid might have something, a few people deduced – so long as Beethoven didn't mind, of course. (They checked – he did mind – Schubert would never buy ear trumpets in this town again.) Thus the name of Franz Schubert became *slightly well known, but not much really*.

Schubert wrote over 800 of these songs, setting well-known poems to music. It's what he's famous for, except for his Eighth Symphony, which he was working on right up until his emergency dash to hospital with syphilis in 1828 that killed him at thirty-one years of age. The Eighth is otherwise known as the 'Unfinished'.

As I prepared to dismiss the man into the insignificant classical dustbin of history, somewhere at the back of my mind I seemed to recall that my mother had a fondness for Schubert. I phoned to check. We were both well. I had been eating properly.

'Do you mind if we have a quick conversation about Schubert?' I asked.

'Schubert? Schubert!' She sounded slightly hysterical. She said *yes*, she loved Schubert. She spoke some more, but I was trying to think.

I butted in: 'So maybe I could come down and we could have a sort of "Schubert Day" together?' I said.

She paused. 'You mean Schubert only gets a *day*?'

'He was a minor composer, Mother,' I replied sternly.

'Says who?'

I mumbled something incomprehensible and quickly changed the subject.

'A day sounds about the right length of time to me,' I replied; it was all I could bear, to be honest – the wet-lipped little fucker. Down the other end of the line I could hear my mother and stepfather muttering to one another. My stepfather was saying that, although he gave us his blessing, he would not be participating in Schubert Day himself; indeed he might go for a walk or something instead. My mother gave him a good dressing-down, and then we set a date for the following Thursday.

Schubert Day

Winchester, England, January 2005

I arrived in Winchester late in the morning. Schubert Day was overcast and cold, with those occasional showers that make your car dirty. My mother was waiting inside with a boiled kettle and a pile of food on the kitchen table. We drank coffee while she offered me the food, tentatively avoiding any mention of Schubert until my stepfather came downstairs bearing a green manila folder.

'Here he is!' announced my mother. 'He's got something to show you.'

'Ah, you've arrived,' said Pete, passing me the folder. It had a white sticker on the front, with 'Funeral' written on it.

'Hi, Pete. Yep. Here for Schubert Day. What's this?' I opened the folder and pulled out a solitary piece of paper.

'It's a list of the music for my funeral,' said Pete.

He lifted the piece of paper from my suddenly limp grasp. 'And there's definitely some Schubert here somewhere.' He scanned slowly down it. 'Ah, here it is. String Quartet in C. Second movement. That'll be nice.'

He smiled and handed the sheet back to me. I read down the list but wasn't sure what to say. 'So, but I mean, you're not planning to, erm . . .'

'OK, let's get started!' exclaimed my mother, and the three of us filed through into the living room. I glanced at the funeral music and noticed that each of the four pieces had their length jotted down alongside. The total at the bottom of the page came to about forty-five minutes.

'Forty-five minutes?' I politely commented. 'Isn't that rather a long sort of, time, to sort of take with, something quite tricky like . . .'

'This is neither the time nor the place,' my mother growled, plainly horrified by the prospect of Schubert being edited down to a more realistic couple of minutes, say.

My stepfather frowned and began to say something, but the stereo was pumping out Schubert's Fifth Symphony. I decided to keep quiet and just go with the flow.

'This is rather bland Schubert,' called my mother over the music. 'Though I'm sure it's absolutely perfect in its construction.'

At this point I realized my mother was going to be rather biased in her Schubert appraisals today; this wasn't a very level playing field. We sat and listened to more of the Naxos *Best of Schubert* CD that my mother had selected as a gentle introduction. As we listened, I made some notes while my mother, an artist, worked on a painting. Pete dutifully munched at a cereal bar, because he's diabetic, and my mother said he'd got rather overexcited talking about his funeral like that.

'Typical Schubert bass,' said my mother. 'This is for virtuosos.'

Then a few moments later she cried, 'Key change!'

The key had changed.

Then, 'Minor key!' It had gone minor.

'Beautifully light,' she whispered. 'Like a *soufflé*.'

Soon, we came to the 'Piano Quintet in A Major', otherwise known as the 'Trout Quintet'. A piano ran riot.

'Without my hearing aid, I can't really hear the water swirling around. Can you?'

'The water?'

'The water, with the trout.'

'You mean it's called the "Trout Quintet" because this is meant to represent an actual trout?'

My mother looked at me like I was a complete idiot. 'That's right.'

The piano/water boiled up even more, went minor and changed key.

'Minor! Key change!'

'I know, I can *hear*.'

'I wasn't sure whether you knew or not what that was.'

'Well I did, so there's no need to patronizingly shout it out like that.'

'But I didn't think you . . .'

'I said I *did*.'

The 'Trout Quintet' progressed with the three of us now sitting in silence.

'What happens to the trout at the end?' I asked.

'He gets caught.'

'I see.'

Next was an 'Impromptu in G-flat Major'. Pete's eyes were closed, and his slippers swayed with the music. My mother gestured towards him, signalling *look how rapt he is by this*. Pete suddenly opened his eyes and noticed us staring at him. He mouthed: *what?* My mother smiled encouragingly, but he refused to close his eyes again. His slippers stopped swaying.

Up next was something called a 'musical moment'. What the hell is a 'musical moment'?

'Just for fun,' smiled my mother.

'String Quartet 14' – 'Death and the Maiden'.

'Ah. Hmm. This is one with rather a plain tune which then develops.'

It was sad. Wintry. I pictured snowy boughs. Then Schubert Day broke for lunch. We had spinach soup and garlic bread, over which my mother informed my stepfather and me that Schubert had been much better-looking in real life than is often portrayed in his portraits.

'People tend to subscribe to a type of ugly Schubert

caricature. I don't know why, but they do. He was so much handsomer than that plump little man-with-glasses we unfortunately tend to get lumbered with in pictures.'

We washed up, and the *Schubertathon* kicked back in with a pair of song cycles: *Die Schöne Müllerin* and *Winterreise*. As the music began, my mother placed a heavy, yellowing music book into my hands – it was all the musical notation, the complete score, for the song cycles, even though she knows I can't read music.

'Just in case you need it,' she said when I complained. In case of an emergency or something, thankfully, I'd be sitting here with the music. If anyone were to ask.

'You can follow the words, at least,' she said. I opened the book and attempted to look pleased.

'It might be easier if you turn to the right page.'

The song cycles were different. They didn't sound much like classical music; they sounded more like folk songs, or blowsy cartoon vaudeville. Just a piano and a male tenor singing in German, the songs gripped me immediately. They were passionate, dramatic, bittersweet, *tuneful*. I liked *Winterreise* (*Winter Journey*) especially. Through the piece, we follow a lovelorn German gentleman's physical and *meta*physical voyage through a snowy landscape as he rues the loss of his beloved, who appears to have dumped him. It features lines of quite titanic misery, such as: 'Many a tear from my eyes / has dropped into the snow / its chilly flakes suck / thirsting up my burning woe'. Onward he trudges, through the wintry forest, until he notices his hair has turned white. He's pleased. This means he must be old; this suffering won't go on much longer; he'll soon die. But then the snow on his head melts; he sees his black hair underneath and curses his youth, and how long he must now wait until the blessed relief of *death*.

Die Schöne Müllerin is the same, except with a few more chinks of light. A sell-out, in other words.

I followed all these songs on the page, galloping along wild-eyed with the thick black scuds of notes. (This felt extremely professional – you can imagine.) These songs are so distinctive because there are no orchestral star-destroyers in the way – it's just one supertuned piano, one carnage-laden poem and two German guys to get it all out. Its beauty is in its simplicity. Schubert's song tricks are the disarming major chord; the tempo crash; the diaphragm punch; the piano squall; the quavers' quaver. I looked up from all this to see my mother clucking smugly in her armchair.

'Enjoying it, are you?'

'Might be.'

'You are, I can see you are.'

I was – it was solid four-ambulance stuff. And goddamn, did it hurt to admit this to my mother. I suspect this is because, no matter how hard we try, or how grown-up we like to think we've become, we can never truly escape the evil clutches of the unwittingly competitive, childish be-havioural impulse that kicks in whenever we return to our familial bosoms. And oh, what a tiresome state of affairs this always proves to be. You think you can rise above it but you *can't*.

Fiona emails to tell me that Schubert's turning into a bit of a modern-day gay icon. A gay icon? I can't quite get a fix on that, so I investigate further by typing 'schubert gay icon' into Google. Fiona's quite right – 920 search results pop up in response. I warily browse them; not all are wholesome.

'My mother will be devastated to hear about all this,' I write to Fiona, 'as she seems to have a crush on him.'

'Your mother sounds very wise,' Fiona replies, telling me

off again for missing out Haydn and for not knowing about the trout.

Next it's Hector Berlioz. He looked a bit like Liam Neeson.

Deliver Me from the Tyranny of the Fingers

Hector Berlioz was a true hero; a god amongst composers. Born near Grenoble in 1803, Berlioz realized he was a musical genius from an early age but decided not to bother to learn to play a musical instrument – since he was a genius already, why ruin his muse with the fetid dogma of applied practicality? *Pourquoi?* The fact that all composers so far through history and this book have been child prodigies, or at the very least mastered *one* instrument, was all a pointless, steaming pile of *merde*. 'When I consider the appalling number of musical platitudes to which the piano has given birth, I feel grateful to the happy chance that forced me to compose freely and in silence – this has delivered me from the tyranny of the fingers!'

Moving to Paris to take up his natural-born role as *automatique composeur d'éminence générale*, Berlioz went to the theatre and fell in love with one of the actors – an Irish singer called Harriet Smithson. He was smitten, gone, unable to function, screwed by wantage. Harriet soon left Paris for London; thus poor Berlioz began despatching love-letters. Quite full-on love-letters. Indeed, they were completely hysterical. Harriet, who'd never actually met Berlioz, assumed he was some kind of diseased headcase and ripped them all up whilst laughing. In response Berlioz composed his *Symphonie Fantastique*. (Didn't call it his 'First', mind, but his 'Fantastic'.)

The *Symphonie Fantastique* relates the story of Berlioz's

Harriet obsession through music. It's the first time anyone had attempted this – the symphony as pure emotional land-scape – expressionistic autobiography and nowt else. The symphony boldly rejects previous notions of structure, melody and knowledge of musical instruments; it's a self-supporting tone poem – an opera without words. This was totally radical; entirely unprecedented. Trembling with vague excitement, I went and bought a CD of the *Symphonie Fantastique* at HMV for the similarly radical price of £3.99 and cued the bitch up on my stereo preparing to reel with Hector's punches of love bitterly unrequited. I had no idea what to expect, but I was proper pumped up for it. Harriet – you *bitch*.

It was a disappointment. It sounds like, you know, tonality-fuelled (feel it) oompa-classical music. It's fine. There are five movements. The first one's loud, the second's quiet, the fifth (the sound of Berlioz dealing with Harriet's rejec-tion) cranks up into a gangly, twisted firestarter, but frankly it's too little, too late. Where's the whammy? Where's the radicalism? Where's the effing *fantastique*? 🎵🎵🎵

Three years later, Berlioz finally persuaded Harriet to marry him. It went badly; she turned out to be a miserable alcoholic and he stopped fancying her almost straight away. Instead he decided to fall in love with someone else, the Italian pianist Marie Moke. But Marie Moke spurned Berlioz at the last minute and ran off to marry someone else. Berlioz decided to murder her, her mother, the husband and then himself. The usual kind of thing. He purchased a set of pistols and some bottles of poison and took a carriage to Nice, dis-guised as a woman, to sort the bastards out. By the time he arrived, however, he'd forgotten exactly what he was doing there, but stayed for a few years anyway and wrote some more, you know, music and stuff. He wrote for up to thirty pianos at a time. Giant, unwieldy five-hour operas. Everyone thought he was mad, but it turned out he was a preternatural revolutionary. He wrote an autobiography, and it's brilliant and deadpan and hilarious.

Berlioz, the first pure, 100 per cent Romantic – cut him and he bleeds blood. Other Romantics followed swiftly behind.

Frantic Sycophantic Antics from the Early Romantics

In the middle of the 1960s, a mystical confluence took place in English pop music. Astonishingly, for a short while English group the Yardbirds almost featured in their ranks three of the greatest electric guitar players of all time: Jimmy Page, Jeff Beck and Eric Clapton. Had Jimi Hendrix taken a little more acid and decided to join the Yardbirds too, the holy circle would have been complete, thus we might also remember more of their songs (though they did have 'For Your Love' and 'Shapes of Things'). And the world would probably have exploded.

A similar situation had occurred a hundred years beforehand. In Paris in the middle of the nineteenth century, there was a gunslinger vibe going down with a decadent bunch of outlaw musicians who'd hitched up in town with only two things on their minds: chicks and pianos. These were Franz Liszt from Hungary (piano), Fryderyk Chopin of Poland (piano), Robert Schumann from Germany (piano) and Felix Mendelssohn, also German (piano). They wore crushed velvet. They had long hair. They had long spindly fingers. They got fucked up on opium. They had consumption on purpose (it was a chic disease). They wore diaphanous white shirts with frilly, red wine-stained cuffs, and they were all too cool for school. *Almost.*

Just as Pagey and Beck were eventually let down by Clappo's 1980s ('Wonderful Tonight', etc.) and then 1990s ('Tears in Heaven' et al.), so these Early Romantics were let down by Robert Schumann. He was a complete wet blanket. Sensitive to the point of absurdity, Rob had a terrible habit of suddenly bursting into tears for absolutely no reason whatsoever. Everything moved him, even nothing. As a child, just playing a couple of piano chords could trigger floods of anguished tears. When he heard about Schubert's death, he wept the whole night, even though he'd never even met him. Robert Schumann became, overnight, the unacceptable face of this new Romanticism (nothing to do with the new New Romanticism that came later). He was so oversensitive that he kept trying to kill himself, and eventually had to be put in an asylum for his own safety, where he soon died anyway. It's a sad old business sometimes, this classical music.

The remaining three Early Romantic pistol-packers were

Schumann.   *Clappo.*

upset at Schumann's death, though they kept themselves occupied taking opium and shagging countesses, or threatening to, or looking at them all steely and ravishing, coughing blood. Chopin was particularly miffed, as Schumann had recently given him rave reviews in a streetwise fanzine he'd been editing, *Neue Zeitschrift für Musik* (*New Musical Zeitschrift*). Even though he despised Schumann, Chopin felt he owed him, since his own star was rising much faster. (Chopin also despised Liszt: 'a binder who puts other people's work between his covers . . . pah!' Berlioz? *Chujek*. Mendelssohn? *Gowienko*. You're lucky you don't speak Polish. These Early Romantics were all very nice to each other face to face, but in private? *Cholera jasna*.

Fryderyk Chopin represented a whole new way of approaching the piano; of approaching music. Compared to the heavy-duty, epic and thick-set style of Beethoven's piano compositions, Chopin's business was akin to light, florid poetry – he was the first to truly caress his instrument. Born in Warsaw in 1810, Chopin did all the usual child prodigy stuff and then moved to Paris (which had taken over from Vienna as the happening town for music) in 1831. There his feathery technique took everyone by storm; his flyaway fingers and tremulous toes danced over the keys and pedals like nobody before. He was basically *Tommy*, except fully sighted, not deaf and he could speak. That he was the greatest pianist ever thus far to have lived was straightaway beyond any reasonable doubt – this droopy-lidded fop Fryderyk is a mystical Polish genius, agreed Parisian society, and Poland. Soon he became massively famous and had an affair with the writer George Sand and they became the Posh and Becks of their time, before it all went horribly wrong, and Chopin died sluicing blood all down his front.

Though Chopin occasionally composed for the whole

Chopin.   *Beck.*

orchestra, he was, unfortunately, bad at it. He was just too damn Romantic. Chopin's true genius lay in his solo piano music. This came in the form of nocturnes, études, impromptus, waltzes, polonaises and mazurkas. These last two are especially Polish, which means they sound a bit brackish and folk-exotic, although personally I can't tell the difference between any of them – they all sound nice to me, like heavenly roundabouts!

Chopin's piano music is sweeping, swoonsome, swish yet swampy. It's beautiful, lilting stuff, but it makes me feel a bit ill. It's so charming, deft, rich, autumn-tinged and achy that it's like slightly over-ripe fruit. Its physiological effect is mild nausea. I'm surprised and disappointed by this, as I have a history with some of it – when I was young, my father used to drape himself over the piano and play Chopin in the middle of the night; I lay in bed listening to the music wafting up through the house and fell asleep and dreamed oddly to it. But hearing it again now, I find this music hard to love, to hold close and dear. I admire it, but I don't entirely trust it. Or maybe it doesn't trust me. That would make more sense. As Oscar Wilde put it, 'After playing Chopin, I felt as if I had been weeping over sins that I had never committed.'

It wasn't just Chopin who didn't like Franz Liszt; a lot of people couldn't stand him. Mostly this was because they were jealous. Liszt had it all. Amazingly for a composer, he wasn't short; he wasn't ugly; he wasn't a moribund manic depressive; he didn't stalk fervidly along riverbanks; he didn't get syphilis or die young; and this meant everyone thought he was weird. He was just too good to be true. Even today, people remain suspicious of the music Liszt composed. He's considered a bit of a charlatan. This is probably for a number of reasons:

a) He was very good-looking.
b) He was even better at the piano than Chopin – in fact he was quite probably the greatest pianist ever to have walked upon the face of Planet Earth. This probably got him beaten up a few times, especially by friends of Chopin.
c) After a lifetime of shagging around and being an effortless genius without having to lift too many fingers, he then became a priest, while continuing to shag around. People smelled a rat. Even I smell a rat actually.
d) He blotted his copybook by arranging super-cheesy karaoke cover versions of old classics like Bach and Beethoven but with added virtuoso tricks and gimmicks. This wasn't such a great idea – maybe a bit Liberace.
e) He invented the idea of the piano 'recital' – the one-man solo performance. *Recital?* scoffed the public. What a pretentious *wanker*. Not only that, but he played it really theatrically – arms waving in the air, hands crashing down.

All very physical and unnecessary, said the critics, while punters just swooned. Soon, of course, everyone was copying him.

f) He was the first classical performer to have genuine groupies. Women flocked hysterically around, wherever he went. They would fight and faint over the white gloves he theatrically tossed aside on stage. This came to be known as 'Lisztomania'. Seriously, that's what they called it, even back then.

g) He didn't die young, indeed he died very old, still with a mischievous twinkle in his eye.

h) He was very good-looking.

Liszt.   *Pagey.*

Liszt was born in Hungary but was such a dandy already he didn't bother to learn Hungarian. Why bother? Who speaks Hungarian?! Hungarians became angry almost at once. So he spoke German and emigrated, away to follow the well-worn child prodigy path around Europe, ending up in Paris at sixteen years old, a disillusioned, exhausted shell of a strutting peacock gone lame.

Young Liszt was ill with the perpetual musical hamster wheel. He was all ready to throw in the pianist's towel and go get a proper job when, one murky night in Paris, he stumbled upon the Jimi Hendrix of this equation – the unique, über-Satanic figure of the great, the terrifying, the worship-me-or-die spectral figure of Nicolò Paganini. There really was something of the night about this guy.

The Devil's Trill

Like Hendrix, Paganini wasn't interested in the Yardbirds – he was much too singular, cut from a darker cloth. Although it was Beethoven who was chief musical inspiration for the Early Romantics, when it came to performance, they learned everything they knew – got all their moves – from Paganini. A mysterious Italian with giant, full-ham sideburns who used to regularly practise for fifteen hours every day, Paganini was to the violin what Liszt turned out to be to the piano – probably its greatest-ever master. He was so good at it that there was no music complicated enough for him to play with the sufficient degree of amazingness, so he wrote his own. It wasn't all that great, which is why he's not remembered as a composer of much merit, but my, was it fast and furious!

Paganini *shredded*, everywhere he went: Parma (easy), Vienna (five minutes), all Germany (a week), London (ages – cynical bastards), Paris (*à vitesse*) – he got through over forty cities, collapsed in a gibbering, worshipful mass before his pointy black winklepickers. Paganini's performances were necromancing, *Their Satanic Majesties Request*-style black

night incense slash 'n' burn spectaculars. He'd stand on stage
– legs spread – surrounded by gaseous blue light, tossing off
some technical impossibility, then rip out a violin string and
keep on playing. Then he snapped another, then another,
until he was playing the whole goddamn arrangement on a
single string. And he used all manner of lunatic bowings and
finger-techniques, all designed to mess with the audience's
heads. And so it did. Often punters wept, sometimes they
fainted, once or twice people claimed to have become pos-
sessed by the Devil as they watched him play, so cracked
was Paganini's technique (these individuals were discreetly
escorted from the building). Indeed, so profound was Paganini's effect that it became common consensus throughout
Europe that the guy had genuinely done some sort of deal
with Lucifer. How else could people explain the whirlwind
raptures he somehow managed to summon? (The actual
reason was 'absinthe'.)

In private, however, Paganini was a gambler and a mope.
As soon as he hit thirty, he gave up practising and slid
into debt and misery. His sideburns turned grey, he lost

all his teeth, and his jaw went wonky (a cowboy dentist), and he could only watch, dejected and in considerable pain, while his performance techniques were ripped off by the Yardbirds. To mollify himself, he tried to open a casino in Paris, but it came to nothing and swallowed up the remains of his cash. He died in May 1840, of disinterest; and to this day nobody knows what the hell he was doing, back there, to his axe. Except mauling it somehow. Devilishly.

But whoah, hold on – the very least this dandy dark knight deserves is an honest attempt at reappraisal; I'll listen to some of Paganini's violin compositions and try to cling on for dear life. To begin, here are some Caprices in A Minor. I'm surprised to discover the very first one I listen to is the melody for the theme music to television's *South Bank Show* (but faster, *much* faster). Melvyn, you plagiarist!* But these caprices: they're squeaky. The violin whistles; there are lots of yelping harmonics and juddering scrape-stops. It sounds like the cat fighting against the guy trying to take it apart for its guts. Or birds; a piercing flock of attack-birds. At least it doesn't mess about or pretend to be anything it's not. This is gratuitous violin excess. If you like the sound of prolonged, roaring, tyre-screech violins, you'll love it. However, now I have a headache, so let's get back to Liszt.

Liszt's appropriation of the OTT panto stylings of Paganini led to a whole new way of performing classical music: pure showing off. Liszt was such a supervirtuoso that he scored some of Paganini's most impossible-to-play caprices

---

* I have since learned that the show's theme tune was actually 'created' by Andrew Lloyd Webber, though Fiona has warned me that if I call Mr Lloyd Webber a plagiarist, he'll probably sue.

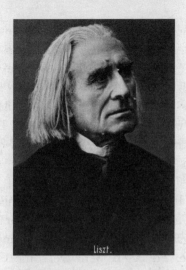

They've invented cameras at last.

for the piano and played them in concert. There was yet more fainting. These pieces are so fiendish to get your fingers around that nobody's ever been able to play them properly since. That's how talented Liszt was – and that's why so many other musicians considered him a charlatan: *pique*. One critic, describing a Liszt performance, wrote breathlessly of his 'magnetism and electricity; his contagion in a sultry hall filled with innumerable wax lights and some hundred perfumed and perspiring people; of histrionic epilepsy; of the phenomenon of tickling; of musical cantharides; and other unmentionable matters!' Forget Elvis, surely this is the birth of rock 'n' roll, right here?

The music he wrote as a young man was pointless. Like Paganini's, it was only so much hot air. But his later work is fantastic. Sure, its virtuosity still dazzles, but it's got a big bright heart and a radical soul, and *solid scaffolding*. Chopin's scaffolding lurches way too much. You get motion sickness. Liszt's preludes, piano concertos, sonatas, Hungarian rhapsodies, all this stuff is fantastically exciting to listen to – modern, fresh and alive inside itself. Though the rhapsodies smell faintly of cheese. He wrote it all as he flitted around Europe, rolling through prestigious musical positions having scandalous affairs with noblewomen. It was a good life. Such was his pre-eminence that musicians, young and old, flocked to hang out and beg him to have a burn-through of their material on his flaming joanna. He pretty much always said, *yeah, sure – and this is your sister, you say?* In his dotage he grew facial warts, like Lemmy from Motorhead. He was surrounded by sycophants and hangers-on but he was cool about it. He always kept his hair long. He was the ultimate Romantic. I like him very, very much.

In 1729, Mendel Heymann begat the Jewish philosopher Moses Mendelssohn. Moses begat Abraham in 1776. Abraham Mendelssohn begat Fanny in 1805, while Felix was begat in 1809. This devout Mendelssohn household, all now begat and living in bourgeois luxury in downtown Berlin, were ultra-conservatives with their own private family orchestra. It was only natural, then, that both Felix and Fanny should blossom into a charming little pair of pianistic genii before they reached, say, three.

Though Fanny was no slouch (she composed three tasty pieces herself, which she named *Three Pieces*), extra-special Felix seemed to be as good at everything as little Mozart had been – maybe even better – so Mater and Pater had no choice other than to encourage their son with his first wee operas, symphonies, concertos and sonatas, all before his balls had dropped, indeed possibly before teddy time. (Is it just me who's tired of tales like this?) Yes, Felix was a genius. Splendid. And off he went to be brilliant everywhere and win prizes and have his violin concerto performed at the Proms every year on the second Thursday in August, right before something a bit zestier, like any old bastard, let's say Johann Strauss (the waltzer). Jesus.

Felix Mendelssohn is the fourth Early Romantic of our slightly tired Yardbirds metaphor.

Felix Mendelssohn.   *Paul Samwell-Smith (bass).*

The tragic thing about Mendelssohn was that for all his promise and technique, he peaked at seventeen, with his ultra-divine 'Midsummer Night's Dream' overture. After that, he was treading water – a busted flush. Talented, *sure*. Bags of potential, *absolutely*. Rhapsodized over by Schumann, Chopin and Liszt, *almost every day*. (They were impressed by his general musicianliness.) Owt worth listening to? *No way, José*. In fact, Mendelssohn's music was so straight-ahead, uninspired, dull and conservative that he became a big draw over in England. As a conductor he was second to none, and he conducted orchestras to huge public acclaim in Birmingham and Manchester. So taken was he by our green and pleasant land, and were we by him, that he composed a few pieces of music in our honour, his *Scottish Symphony* and famous *Hebrides Overture* (featuring 'Fingal's Cave' – not baaad). One day, Mendelssohn was invited/summoned to Windsor Castle by Queen Victoria, who claimed to be a big fan.

'Your music pleases me,' announced the queen. Mendelssohn bowed, and stayed down. 'I am particularly enamoured of this one . . .' Queen Victoria sat down at her piano and bashed out a snippet of *Three Pieces*.

'Ah,' stammered Mendelssohn, still bowing. 'That particular piece, your Majesty, delightful though it undoubtedly is, was written, um, by my sister Fanny.'

'Oh,' said Queen Victoria. And she stopped playing. 'Do you want to play something for us anyway?'

'Yes, all right.'

He sat down and played for about five hours. It was so mushy and boring they invited him back again, time after time after time.

Mendelssohn despised the other Early Romantics. As a hardcore old-skool classicist he was deeply suspicious of all this swashbuckling new harmonic daring and pyrotechnic fingerbobs. He thought they were all vulgar, excessive, and off their heads on ego, booze and damnation. He was right.

Unlike the actual Yardbirds, these Early Romantics were harbingers of the sounds of the future – music was about to get even richer, and twisted and colourful and out of control. Actually, maybe it was like the Yardbirds after all; when they latterly morphed into the *New* Yardbirds and then changed their name to Led Zeppelin. I think my metaphor's back on course. If Mendelssohn thought this lot were bad, wait till he saw who was coming next!

*

Franz Schubert scores:

Sex: 7. I can't get over the fact that Schubert's a bit of a gay icon.

Drugs: 4. Look how I avoid the obvious amyl nitrate joke here.

Rock 'n' roll: 6. And any clichés about disco-dancing and stuff.

Hector Berlioz scores:

Sex: 8. Oh, Harriet.

Drugs: 6. Oh, Marie Moke.

Derangement: 9. Damn that woman (and that one too).

Chopin, Liszt and Paganini score:

Sex: 9. As much and often as possible – they'd sometimes even get serviced as they played.

Drugs: 9. Heroin, please, but whatever's lying about will be fine.

Rock 'n' roll: 9. Klavierhammer of the gods.

Schumann and Mendelssohn score:

Sex: 2. John Paul Jones.

Drugs: 2. John Deacon.

Rock 'n' roll: 3. Paul Samwell-Smith.

Seb suggests:

Berlioz: *Memoirs of Hector Berlioz (from 1803–1865)* by Hector Berlioz (Dover) 🚐🚐🚐🚐
(Large print. Funny. Cheap.)

Schumann: *Vladimir Sofronitsky Plays Schumann* (Vista Vera) 🚐🚐🚐🚐
(Fraught but tasty. This stuff illustrates how freakishly

oversensitive Schumann's disposition really was. Some of this music's so overwrought it actually quivers.)

Liszt: Anything he wrote for solo piano. Sorry to be vague, but hey. 🎹🎹🎹🎹

The following listening suggestions are in my mother's own words. I was specifically not allowed to edit them; nor indeed was my editor; nor the freelance copy editor. *

Heather Heaven:

To experience Schubert's lieder at their best, hear the song cycle *Die Schöne Müllerin*, D795. Deutsche Grammophon do it with five other exquisite songs – Dietrich Fischer-Dieskau sings, with Gerald Moore. Of course. 🎹🎹🎹🎹🎹
Who but Schubert could portray water more wetly or the wind passing through an abandoned lute more poignantly?
Rejoice with the lovelorn wanderer!
Ache, in 'Troch'ne Blumen', as the summer fades and the ghostly elfin footsteps walk over the cold grave : . .
Be enraptured.

For typical Schubert, beautifully played, listen to *Music for Violin and Piano*: Adele Anthony, Violin; Jonathan Feldman, Piano (Naxos Laureate Series) 🎹🎹🎹🎹🎹
'Duo Sonata in A Major' (Op. 70, D895) is a joyous, fond conversation between old friends, with a touch of bitchiness in the scherzo.
'Rondeau Brilliant in B Minor' (Op. 159, D934) goes on a bit. Think, I'm afraid, Dudley Moore.
'Fantasy in C Major' (Op. 159, D934) – ah, bask in this!

---

* Note to copy editor – I hope this is OK.

After tremulous, then exuberant, anticipatory delights, there is That Tune, with its heart-tearing lurch into the minor and back. Witness thereafter the most masterly example of variations on a theme – the fourth so gleefully frenzied it threatens to escape its confines and twinkle off into the ether.

Franz Schubert, by my mother, Heather Bowering.

11. Fascist Dwarf Has Big Ideas

'Wagner? A genius. Without question!'
David Mellor

'I love Wagner, but music I prefer is that of a cat hung up by
its tail outside a window and trying to stick to the panes of
glass with its claws.'
Charles Baudelaire

Even over a hundred years after his death, Richard Wagner
still winds everybody up. There's no in between with this
guy; there's no 'I can take it or leave it'. You're either a
passionate Wagnerian or you're a fervent anti-Wagnerian.
Except me, I'm neither. Not yet. By the time you come to
the end of this chapter, I'll have changed – I'll be either/or.
Which will it be? I'll bet you absolutely cannot wait to find
that out.

Here in the early twenty-first century, Wagner has just
about made it up there with Bach, Mozart and Beethoven.
He's the fourth face up there on the classical Mount Rush-
more. He's that big. The only thing holding him back from
100 per cent permanent acquaintance with the untouchables
(apart from the fact that half of all classical music lovers
despise him) is that, to all intents and purposes, he only ever
wrote opera.

Oh God.

Let's ignore that for a while and begin with Wagner the

man. He was awful. I know that elsewhere in this book I've undertaken a little spurious subjective character appraisal (I mean – Bach wasn't *that* much of a wanker), but consensual consensus of Wagner the man is all mercilessly consensual in its brutal assessment of the personality of Richard (always pronounced 'ree-kard') Wagner. So much so that, when I use the phrase 'complete and utter cunt', I'm actually being quite charitable, and very few classical scholars would argue with me. About that particular fact.

Let's take a look at the evidence.

a) He was a terrible racist, especially with regard to Jews, and believed the Aryan male (German model especially) to be the ultimate manifestation of perfection in humanity (you can see where this is going already, right?).
b) He had a narrow, vertical black moustache and a fondness for Alsatians, side-partings and world domination. (This point is all lies, I apologize.)
c) He kept on seducing married women.
d) He got into debt.
e) He was right up himself.
f) He wasn't very nice to Ludwig, King of Bavaria.
g) Adolf Hitler idolized him. Not terribly fair on Wagner, this one, I know, but they all count, come on.

It's only really point a) that's the problem; most of the rest are typical of most composers. A similar list of Beethoven's personality shortcomings, for example, would be way longer than that – i.e. he kidnapped his nephew – who then attempted suicide – without apologizing to his mother; in fact he threw books at her head.

Another reason people get wound up about Wagner is

because of what he was actually attempting to do. He couldn't care less about anything as facile as symphonies, songs or sonatas; he was way more ambitious than that. Wagner set out to single-handedly *unify the arts.* Yes, modest Wagner's ambition was to invent some ultimate hybrid blending literature, theatre, music, poetry, performance, visual arts, the whole blinking caboodle into one, all-encompassing and definitive art form. And his masterplan, his solution for achieving all this? *Opera that goes on for ages.* Bit of a let-down, that payoff, isn't it? How depressing, that unification of all art equals a large opera. Oh, well.

Wagner's early works were not nearly long enough. These were a bunch of production-line operatic juvenilia composed on the run from the mass of creditors who were forever on his tail. Indeed, his life uncannily mirrors that of television's A-Team – bounding around the place being heroic on a shoestring while avoiding the no-fun forces of law and order. Wagner's love of – nay, insistence upon – luxury at all times, at all costs, compounded this ongoing manhunt. If you lent Wagner £20, for example, no matter how hungry or thirsty he was, or in need of imminent transportation elsewhere, he couldn't help but spend the money on a nice bit of mink, or some expensive perfume, or a pretty silk scarf. Then he'd run away, so you'd have to chase him all over Europe to try and get your money back. Thus, if you close your eyes and picture a midget Barbara Cartland struggling to unify the arts in the back of the trademark black van alongside B. A. Baracas, Hannibal and Face, you've got a pretty accurate portrait of Richard Wagner – the man, his motives, his height and his hay bale-firing combine harvester featuring unnecessary welding.

The strange and unique thing about Wagner is that, unlike many artists with any number of character defects, people aren't willing or able to separate Wagner's art from his personality. This is because his music is so completely 360-degrees, all-consuming, far-reaching and full-on. There's no subtlety here whatsoever. Such is its impact that Wagner the man becomes omnipresent throughout his work in a way that, say, Shakespeare managed to avoid. Thus the audience becomes complicit to the personality. Thus for an audience member to enjoy Wagner means to embrace the man himself; thus, if you like Wagner, you hate Jews, in fact you're a Nazi – it's as simple as that. Wagner fans, however, resent being called Nazis, so the battle rages on in light-hearted books such as these.*

* *Decoding Wagner; Last of the Titans; Aspects of Wagner; The Birth of Tragedy and the Case for Wagner; From Wagner to Virtual Reality; Wagner's Ring: Turning the Sky Round; Ring of Power: Symbols and Themes – Love vs Power in Wagner's Ring Cycle and in Us; Wagner without Fear; Interpreting Wagner; Wagner: The Terrible Man and His Truthful Art; I Saw The World End: A Study of Wagner's Ring; The Tristan Chord: Wagner and Philosophy; The Case Against Wagner; Finding an Ending: Reflections of Wagner's Ring; Wagner's Hitler; Heritage of Fire; Nietzsche and Wagner: A Study in Subjugation; Richard Wagner's Visit to Rossini; Richard Wagner's Literary Journey; Richard Wagner and the Anti-Semitic Imagination; Wagner and the Greeks; Wagner and Russia; Wagner's Ring and Its Symbols; Curse of the Ring: An Archetypal Translation; Wagner Organic; Wagner in Rehearsal; Ring of Power: Penetrating Wagner's Ring; The First Hundred Years of Wagner's Tristan; The Darker Side of Genius; Ring of Myths: The Israelis, Wagner and the Nazis; Wagner: The Wehr-Wolf; The Worker, the Foreman, and the Wagner Act; Wagner Attack! The Ring Cycle and Perpetual Violence; The Teutonic Mythology of . . . ; The Threat to the Cosmic Order: Psychological, Social and Health Implications of Richard Wagner's Ring of the Nibelung; The Ideas of Richard Wagner: An Examination and Analysis of His Major Aesthetic, Political, Economic, Social, and Religious Thoughts; The Abandoned Child, the Authoritarian Father, and the Disempowered Feminine: A Jungian Understanding of Wagner's Ring Cycle; Richard Wagner Allzu Menschlich: Der Meister, die Frauen und das Geld, unter Verwendung von Selbstzeugnissen, Lebensberichten, Briefen und Dokumenten.*

Because no opera house in the known universe wanted to stage his operas (a few had tried before; they'd been a disaster, and Wagner had fled the scene), in 1851 Wagner came up with a cunning plan to circumvent this despotic cynicism – he'd build his own. In fact his plan was even better: he'd not only build his own lavish, state-of-the-art opera house, but he'd also create his own music festival to go with it. Yes, a huge musical extravaganza featuring nothing but his own opera, which the European public, so far, had been perfectly happy to ignore. What a brilliant idea! He asked his mates if they'd mind lending him a few more quid, and they all turned green and ran away. Further away.

However, by 1876 his folly was somehow complete (thanks to young Ludwig, King of Bavaria – though Wagner would soon upset him, and he would console himself building Disney castles throughout the German countryside), and the first-ever Richard Wagner Festival took place in the small German town of Bayreuth that summer, featuring the world première of his epic Ring Cycle. It went well, pulling in over 4,000 punters, although it lost so much money that first year that Wagner couldn't afford to stage it again for six years. There were also many complaints about the toilets. But the festival's sheer audacity and some deft courting of influential music critics broke open the floodgates for Wagner; suddenly his operas were being staged all over the world and they were all the cognoscenti could talk about, and a trip to Bayreuth became *the* essential music lover's pilgrimage. Wagner became the biggest name in music *ever*. A living legend, from out of virtually nowhere. He'd transcended the medium of music into a role of genuine cultural revolutionary, a hero for the age. His ridiculous ambition to unify all art looked like it was going to work out after all. Wagner stood in his lavish study, five feet high in his stockings, dressed in his ridiculous multi-coloured silk outfit and rank floppy hat, smoking his big stupid pipe and talked, for approximately ten years, about nothing except himself.

He wrote millions of letters all about himself, too.

The Richard Wagner Festival continues in Bayreuth to this day. Every year hardcore Wagnerians arrive from all corners of the globe to pay homage to the great man and sit on mahogany benches listening to the entire Ring Cycle, munching vast sausages. In fact the festival is so oversubscribed there's a hefty waiting list for tickets. The average waiting time? Fourteen years. Seriously. And if you're not in the mood to wait, you can snag one off a tout for a couple of grand if you're lucky. For the purposes of this book, I chose not to do this.

You might be beginning to sense that some people take

Wagner quite seriously. Especially, perhaps, the Ring (Rinse) Cycle. Well, yes. They do.

Dive. Dive. Red alert. Brace yourself, we're going down.

Der Ring des Nibelungen

This means 'The Ring of the Nibelung' ('Ring' being an actual ring made of gold; the 'Nibelung' is a race of dwarfs; thus it might make it easier for you to think of this whole shebang as *Dwarfs' Ring*).* It might also serve as a warning; à la 'Keep Out', or 'Danger', or 'RUN FOR YOUR FUCKING LIFE'. *Dwarfs' Ring* is a series (a 'tetralogy' actually) of four rather large operas: In sequence they go:

1) *Das Rheingold* (The Rhine Göld) – 149 minutes long;
2) *Die Walküre* (The Välkyrie) – 216 minutes long;
3) *Siegfried* (Siëgfriëd) – 233 minutes long;
4) *Götterdämmerung* (Twilïght of the Göds) – 245 minutes long.

These minutes are not cumulative. In fact when you add them all up, the whole Ring Cycle lasts over fourteen hours. Fourteen hours and five minutes, to be precise. (That's an incredible symmetry, don't you think? Waiting fourteen years for fourteen hours?) That's without any intervals, breaks, births, deaths or general elections. To put this into context, in the time it takes to listen to the entire Ring Cycle, you could listen to The Beach Boys' *Pet Sounds* album twenty-eight times. You'd get through 250+ playbacks of

* Interesting fact: the plural of 'dwarf' was 'dwarfs' until J. R. R. Tolkien wrote *Lord of the Rings*, in which he changed the plural to 'dwarves'. Nowadays everyone says 'dwarves'. Crazy, huh? Bearing in mind what's coming up next, I can only apologize that this footnote's not longer.

Kylie's 'Can't Get You Out of My Head'; 1,200 of Nuclear Assault's 'Hang the Pope'; almost halfway through 'Supper's Ready' by Genesis. *Der Ring des Nibelungen* is Wagner's crowning glory – his definitive lifetime's achievement. And possibly the most intricate and convoluted practical joke in the whole, wide world, except for Ben Elton's musical about Queen, *We Will Rock You*.

Obviously, I emailed Fiona in a state of considerable panic.

'This sounds like a Big Conversation. I can't do Wagner in three lines,' she wrote back. 'We ought to meet for lunch and go through this properly.'

I allowed myself to relax; lifejacket Fiona was going to helicopter rescue me out of the boiling oceans of gross-operatic whiteout yet again. Thank Christ. As I waited for our allotted second date to arrive, I ploughed my way through *The Abandoned Child, the Authoritarian Father, and the Disempowered Feminine: A Jungian Understanding of Wagner's Ring Cycle*, which I found incredibly interesting. But several days passed and we kept missing each other; I feared this meeting wasn't going to happen after all. And it was then that I remembered the heavy, mildewed package I'd innocently placed into my car boot on leaving Winchester the day after Schubert Day. It was some old heirloom that belonged to my stepfather Pete that he'd said I ought to borrow. At the time I hadn't paid it much attention, so keen was I to escape the Schubert.

'You'll be needing this soon,' he'd said, his voice full of a strange sort of sympathy. 'And you can keep it for as long as you like.' He patted me conspiratorially on the back. 'Really. For as *long as you like*.' But I'd ignored him, and not given it another thought. That was, until now. Perching on the edge of my sofa, I nervously slid the ancient leviathan out of its complex sheaths of vintage carrier bags, gasping as its full tonnage pressed down into my jeans. I stared at the giant off-white, gold-lettered reinforced canvas container disbelievingly for a full ten seconds. Stars pricked the edges of my vision. The room began to spin. My mouth dropped open and everything went slow motion. The package nestling on my lap was an eighteen-disc, 1953 vinyl box-set of *Dwarfs' Ring*, conducted by super-famous dead conductor Wilhelm Furtwängler.

'*NOOOOOOOOOOOOOOOOOOOOOOOOOOOOO.*'

Tangled Up in Glue

I planned it like a military operation. Actually I planned it exactly like the scene in *Trainspotting* when Renton locks himself in a room trying to kick heroin with just a bucket, a blanket, some food and a bolt on the door. I was going to apply the same principles to my appreciation of Wagner's Ring Cycle. It would just be me, a bucket, the record player, the box-set, the opera texts, some water, some crackers (I like crackers), a blanket and a notebook. I do have a toilet by the way, I just thought it wise to have the bucket too. I wasn't able to lock myself in since our back bedroom doesn't have a lock; otherwise I would've. The plan was to start at 8 a.m., and, allowing for the fourteen hours of music plus the time it would take to flip thirty-eight sides of vinyl, I was looking at an endzone of approximately 11 p.m. About fifteen hours in all.

'If you make it beyond eight hours, I'll be amazed,' said Faye the day before, as I stood in the kitchen doing breathing exercises and some kung fu.

'I'm at work till late tomorrow, so you'll be on your own. Good luck.'

'Thank you, but I'm sure I'll make it through. How hard

can it be, sitting on a chair listening to music all day? It'll be a piece of piss, I guarantee it!'

Later that day, Fiona emailed to apologize for lunch, and to say that she thought what I was doing was excessive.

'READ the text first, even if you don't understand it. You'll never keep up if you try first off to do it with music. You should be gentle on yourself – Wagner didn't expect it to be heard in one day (in Bayreuth it takes a week, with a couple of evenings off . . .). And I have to say that I do think Wagner's a GENIUS, and I'd probably take the *Ring* to my desert island.'

No pressure, then. But why did nobody have any faith in me? *I'll show 'em*, I thought. *I'm a music lover! Fourteen hours of opera is child's play.*

A brief defence of the listening format. Agreed, it's not wholly fair covering opera without the visuals; after all, it's conceived as a multi-sensual art form. However, this book was never intended to be a guide to sodding opera – this is about classical music, not music plus woman in Viking helmet and fat man in beard and eyepatch with sword on one knee, yelling *blah*. Quite frankly, I feel there's been quite enough opera already as it is. Much as I'd love to omit Wagner, I can't, though I can tell you now that we're not going to be doing any more of the big opera-only guys, i.e. Verdi, Rossini, Puccini, Bellini, Bizet or whoever. Mine is a quest for the ears, not for the patience, so if you want more opera than this, you shouldn't really be here in the first place, should you?

Let There Be Ring

08.00: I am still in bed. Faye attempts to wake me, but I am already awake, just pretending not to be.

'Wagner Day!' she announces gleefully, tugging the curtain wide open.

'I *know*,' I snap. 'I need *sleep fuel*.'

Faye then leaves for work. I remain in bed, lying on my back for half an hour, and then fail all my deep-breathing exercises.

09.00: I drink coffee and stare at the box-set.

09.15: Stupid box-set, fuck off.

09.30: I reluctantly open the box-set (there is creaking and dust) and regard my poor, innocent record player. I pat it. Then I unpack the box-set (more dust plus several old newspaper clippings which then crumble into dust as well) and slip out the first disc. Here it is, boys and girls:

For any younger readers, these circular black things are called 'records'.

09.45: I admire the silky black side of vinyl and spin it around in the light. This is disc one of eighteen; side one of thirty-six. I am as yet unable to comprehend the immensity of all this laminate recorded sound. Finally I lower the record on to the rubber turntable and lay the crisp, yellowed libretto open on my desk in front of me. For what we are about to receive . . .

10.01: . . . may the Lord make us truly thankful. Amen. We're off! Not to see the wizard unfortunately. The sound that emerges from the speakers is incredibly tinny; not even stereo. Ancient scratches pop and crackle as the 1953 guys scrape up some woozy, swirling vibes. The lo-fi recording quality is actually pretty cool; it gives the music an other-worldly, murky atmosphere.* Before long, a clutch of women begin to twitter. These are Rhinemaidens – mermaids – they are defending the Rhinegold – some magic gold, in the Rhine. Well, so far, so good. I look out of my window. It's a beautiful sunny day. God, you bastard, couldn't you at least have made it rain?

10.30: An embittered dwarf joins the tedious, hollering Rhinemaidens: yes it's a Nibelung; indeed it's Alberich, King of the Dwarfs. Surely all we need now is a ring to appear from somewhere and we can all go home happy and not get too caught up in the rest?

11.00: Act Two. Some gods. There's Wotan (chief god), Fricka (his wife), Freia (his sister-in-law), Loge (the Dale Winton of gods), plus a pair of giants. Phew, that's enough plot!

11.05: Now everyone is singing. The only way I can tell the voices apart is by reading along with the script. The music itself is pompous and cheesy-sounding, and each section repeats itself mercilessly (these recurring melodic blocks are called 'leitmotifs', and Wagner specialized in them: it's like building music out of Lego). Gods-wise, not much is happening. There is some complaining. A pigeon lands on the

---

* I love a party with a happy atmosphere; I want to take you there; then you and I'll be dancing in the cool night air.

roof directly outside my window. The pigeon is grey and white. It pecks at some things. Please don't go, Mr Pigeon!

11.20: I miss him.

11.45: Not long now till lunch. Mood: optimistic.

12.05: I have to tell you, listening to opera is tiring. It manages to drain one's energy amazingly effectively. I've already yawned today – and rubbed my forehead and stuff – much more than usual; maybe more than ever before. Keep on flipping the discs, flipping discs. The music sounds like the soundtracks to old silent films – jaunty; swollen; irritating.

12.15: Why not have an early lunch as a special treat? By the way, those two giants have taken away Wotan's sister-in-law. To Giantland. Yonder. A bit further. Left a little. That's it. *Stay there.*

12.32: Well, I ate a tuna sandwich and it brought a small ray of sunshine into my life. Sadly it was over too soon, and now we have . . . what do we have . . . we have side six; disc three. A bunch of yoked midgets have forged the stolen Rhinegold into a ring. The ring is magic. One giant murders the other because of greed, I think. These greater 'life metaphors' are really quite profound when you think about it. Mood: patronizing.

13.00: Oh, right. The ring is cursed. Gods wander around (gods wandering around is an important part of the Ring). Holy mackerel, this is boring. Oh, hang on, the opera just ended; that's the end of Part One. Now it's time for Part Two – *Die Walküre*. Can the stakes rise any higher?* Can the gods do one single exciting thing?† Who will the ring curse next?‡ Perhaps even Wotan himself?§

* Possibly.
† No.
‡ Who cares.
§ Yes, that's it.

14.00: Hi there. Not much happening at the moment. I have a sore neck and need to urinate, but apart from that things are much as they were an hour ago. I feel like a night watchman. *Who goes there?* Ah, a dwarf and a giant. OK – continue on your way. Hail.

14.30: I warn you, I have just been reading the libretto again and there is incest in this opera. Mood: wary.

15.00: There's definitely incest in this opera. Between Siegmund (illegitimate son of Wotan) and Sieglinde (illegitimate daughter of Wotan).

15.20: And it's consummated! Things are looking up, or down, depending on your moral viewpoint. I am just pleased that something's happened. What's this, side ten or something? It's all starting to blur into one. I go and fetch a glass of water. I look at it. Drink it. Every second counts. Mood: less thirsty.

16.00: I can feel myself fading, losing my sense of humour. Doubt's seeping into my mind for the first time; I'm not convinced I'm going to make it to the end. This sudden idea of stopping before the finish line delivers me a mighty rush of serotonin which keeps me going through another protracted bout of everyone standing around saying metaphysical things in a warbling style. Wotan and his wife argue about his son and daughter shagging. Oh, well, says Wotan. His wife disapproves. How modern. You see this all has a catastrophic relevance for the way we lead our lives today. Mood: belligerent.

16.30: I pine for a Rubik's cube, even though the best I ever managed was two measly sides; but I could do patterns from a completed one: a star pattern and a cross. Poor old Mr Rubik, who never patented his cube and never made a penny out of it. This tale occupies my thoughts as a fleet of flying armoured horse maiden warriors gather in the dusk for battle. For this section, Wagner steals the music from the helicopter/napalm scene in *Apocalypse Now*. Mood: embittered but ready for flying armoured horse maiden warrior action.

16.45: There's a lot of noise suddenly. Screeching and trumpets and it goes on for ages. I sit and wince through almost twenty minutes of it.

17.15: Slightly quieter now. I take advantage of the lull to do a handstand.

17.22: Why is it that when you're really, really bored, you never receive any text messages from anybody, but when you're busy or with friends or doing something interesting, you always get loads? Could this banal aphorism be the contemporary equivalent of you wait ages for a bus and then two come at once? Mood: paranoid.

17.30: Someone has a fight.

17.45: My eyes hurt.

17.50:

18.00: Eight hours down, eight miles high, less than zero. Somebody named Sintolt the Hegeling has arrived, with Wittig the Irming. I enjoy sucking my teeth yet pine for medication. The minor-key fairground music grinds onward like an incontinent glacier. I am the nappy.

18.15: I forgot Sintolt the Hegeling.

18.20: Well, that's the end of the second opera. Thoughts so far: well, this is undoubtedly one of humanity's greatest artistic and creative achievements; all these Norse myths, Germanic myths, plus the continually witless, self-indulgent prophesying; I've never had as much fun as this ever in my life before.* Mood: exultant.

18.16: *slight dizzy spell*

---

* Except for maybe once or twice.

18.20: pPhysiological response so far: nervvous tension. A lot of nnnnervous tension and some stress and keybard erors.

18.45: I give up on making my listening notes. They'd been becoming gradually more incomprehensible, plus they were shit and completely pointless in the first place. What is this, a fucking exam? Mood: chaotic.

18.50: I worry about Fiona quizzing me about the *Ring* afterwards. I try to concentrate harder but I still can't break through Wagner and Furtwängler's impregnable magma crust. I worry that opera is simply beyond me.

19.00: There's a big difference between hearing and listening, people. And deafness is pretty underrated.

19.15: Another handstand to take my mind off things. M<od: dizy.

20.01: I am lost (again) in the libretto. I think Wotan is now in disguise – dressed up as a humble traveller. This is an excuse to tell the entire *Ring* back story up to this point. This isn't the first time this has happened. Surely *Ring* fans know the back story already and hardly need reminding of it every hour or so? And anyway, it's absolutely appalling in the first place! Don't bother – go for a walk! Mood: incredulous.

19.42: Mood: confused. This isn't getting any easier. I am not developing a taste for it.

20.10: I'd like to go for a walk too, except it's dark outside now. We've been going for ten hours. Any critical faculties I might have been in possession of before today have now been well and truly blasted to bits. I doubt I'd even recognize my own reflection.

20.25: This has perhaps been the most boring day of my whole life. There was one day, back in 1998, when I sat in traffic on the South Circular road for eight hours, but at least then I had the radio and a Grab Bag of Quavers. I am on side twenty-two or twenty-three I think, I don't know. My ears buzz. Dunno if it's fatigue or the record or the orchestra or what.

20.45: *This all sounds exactly the fucking same. AAAAAA-AARRRRGGGHHHHHHHH.*

21.00: Faye comes home. She says I'm acting 'strange'. She stares deep into my eyes, looks briefly troubled and then leaves the room, closing the door behind her. Mood: back to paranoid.

21.00: We are on the last opera, *Götterdämmerung, Twilight of the Gods*. Mood: exhausted and my arse aches.

21.15: Someone sent me an email today with a photo of one of the best bits of graffiti I've ever seen: scrawled haphazardly on to the wall of what looks like the underside of a bridge, somebody has painted in large black letters: CATS LIKE PLAIN CRISPS. It's thoughts like these that are keeping me sane right at the moment.

21.18: What the hell does that mean? Cats like plain crisps. *What?*

21.32: Wotan something. Wotan does something. Mood: sympathetic towards Wotan. It's been a long old day for all of us, and Wotan's had to sing the whole thing. Most of it at least. I think. I'm not sure, to be honest.

22.00: So, twelve hours. I can't take any more; there's no point in listening to any more. This hasn't achieved anything except given me a lifelong allergy to Wagner – I'd rather go to Middlesbrough than Bayreuth. This is just an endurance test – a grisly notch on a bedpost. Are there people out there who genuinely enjoy listening to this bollocks?

22.12: Foam is gathering in the corners of my mouth. I can't keep this going for much longer, I'm sorry.

22.15: You're coming off, in fact you're *definitely* coming off before the end. Feeling weepy now.

22.22: Barely even halfway through the fourth opera, *Götter-dämmerung*, I yank off the stylus and tug out the plug from the record player. I find myself sprawled on the floor breathing heavily. The silence is *magnificent*. Mood: uncomfortably numb.

22.35: I lie in the bath.

22.40: Add water.

22.45: Damn it, take my clothes off.

22.50: Clenched fists/splashing.

23.15: Bed. Sleep. Nightmares. Thanks, Richard. Never again.

Irredeemable Dark Destruction

Next morning, an email from Fiona was waiting in my inbox. 'It's true large doses of Wagner are pretty hard, especially when you're not in the theatre. Not that much happens, or only over very long stretches of time, as you'll have discovered,' she wrote. 'But you can't get away without listening to the whole of *Götterdämmerungnernngern*. It's only when you finish that that you see how the whole thing comes together. PULL YOURSELF TOGETHER. Be a man.'

I'm not kidding – she really did write that!

That same afternoon I received a text message from Owen, informing me that, for the first time in about fifteen years, BBC television were screening the whole of Wagner's Ring Cycle over four consecutive evenings. Was he winding me up, or what?

'When?' I replied.

'Tonight.'

'I'm not going to watch it.'

'But you're on Wagner. You have to.'

'I've just sat through twelve hours of the bloody Ring Cycle and I'm not in the mood for a repeat performance. In fact I never want to hear a single note of it ever again.'

'This is a seismic television event of significant cultural importance. And it's introduced by Michael Portillo.'

Michael Portillo? All right I'll watch it then.

After Michael Portillo's brilliant introduction which I unfortunately missed, *Das Rheingold* kicked off just as it had in 1953, except this time as a full theatrical production from the Royal Opera House in London's Covent Garden, featuring famous Welsh bass-baritone Bryn Terfel as Wotan. The music sounded exactly the same as it had in the fifties, except everything and everyone looked ridiculous. This was a classic example of somebody having the wise idea to 'contemporize' the Ring; give it a little leftfield twist; funk it up a little. The result was a production that was stylistically identical to the film *Chitty Chitty Bang Bang* meets *Dr Who* (Pertwee era) meets Dr Josef Mengele. Especially down in Nibelung; Jesus – was that Auschwitz-style torture-chamber set-up really necessary? These (suspiciously tall) dwarfs were lashed to steel stretchers with their brains half hanging out. And what's with the white coats? It's only meant to be a bunch of dwarf miners. Be nice!

Elsewhere, the giants were short, the Ring was bright red, the magic helmet was a large perspex box. Everyone was fat. Bryn Terfel is not good at acting. His eye make-up fell halfway-off three-quarters through and nobody bothered to stick it back on for him. This is why it's infinitely preferable to listen to opera and not have to watch it.

'This is like a shit pantomime,' said Faye, half-watching, flicking through a magazine. 'It's like a crappy *Lord of the Rings* or something. It's embarrassing.'

'But it's the Ring. You can't say that.'

'I don't care. It's a load of old bollocks. Which one's Widow Twanky?'

Frankly it could have been any of them. But one is not allowed to say such things.

'It's taken me ages to get beyond the "image" of Wagner,' wrote Fiona, who this time seemed less aggressive. 'Or to get beyond the weirdness and male-dominated obsession of self-confessed Wagnerians. There's someone called Denby Richards who's been to something like 300 Ring Cycles all over the world, and counting.' (Using my calculator, I've worked out that Denby is over a thousand years old.) I wrote back saying that, although I was struggling, and had been taken ill with it, and experienced bizarre hallucinations along the way, I would keep on trying, and that, yes, I will get around to *Götterdämmerungnernngern* at some point; just maybe not for a week or two. I had a pile of lithium that needed taking first.*

Wagner is the classical/operatic equivalent of LSD. No matter how strong the dose, it can still screw you up; but there's no end to quite how far out you can choose to go with it – the sky's your limit. Just be careful; and remember it's a ten-hour-plus trip; it won't just end after a couple of hours, like other composers. And when you first listen, make sure you're with someone you trust who's done it before and can guide you through.

There's a overall moral to the Ring Cycle – in fact two

---

* The next evening I tuned into BBC2 for Part Two – *The Valkyrie*. The second half was to be broadcast live, the first half pre-recorded to compensate for the theatre interval. But something else was on BBC2 instead. On my telly at least. Something with detectives. *BBC controllers have seen sense at last*, I thought. But it wasn't that. Bryn Terfel (Wotan) was ill, so they cancelled it. I can hardly begin to express my relief. Parts Three and Four were only ever an ugly rumour.

morals, two principal tenets. They are: power corrupts; and: love conquers all.

Was Wagner's attempt to unify the arts ultimately successful? Sadly not. Though he triggered admirable amounts of confusion. As to whether I've emerged from this experience as a Wagnerian or an anti-Wagnerian, I have *absolutely no idea, leave me alone.*

*

Richard Wagner scores:

Sex: 11. The *Karma Sutra* for dwarfs.

Mythology: 11. All myths are in here somewhere.

Rock 'n' roll: 11. U2 playing Meat Loaf at Neverland.

Seb suggests:

> *Prelude to Tristan und Isolde* (an opera about sex, in case you prefer that to the goblins and Wotan), by the Sheffield Philharmonic (Warp) 🚐🚐🚐

> (At just ten minutes long and featuring absolutely no singing, this is Wagner at his very best; it's a swooningly dramatic slice of romantic assurance and tasty sonority. Once you've listened to this, you can jettison the remainder of the opera with confidence.)

12. Radio Ga-Ga

After Wagner I felt I needed some light relief, so I went and stood next to a road drill on Brentford High Street for three hours. Ahhhhh, that's better. Then I returned home and turned on my trusty rabbit radio and twisted its left back

foot to somewhere between 100 and 102 FM. The sound that emerged from the rabbit's blue belly was immediately soothing, and nice. I recognized this as Beethoven's 'Moonlight Sonata' from chapter nine. In blissful rhapsody, I allowed my damaged consciousness to drift drowsily along with the chordal work and notes, soon becoming entirely contemplative, and relaxed enough to, say, do some housework or take the children to school. My reverie was ruined at the end of the piece, however, when Beethoven was replaced by an advertisement for cheese. The rabbit's foot had landed upon Classic FM, Britain's most popular classical music radio station for attention span deficit disorder-stricken pensioners. So sedated was I by the smoothness of the music and whey that it didn't occur to me to investigate this important cultural phenomenon further until several weeks later, by which time I had acquired several pieces of Cheddar, a whorl of Port Salut and a Stannah Stairlift. Bow down to the terrifying subliminal power of advertising. And bow down to Classic FM. You might as well.

There are two ways to listen to classical music on the radio in the UK: BBC Radio 3 and Classic FM. Radio 3 is the purist's choice; they broadcast through the full glorious spectrum of classical music, from experimental through mush, all the way up to experimental modern composition, world music and even obtuse electronica (late at night when the duffers are asleep). Radio 3 broadcasts all 7,000 Proms live every year, and is perfectly happy to play a whole opera all in one go; or even a symphony; or an old man with a heavy Eastern European accent talking about nothing. Radio 3 has approximately one million regular and discerning listeners.

Classic FM plays the hits, just the hits, and nothing but the hits. It's unashamedly populist; indeed, it's very raison d'être is to be as populist as possible. It was bloody invented to be popular, so there's no point in pretending otherwise. To its credit, it has never done this. This is why it has more than quadruple the listeners Radio 3 has; and why cheese manufacturers hold the station in such high regard. It was the demographic-busting popularity of this relatively recent concept that interested me; to understand and appreciate Classic FM was, I felt, an important part of my journey. Especially since I was scared of Radio 3 sending me to prison.

A Day Out at Classic FM

I emailed station head honcho Darren Henley and asked if he thought it might be OK for me to come into the Classic FM studios and spend a day behind the scenes; to see what it's really like at the commercial broadcasting rock face, to take the pulse of the mogadon nation at stupefied repose.

Darren did not reply. Some days later, however, I received an email from his assistant, Emma, asking if I was free to come and have a chat with Darren in a couple of weeks' time. I was so pleased to get a response that I didn't dare say that I didn't actually want to *chat* to Darren, I just wanted to wander around being annoying and getting in everyone's way. A chat, I eventually decided, was better than nothing, so I wrote back with an enthusiastic *yes please*, with some crass and ingratiating kisses at the bottom.

As Darren Day approached, I determinedly thought up loads of excellent questions, such as 'how many listeners do you have?', and 'why is Classic FM so brilliant?' I hope Darren will be impressed with these, I wondered nervously in a coffee shop on Regent Street just around the corner from their top secret studios in Swallow Place, right off Oxford Circus. *This is gonna be a total grilling,* I cackled, trying to stop my hands from shaking.

In Classic FM's swish, brushed-steel reception area, I sat rigidly on a high stool and stared out the window, smiling. Soon Darren came out and we shook hands. Mr Henley's been at the station almost since the beginning; he started as a newsreader and worked his way steadily up through the ranks to his current position of commander-in-chief, and he looks like a friendly hippo in glasses. He led me through to his sun-streaming office and we took up positions on either side of a round glass table, smiling at one another. Darren told me he'd just finished writing Aled Jones's autobiography.

'How does Aled feel about your writing his autobiography?'

'Well, we're friends, so it's fine. In fact he asked me to write it.'

'How does Aled feel about *The Snowman*?'

'He's pretty sick of it.'

'I think we all are.'

I noticed our eyebrows were raised. We slowly lowered them. That was enough preliminary gossip.

'So, Darren,' I demanded, 'how many listeners do you have?'

'6.2 million.'

'Thank you.'

'No problem.'

I felt the question had gone well. I smiled some more and Darren smiled back.

'And are they all pensioners?'

'No. One million are under twenty-five, one and a half million are between twenty-five and forty-four, and the remaining four million are forty-five plus.'

'Righto.' I looked at my notes. They danced in front of my eyes. 'And how do you choose your playlist?'

'Everything we select to play on the station first has to get through a special group of 250 people. If they like it, we'll play it. If they don't like it, we won't.'

'Like a focus group?'

'It's a rolling 52-week-a-year piece of research.'

'You won't play anything that hasn't been approved by these 250 people?'

'Nothing at all.'

'So there's never any spontaneity?'

'None.'

'Who are these 250 people?'

'I can't say.'

'Where does this take place?'

'Swindon.'

I was quite shocked by all this.

'How often do you get accused of dumbing down classical music?'

'We've been through all that now, and we're tired of it,' grumbled Darren. 'We've been going for ten years already. We're an important part of people's lives. We publish our monthly magazine, we publish books, we release CDs, we stage concerts, we . . .'

I can't write as quickly as he talked. As I scrawled haphazardly into my notebook, Darren spread a selection of CDs out over the table, saying I could take them home with me if I wanted, which of course I did – I'm not stupid. Which of these Classic FM albums are real, and which do you think aren't?

a) Music for Mums

b) Music for Cool Teens

c) Music for Granny and Grandpa

d) Music for Babies

e) Music for Illness

f) Music for Sex

g) Music for Driving

h) Music for the Blind

i) Music for Fitness

j) Music for Pets!

k) Music for Rainy Days

l) Music for Dinner Parties

m) Music for Prince Charles

You can check the answers by logging on to the Classic FM website and following some links. And Classic FM plays music that all the scenarios and age groups listed above will enjoy anyway; so long as it hasn't got a beat and the 250 people in Swindon like it, they'll play virtually anything you like. 'We do not frown upon Paul McCartney as a composer,' says Darren.

'You mean his *classical* stuff?'

'We do not frown upon it.'

Back in Darren's office, my questions were getting downright impertinent.

'Do you think there's a two-tier system with classical music on the radio in this country? Radio 3 gets the intellectuals and you get everyone else?'

'Well let me tell you this. Fifty per cent of the Radio 3 audience listen to Classic FM too. Or, as I prefer to look at it, one-sixth of our audience also listen to Radio 3.'

Darren had fucked me with maths. I scribbled down some random fractions and looked up with a smile of deep understanding. I then asked Darren how classical music could (or should) compete with pop music. He said, yes, of course it should compete – it *does* compete – and anyway, classical music's much better than pop music. All pop songs are ripped off from classical tunes in the first place.

'Really?'

'Yes of course.'

'Which ones?'

'All of them.'

'Do you like any pop music?'

'Oh yes, I have a totally broad range. I like everything.'

'Everything? Is there anything you listen to that would surprise Classic FM listeners?'

Darren paused for some time. 'Swamp rock,' he finally said. 'And Showaddywaddy.'

What's swamp rock?

'Where next for Classic FM?' I insisted.

'We recently launched Classic FM TV (similar to MTV except with more candlesticks in the videos). And we sponsor orchestras and do lots of all good things and stuff like that, really impressive, *what a brand.*'

This was the gist at least. I have to say I was extremely impressed by Darren's blue-eyed evangelism; it was infectious. As he spoke on, getting more excited and breathless by the minute (as was I), he continued to shower me with free gifts: magazines, more CDs and a promise of two tickets to a forthcoming Classic FM Live event at the Royal Albert Hall.

'Have you been to one of our concerts before?' I hadn't. 'Ah, well, you'll have never been to a concert quite like one of ours.'

'What do you do that's different?'

Darren's eyes blazed like fire. 'You'll have to wait and see!'

I decided to wind up the interview. Or rather, Emma was discreetly gesturing that it was time for me to leave. And not that discreetly either.

'One final question please,' I said. Darren nodded.

'What's the worst thing about Classic FM?'

'The *worst* thing?'

'The very worst.'

Darren scratched his chin. 'Nobody's ever asked me that before. I'm a little thrown. *The worst thing?*'

'The absolute totally worst thing about it.'

He looked at his shoes. They were shiny. One tapped impatiently.

'Nope, can't do it. I can't think of a worst thing.'

We smiled somewhat hysterically at one another.

'Thank you, Darren.'

'It's been my pleasure.'

'Are you sure I can take all this stuff?'

'Of course.'

I scooped it all into my rucksack and was preparing myself to depart when Darren suddenly asked, 'So what have you learned?'

'What, just then?' I scrambled to open my notebook again. Dammit, a test.

'No, I mean for your book. Tell me what you've learned about the world of classical music.'

I stared at him and blinked.

'I've learned . . . a lot.'

'Give me an example.' Darren smiled broadly; encouragingly; it looked as if he really cared.

'I've learned that . . .' He was proper beaming. The gap between his front teeth was mesmerizing, and my blank mind bleached gradually blanker. '. . . people are *nice*.'

We stood absorbing this for a few moments, then Darren's face glazed over, and Emma stood too and smoothly ushered me out of the building. Darren's one of the nicest and most charming people I have ever met; he's brilliant – the right man for the job. Feeling slightly humbled, I caught the tube home and switched on the rabbit radio and sat listening to Classic FM for an hour. After that I read the latest edition of *Classic FM Magazine* all the way through until Faye came home and very gently removed my overflowing colostomy bag, replacing it with a fresh one. I smiled up at her with my gums.

Some weeks passed without the free tickets Darren had promised arriving; and I began to suspect it had just been a clever ploy to get rid of me a bit faster. I didn't really mind – I was a bit sick of the Royal Albert Hall from the previous

summer anyway, plus I respected him for the deceit. But then a letter arrived with the tickets and a note from Emma: 'Drinks and canapés will be in the box from 6.45 p.m. Enjoy!' The *box*? Sweet holy mother of Jesus, where did I put my monocle? My opera glasses? My faith in human nature?

Classic FM Live

Even outside of the Proms season, people still go to classical music concerts in the United Kingdom on a regular basis. I know – it's amazing. On Thursday, 21 April 2005, the night of the Classic FM live extravaganza, classical music concerts were also being staged elsewhere in London (Smith Square, the Royal Festival Hall, Handel's House (get in!), the English National Opera, the Royal Opera House, Queen Elizabeth Hall, Sadler's Wells, St Martin-in-the-Fields, Jerwood Hall, St John's Church Waterloo and Wigmore Hall) as well as in York, Upper Norwood, Lincoln, Cheltenham, Manchester, Chatham, Glasgow, Cardiff, Edinburgh, Poole, Plymouth, Hereford, Penrith, Leeds, Mayfield, Truro, Belfast, Gateshead, Oxford, Brecon, King's Lynn, Portsmouth, Tetbury,

Chester, Nether Wallop and Warwick. And there were more on top of those – that's just a selection of the bigger ones. This isn't bad for a rainy midweek in April. In fact, it's almost as if classical music were thriving; or at the very least stumbling around the place with its arms outstretched like a zombie in ducktails.

Classic FM – the Nation's Favourite Broadcaster by Absolutely Miles

Faye and I were standing outside the door to our box at 6.45 p.m. precisely. Unfortunately the door was locked. We chased down an usher.

'Please open this door.'

The usher was small and dressed in red. He looked at us and checked our tickets; then looked at us again. Then he checked our tickets.

'Look, we're legit. Please just open the door.'

He opened the door very slowly and peered inside. We barged past him. The box had seats for eight, and a small anteroom behind with a table full of bottles of wine and party food.

'Right,' I said, reaching for a glass, a plate and a corkscrew and trying to unpeel the clingfilm all at once. 'Let's get started.'

'Are you sure this is meant for you?' asked the usher, nervously jangling his keys.

'Yes it is; now please close the door behind you.'

He left, and Faye and I started to unwrap everything.

'I don't like this,' said Faye, tucking into a chicken satay stick. 'Is this really all for us or are we about to be joined by a bunch of complete strangers?'

'Ngchw. Ggmnaw, mmf nga mmrgh.' The beef ones were quite tasty; less so the salmon. The red wine, much of which streamed down my chin, was a cheeky little number. And I will not be letting the fact that Darren provided all this for nothing – out of the kindness of his heart – influence my merciless reportage of the evening's proceedings. I'm bigger than that.

'I'm not,' said Faye. 'I think you should say this is brilliant, even if it's shit, which it probably will be.'

'I thought you were supposed to be being bigger than that.'

'Oh, yes, sorry, I forgot. It will undoubtedly be superb.'

'That's better.'

'Despite all the pensioners.'

'Be big.'

'Who are all great.'

'Bigger.'

'There aren't any pensioners here at all.'

'Perfect.'

Then the door opened and two respectable ladies shuffled in. We all stared at each other with wild, animal eyes. Faye and I chewed madly.

'Gmgnngh!'

This turned out to be Anne, an arts consultant, and her mother Elizabeth, who was here to celebrate her eighty-fourth birthday. They were here on a freebie too. We relaxed slightly.

'Happy birthday, Elizabeth.'

'Ooh, thank you.'

I turned to Anne. 'Erm, Darren . . . ?'

'Oh, Darren, yes, Darren!'

Phew – we both knew Darren; we relaxed even more; and Anne and Elizabeth got started on the booze 'n' nibbles.

Just as we were beginning to make a proper dent in the canapés, two more people burst in. This was Anne's colleague Stephen and his wife Julia. This was all terribly super; I was beginning to wish I'd worn something smarter. Next to enter our tiny chamber of delights was Classic FM's marketing director, Giles Pearman, accompanied by Classic FM's official masseur, Bernie.

'I've just been backstage and done that Julian Lloyd Webber,' announced Bernie, who was short, salt-of-the-earth and in his fifties and a polo shirt. 'Hunched right over, he was. In a right old state. But a bit of this, a bit of that, and he was right as rain. Now he's fit to play his whatever it is that he plays.'

'The cello,' said slick Giles, giving the room a professional once-over.

'That's the one.'

We were all rapt by Bernie. Giles was trying to wrest control, but Bernie wasn't having any of it.

'And that conductor – he could barely walk! Came in like this.' Bernie did an impression of a staggering, robotic cripple. 'Soon sorted him out, though. Bit of a knead.' He motioned the knead. 'And that bird – manager of the orchestra or whatever . . .'

'Helen,' said Giles.

'That's the one, yeah. Bloody sciatica! Bit of a tangle, to be honest; there I was with my hand, you know, on her . . .'

'Behind,' said Giles.

'My hand right up her arse. Pushing right up there – it's the only way, you know, really giving it some – that's the only way to do it.'

'It was quite a sight,' said Giles.

'You're telling me,' agreed Bernie.

There was a definite shade of the *Fast Show*'s Ralph and

Ted about these two. As Bernie continued with his backstage tales of tendons, Giles sidled up beside me.

'So who are you, sorry?'

I swallowed a lot in a hurry. 'A book thing? I, um, I interviewed Darren? And . . .'

'Darren! Ah, right . . . right. I thought you'd just walked in off the street! Haha!'

'Haha! Really, though, I promise I haven't. Look, here's my ticket.'

Giles checked it. 'OK,' he said.

It was time for the concert to begin, so we all took our seats; the hall looked rammed; shades of pastel and grey. And ties; navy blue ties. Simon Bates came out in a spotlight and told some jokes and pointed out some weddings, anniversaries, etc. in the audience – his usual kind of patter (sadly the orchestra didn't play his 'Our Tune' music). Finally he departed, and the music started up. The less said about that the better. In the interval, Bernie continued his tales of life as a masseur to the classical stars. Though he tried damn hard, Giles still couldn't get a word in edgeways. And the less said about the second half the better, too; though it was a marginal improvement on the first – no 'Theme from E.T.' or 'Greensleeves' this time; and Julian Lloyd Webber made a sweaty, honest fist of Elgar's weeping cello concerto, despite coming out as a grimacing deadringer for a Dickensian jailer in a heavy metal headband.

'Mr Lloyd Webber was looking extremely supple, I must say, Bernie,' I commented as fierce applause swept the hall and Julian swept back on for much bowing and waves. Bernie laughed, and nodded, and flexed and cracked his fingers in satisfaction. His fingers of magic; fingers of fame.

As we were all saying our goodbyes, because I hadn't had

an opportunity to speak to Giles properly, I asked if he'd mind doing a very brief interview.

Stupidly, he said yes. I asked if, like Darren, he was a blue-eyed classical music evangelista.

'My background isn't classical music,' replied Giles. 'I used to work for Unilever on their ice cream brands, like Magnum and Solero. I really do like classical music, but I'm not an expert, although I had bought a few compilation CDs before I started working here. My favourite piece is Barber's *Adagio*, and my two-year-old son even listens as part of his night-time routine to the station – that's a hot tip, as Classic FM is great for getting babies and toddlers to sleep at night!'

I asked Giles if he liked pop music.

'My music tastes are very varied. I am currently very into Keane and U2's new album. My wife does get rather upset when I put on Barry Manilow's *Greatest Hits* album, which is also in my collection.'

Then Giles said this: 'Classic FM is a bit like an open family; we want as many people as possible to join and discover the music. The good thing is that nowadays it's much more acceptable to have broad music tastes, so it's OK to say you like Eric Clapton and Mozart in the same sentence. It does give me a big boost when I see the Albert Hall full to capacity with people loving the music and to know they all came through the door because they heard it advertised on the station. I am also very proud of the way that Simon Bates comperes the evening, making it warm, friendly and informal but still at the same time keeping it magical.'

I asked him what he thought of tonight's concert.

'I loved the last piece as an encore – "Pomp and Circumstance March No. 1" by Elgar, best known nowadays as

"Land of Hope and Glory". It always sends a shiver down my spine.'

Where next for Classic FM?

'We want to spread the word and get more people out there discovering classical music. Our latest project, "Classic FM Music for Babies", is about that. Talking to pregnant mums and dads about how the music can benefit their babies' development and help them sleep at night . . . that's good news for the parents too!'

Holy Christ. Giles had unwittingly revealed one of the answers to the 'guess the real CD' game earlier on. Never mind.

13. The Waste Land

In the levelled, post-apocalyptic wilderness that was nine-teenth-century Europe après-Wagner, the few composers that were left sat in their garrets and wept. As did I. Wagner had ruined everything. No longer was there a Western musical tradition to follow; no thread to lead them; nor me either: Wagner had turned everything up to eleven, poured on nitro-glycerine and blasted all subtlety and progress to Kingdom Come. What was everyone supposed to do now?

'Do you like Funkadelic?' I emailed Fiona hopefully.

'Who? What? *Why?*' she angrily replied.

'Never mind. I suppose I should be getting to grips with something?'

'*Have you got to grips with Wagner yet?*'

I decided the best policy at this particular time was to sulk.

Though it didn't much help with the rebuilding, there was, at least, a Wagner antidote on the market – Johannes Brahms. Brahms, a fat, bearded and ill-tempered German gentleman, ploughed the furrow of reason and sanity throughout the Wagner era while all around were losing their heads in the kitchen sink. Brahms wrote modest, lyrical pieces in an old-fashioned classical style, and was ridiculed for it. But he became a sort of safety net for those falling out of Wagnerian love; Brahms caught and collected the increasing number of defectors, methodically turning them back against their former mentor. Even today, those listening to Brahms are doing so pointedly so as not to be listening to Wagner. Listening to Brahms is a Wagnerian protest vote, thus his music has remained extremely popular. While audiences continue to endure Wagnerian opera, so too will music lovers take refuge in Brahms; their yin/yang meta-physical face-off is one of the most fundamental cosmic balancing acts facing humanity today.

Brahms is interesting in that he burned more of his own musical manuscripts than he published. This was less common sense (or psychotic pyromania) than rigorous quality control – and it meant that we've ended up with just four symphonies from Herr Brahms, which has made life easier for all of us. I have found listening to Brahms akin to lying in a flotation tank: there's a feeling of sensory depriv-ation plus a queasy awareness of the earth revolving beneath. It's music made of sky – light, light blue.

How monstrously poetic.

'Can someone please help . . . superglue, you say?'

My Country Is More Sonorous than Your Country

Having snorted down their Brahmsian smelling salts, European composers awoke and sensibly decided not to attempt to outrun or outgun Richard Wagner; instead they took a collective step sideways into their own national folk songs, dances and traditions along these lines. This meant two things: 1) all these new influences meant that classical music became much *zingier*, and 2) the long-established urban power centres (Vienna, Paris, Rome) decreased in importance as other European countries got a chance to prove they weren't just lowly peasant-stuffed provincial backwaters. Though they were. Navel-gazing nationalism might sound like a regressive step, but it was like opening all the cupboards; and it meant that by the end of the nineteenth century, a huge melting pot of musical ideas and influences had become available for all to plagiarize or be inspired by (especially if you were a gypsy). Each country had its own composer – or several composers – trying evoke their own specific national consciousness via music. Soon they made it on to the front of stamps; even coins; some even hit the giddy heights of the back of their banknotes. If they had banks, that is.

In Bohemia, Dvořák and Smetana evoked the spirit of the gypsies and gypsy dancing.

In Hungary, Bartók evoked traditional Magyar folk, and gypsies.

In Moravia, Janáček evoked traditional Moravian folk, and gypsies as well.

In Norway, Grieg evoked snowy forests and polite desolation.

In Finland, Sibelius evoked similar wintry scenes, except better, as Grieg is generally held to be a mawkish, sentimental loser (with a seriously crap moustache) and I can't be bothered to go and buy any.

In Denmark, Nielsen evoked roll-mops.

In Great Britain, Elgar, Britten, Holst, Delius, Walton, Tippett and Vaughan Williams evoked our naval superiority, stately stiff upper lip and no bloody gypsies, thank you very much

In Holland, Diepenbrock evoked an early template for the art of the one-hit wonder.

In Spain, Albéniz and De Falla evoked bullfights, delicious chorizo and ultimate obscurity.

And in Russia, five self-taught pissheads gathered in a St Petersburg tavern, downed seventeen bottles of vodka and drunkenly christened themselves *Moguchaya Kuchka* (the Mighty Handful). They evoked almighty hangovers, being late for work and an inability to compose properly, as they didn't really understand music. But they weren't about to let trifles like these stand in their way – they were the *Mighty Handful*. Get out of our way, we have bushy black beards!

Russia never had an Early Romantic period. Nor a Classical, nor a Baroque. There was nothing to have a Renaissance of either. While Europe plunged through the epochs, the great motherland remained resolutely Medieval. Therefore, when a short Russian man with palm-tree hair and glasses named Mikhail Glinka composed an opera entitled *A Life for the Czar* in 1836, the country had no idea how to react. There was a lot of musical history to work through in a very short amount of time. Having cribbed it, Russia promptly hailed Glinka a national hero and a genius of Beethovian stature. Here was the beginning of the epic, tragic tale that is the story of classical music in Russia. I flew to Moscow to investigate almost immediately.

It Seemed Like a Good Idea at the Time

Moscow, Russia, April 2005

My advice is: fly Aeroflot. Honestly. Initially I was searching for the cheapest direct flight to Moscow from all airlines other than the Russian national carrier (Aeroflot has a bad reputation, a reputation involving mechanical failure and crashing). However, all the flights were ridiculously expensive, so in the end I thought to myself, OK, I'll just *check* and see how cheap Aeroflot are in comparison to these others.

'We're flying Aeroflot,' I informed Owen over the phone.

'The planes made out of elastic bands and balsa wood that crash? *No thanks.*'

It was too late, though, as I'd already bought the tickets. Next I had to sort out an invitation. To enter the Russian Federation you have to be invited by somebody already inside the country, so I'd like to give a big shout out to Mrs Olga Leninovsky of Kremlin Heights, Moscow, for the letter; only next time please don't send photographs, OK? I'm married.

Actually our Aeroflot airliner didn't crash: it had seat belts and trays, just like normal, and stewardesses and drinks and everything – really a lot of drinks, so many that arrival in Moscow can be an extremely jolly affair, exiting the plane arms linked with your new Russki pals singing patriotic songs and shouting. That is, until you hit customs, where if you smile you aren't let in.

I'd had problems finding a hotel room, as Moscow was

hosting a big trade expo during our whole five-day visit and everywhere was full; but in the end I got lucky – a whole flat to ourselves on the eighth floor of an old Soviet apartment block. It was ace – it had wood-tiled floors, two balconies, a view of the (admittedly distant) Kremlin and three bedrooms.

'There's no furniture,' said Owen.

'The oven doesn't work,' said Owen.

'The TV doesn't work,' said Owen.

'There's nothing to cook with,' said chef Owen.

'But if the oven doesn't work, then . . . ?'

'And there's a leak under the sink,' said Owen.

'Would you like some vodka?'

'There are no glasses.'

We sat on the floor and listened to selections from the Mighty Handful through my portable speakers.

'Can we listen to something else now?' pleaded Owen after five minutes.

'*Nyet.*'

The Mighty Handful was:

Mily Balakirev (job: leader of the Mighty Handful; musical training: none);

Modest Mussorgsky (job: civil servant; musical training: no);

César Cui (job: military engineer; musical training: none);

Alexander Borodin (job: chemistry professor; musical training: zero);

Nikolai Rimsky-Korsakov (job: naval officer; musical training: *nyet*).

The guys all sat around in Mily Balakirev's flat, drinking vodka and trying to compose a specific new kind of music – music that represented what it was like to be Russian;

323

there was to be none of that Germanic, European bullshit: this was about unpolished patriotism – true grit. They argued fiercely among themselves until Balakirev restored order with a heavy oak stick.

'Silence!'

The Handful murmured to themselves.

'Who has a composition to share with the group?'

Mussorgsky timidly raised his hand.

'Let me see!'

Balakirev's dark eyes ran urgently over the manuscript.

'Terrible!'

The Handful all giggled.

'This is not Russian enough! Make it more Russian!'

'How?' sulked Mussorgsky.

'I don't know. Let's have a discussion!'

So they sat at Balakirev's feet and argued into the night. This pattern continued for several years, until Mussorgsky emerged blinking into the St Petersburg daylight clutching his opera *Boris Godunov*. It was a nationalist masterpiece, evoking peasants, vodka, horses, mud, the Czar and gypsies.

'Well done, Mussorgsky!' bellowed Balakirev, who was green with repressed envy and red-faced from vodka. 'Who else has something?'

Cui raised his uniformed arm. He'd written a small, relatively worthless piece entitled *Orientale*. Balakirev snatched it out of his hands.

'Is this the best you can do?' Balakirev thundered.

'Yes,' said Cui, staring miserably at his cheap leather shoes.

'You are useless! Henceforth, you shall not compose. Instead, you can be our propagandist!'

'Oh bloody hell.'

'Silence!'

Borodin had composed an opera too: *Prince Igor*. It had taken him twenty years to write. Balakirev flipped through it, admiring its folksy stylings.

'There is much truth in this piece,' cried Balakirev. 'Well done!'

'Thank you. Phew,' said Borodin.

'But where is the ending? This opera is not finished!'

Borodin never managed to finish it. The rest of the Handful had to finish it for him.

Nikolai Rimsky-Korsakov nervously handed over his own efforts: the operas *The Czar's Bride*, *The Story of the Czar Saltan* (including the famous 'Flight of the Bumblebee'), *Christmas Eve*, *The Golden Cockerel* and *The Legend of the Invisible City of Kitezh*.

'Is this all?' growled Balakirev. Rimsky-Korsakov shook his head and passed over some further sheaves of orchestral music: a Symphony in E-flat Minor, a Symphony in C, and the *Capriccio Espagnol*.

'*Capriccio Espagnol*?' harrumphed Balakirev. 'That doesn't sound very Russian!'

'Well, I've been taking lessons from . . .'

'Taking lessons?!' The Handful all gasped.

'. . . and I've got a job at the St Petersburg Conservatory as professor of music.'

'Traitor! The Handful is about amateur, unlearned, honest expression! You have brought shame upon our group!'

Rimsky-Korsakov became irritated. 'So what have you composed, then, Balakirev?'

'Me?' roared Balakirev. 'I have composed many things!' The Handful eyed him suspiciously. 'For example, my charming and extremely Russian piece for piano, *Islamey*.'

'*Islamey* is very short, Balakirev. What else?'

'My First Symphony!'

'Your only symphony,' muttered Cui.

'Insubordination!'

'How many other symphonies have you written?'

'I have been busy supervising all of you! I have no time for bourgeois symphony-writing!' Then Balakirev stormed out, never to return. He filled the hole of the Handful with religion. The remaining Handful drifted away too, one by one. Mussorgsky drank himself to death; Borodin threw himself back into science; Cui just disappeared. Rimsky-Korsakov started his own circle of composers, whose ranks included a young man by the name of Pyotr Ilyich Tchaikov-sky, who went on to do a bit of gear, yeah, but it was the Mighty Handful who invented Russian music. And their leader, Mily Balakirev!

'The freezer doesn't work either,' said Owen, who was on a diet again.*

'Comrade, you are cool enough already,' I lied, but it shut him up long enough for us to leave the flat early the next morning, to explore Moscow and do some classical music fact-finding. The first thing we had to do was find the agent for our apartment and pay for our entire stay in advance, in cash. Elena, our contact, had told us that any currency was fine, but she'd rather it wasn't roubles.

'Is paying for everything in advance in mixed currency normal?' asked Owen, as we stood in line for a cash machine on Попянка Мап. The sun shone hard, melting seven months' accumulated snow into fast-flowing streams of grey sludge. We were overdressed and underbooted.

'No, this is sheer anarchy, but I think we'd better get used to it. We should prepare ourselves for *continual lawlessness*.'

---

* This time it was wheat-free, dairy-free, sugar-free plus 'four or five Carol Vorderman exercises every day'.

I withdrew a couple of hundred dollars, but Owen's card was rejected before he'd typed any numbers in. This wasn't a good sign. As we worked our way up through screaming traffic to cross the Moscow river and pass up beneath the west wall of the Kremlin, every cash machine we tried along the way spat Owen's card out; but he kept trying. I was deeply moved by this dogged yet pointless charade.

'Have you actually got any money in there?'

There was a barely perceptible pause, and then a half-arsed 'I think I do.'

Elena's plush office reeked of New Russian money. Must be mafia, I thought to myself, since she had a computer on her desk as well as a calculator and an AK-47. I handed over all my dollars without even being asked.

'This is not enough,' she said. It did look rather risible, lying there in her frigid, upturned palm. We turned towards Owen. He slowly reached into his jacket.

'Do you take a cheque?' he asked. Elena laughed coldly, and proceeded to strip my wallet clean of everything – even my Donor Card.

'There is a big market in Russia for internal organs,' she hissed.* Promising to come back with the rest very, very soon, we were eventually allowed to leave. Outside in the sunlight, Owen asked if *I* would take a cheque, except I was in the middle of being bothered by a beggar. But then I laughed coldly too, and we walked towards Red Square in silence.

Upon reaching Red Square, which is vast, cobbled, full of policemen and tourists and is terrifying, but in a good way, Owen posed like Bruce Forsyth.

* All right, all right.

To the right of Owen you can see the walls of the Kremlin and Lenin's marble tomb, inside which he lies embalmed. Above Owen's head, just to the right, you can see St Basil's Cathedral. To his left, you can see Государственный Уинверсальный Магазин.

'Can I borrow some money?' asked Owen.

'But Elena took it all.'

'You must have some left.'

'Only a tiny bit. I'll lend you some money if you go over there and pretend to be storming the Kremlin walls.'

'What, over here?'

'Yep. Now try and make it look like you're storming it.'

He sort of, raised a leg.

'Put some effort in – you're meant to be sacking it not leaning on it.'

He raised an arm, paused, and then came back over. 'How much can I borrow?'

'Twelve quid.'

'Is that all?'

'It's all there is.'

Next morning, despite further symbolic cashcard rejection

Ahead of Owen is the looming Kremlin. Nobody was shot during the taking of this photograph.

from Owen, I extracted some money, and off we went in search of some classical music; specifically Moscow's Tchai-kovsky Concert Hall up by Маяковская metro station. Here we ran into trouble. Moscow's underground system is a mighty feat of engineering: its stations are marble-clad marvels; its escalators plunge deep into the bowels of the earth; a train always arrives within a minute; the system carries more passengers every day (nine million!) than the London and New York systems *combined*. The problem is that at intersections with other lines, stations change their names. So one busy intersection can have as many as four separate titles. This can be confusing, especially when your Cyrillic's not great and you're having to count your way in stops in the first place. But we made it to Маяковская eventually, having got horrifically lost at Пшкинская; or rather Чеховская; or was it Тверская? We were glad to get the fuck out of there, to be honest.

In the brown lobby of the Tchaikovsky Concert Hall, Owen and I perused a number of different posters, attempting to identify which was the one with the programme of the week's events, while being glared at by roll-necked security. Briefly waylaid by the toilet-cleaning schedule, we finally deciphered the correct poster and immediately came up trumps: a bunch of Prokofiev, playing tomorrow night (with some Ravel and Beethoven's Third too, but screw that). Not only was that most Russian of Russian composers Prokofiev on the bill, but it was also the *National Première* of his 'Queen of Spades' suite. This sounded like an event of vital national importance, so I rushed to buy tickets from the old lady knitting in the booth, and it didn't take too long actually – only about a half an hour, after she'd switched on the intercom – to get my point across and two tickets in return. We were delighted, so delighted, in fact, that we headed straight to the Bolshoi to buy tickets for there too. For the remaining nights we had free, there was a choice between either ballet or opera.

'I hate ballet,' said Owen.

'Even though I've never seen it, so do I. Does ballet really have anything to do with classical music?'

Picking up my negative suggestion well, Owen replied, 'No, nothing.'

'And there's no *way* I'm going to the opera. I'm through with opera for ever.'

'Which leaves . . . ?'

'I think we can go.'

We couldn't find the entrance anyway. Instead we strolled down Тверская and stood in Red Square again. We never got bored of it.

Pyotr Ilyich Tchaikovsky never really got on with the Handful.

'The Mighty Handful,' he wrote, 'are afflicted to the marrow with the worst sort of conceit and with a purely dilettantish confidence in their superiority over the rest of the musical world. This is my honest opinion of these gentlemen. What a sad thing!'

Thank God the Handful were wankered on booze when he said it, or they'd have paid Pyotr Ilyich a visit that very afternoon.

Unlike the Handful, Pyotr Ilyich was a sensitive man – a man of refinement and style. His beard wasn't black and heavy, it was grey and neatly trimmed; his music wasn't raw and earthy, it was florid and exquisitely nuanced; his tipple wasn't meths and lighter fluid, it was vodka, sometimes even with mixer. It figures, then, that Pyotr Ilyich was a raving homosexual whose music was nowhere near Russian enough as it ought to have been. Tchaikovsky was born in 1840 in a godforsaken nowheresville called Kamsko-Votkinsk, but soon escaped, first to St Petersburg, then on to teach harmony at the Moscow Conservatory, where he began to compose in earnest. As well as a few tentative symphonies, which he wasn't very good at, he enjoyed composing for ballet. Nobody had taken ballet music remotely seriously until now; it had been basic music-to-order; secondary to the dancing.* Tchaikovsky changed all that with his *Nutcracker*, his *Swan Lake* and his *Romeo and Juliet*, the score of which he excitedly but ill-advisedly forwarded to the Handful to see what they reckoned. Good, *nyet*?

'It's completely terrible!' raged Balakirev.

'Shit! Shitty shit shit!' pounded Mussorgsky and the others.

Criticism such as this led to Pyotr Ilyich becoming a virtual recluse in his tiny Moscow apartment for almost three years. Then, in 1877, unwisely, he married one of his groupies – moronic nymphomaniac Antonia Ivanova Miliukova – out of pity and just a few days later attempted suicide by throwing himself in a river. However, it wasn't a very deep river, and he was rescued by his brother Modest, and instead of death he got the sniffles. He chose not to go back to Ms Miliukova, who soon went mad and died in an insane asylum.

Fortunately, Pyotr Ilyich was soon befriended by a rich widow named Nadezhda von Meck, who also adored his honey-dripping, effete melodiousness. Like Pyotr Ilyich, Ms von Meck was very shy, and upon her insistence the two never met; they just sent each other hundreds of letters, and she sent money – 6,000 roubles every year.

---

* To be honest, unless I can actually see some diaphanous chicks leaping about, I can't tell ballet music from non-ballet music. Really, I've tried – I've no idea how to tell the difference; in fact I don't think there *is* a difference – ballet is just classical music with lilywhite dancing girls: it's that simple.

'I'm not surprised you don't want to meet me,' wrote Pyotr Ilyich. 'You'll only be disappointed.'

'I prefer to think of you from afar,' she dreamily replied. 'To hear you speak in your music, and share your feelings through it. The more you fascinate me, the more I fear our acquaintance. You're not gay, though, are you?'

'No, of course not! I'm married – to old whasserface.'

But in 1890 Nadezhda von Meck somehow unearthed the truth and abruptly terminated all correspondence and roubles. Pyotr Ilyich never recovered from the blow. Instead, he composed the *1812 Overture* and ran off to America, where he hid in his skyscraper hotel room and didn't answer the phone, as it hadn't been invented yet (well, it had, but it wasn't quite ready).

For our second night in Moscow – 'the city that never sleeps' – we stayed in again. This time, though, we had money; and we celebrated the fact by buying the biggest and most expensive bottle of vodka we could find, taking it back to the apartment and drinking it out of paper cups as we listened to Pyotr Ilyich turned up as loud as possible. We also had a beetroot and a few cartons of yogurt. Before we left London, I'd downloaded a whole load of Tchaikovsky especially; and as we sat on the floor listening to it, I was amazed by how much I was already familiar with.

'I seem to know all of this stuff,' I yelled at Owen, who was playing 'air cannon' along with the *1812 Overture*. 'It's all incredibly famous.'

'Boom!' he went. 'Bang!' And he waved his arms about. 'Tchaikovsky! Brilliant! Total rainbow rock 'n' roll!'

'Rainbow the band?'

'What? No, be quiet. Boom, bang, death!' He downed his paper cup and threw it on to the floor, where it bounced pathetically. He picked it up and refilled it. 'Death or glory!'

'I think you've had enough.'

'I can't hear you! And anyway – I've barely even started!'

The overture trumpeted onward. I worried about the neighbours.*

The *1812 Overture*, arguably the best-known piece of classical music of all time, was written as a (belated) celebration of Russia's victory over France in the Napoleonic Wars. It's programme music – i.e. it's telling a story; and the story here is that *the Russians won, so fuck you, Frenchies*. The French national anthem even makes an appearance early doors, before the frogs are systematically butchered by Czarist infantry and the 'Marseillaise' is buried beneath blasts of Russian cannon fire and the mighty 'God Save the Czar' (the Soviet regime replaced the 'God save the Czar' stuff to a more proletariat 'Glory'). The whole battle's wrapped up inside a quarter of an hour. Good thinking. Next, Owen and I swooned along to the Piano Concerto No. 1. It's so famous – so *funny* – like a cartoon! I had no idea that was by Tchaikovsky!

'Bing, bong, *bash*. Bing, bong, *bash*,' conducted Owen. 'I love Tchaikovsky!'

The vodka was flowing thick and fast; much of it lay in pools on the wooden floor. We steadily hammered our way through the very, very best of Pyotr Ilyich, though my subsequent listening notes are sadly entirely illegible. In truth, Owen threw my notebook out of the window. We watched it flutter to the ground and land haphazardly on a scrap of snow-covered scrubland.

'Thanks.'

'Death or glory.'

---

* Until a few hours later, when I met them and they were even drunker than us.

'Neither.'

'You can't have neither.'

'Oh, for God's sake.'

I can't remember exactly what happened after that, so instead, here are some (much more interesting) Москва Факты – facts about Moscow:

Men wear jeans and black leather jackets.

Women wear (knee-high) boots and too much make-up.

Everybody (young and old) walks around holding bottles of beer.

Everyone is super-friendly.

The food is basic but hearty, unless you're prepared to pay way more.

Mafia, what mafia? Oh, *them*. They travel in blacked-out people-carrier convoys; their minders stand outside the restaurants they're inside with their arms folded and sunglasses on. It's quite sweet really.

Cars go way too fast. Except these cars, which don't.

Booze, fags and the metro are all dirt cheap, which means Muscovites, of whom there are shitloads, are happy enough.

Nobody speaks English. *Nobody.*

Drunk men sleep in their cars with the engine running so they don't freeze to death overnight. The first time we saw this we thought it was a suicide bid, and Owen knocked on the guy's window to try and wake him up. Having established that the exhaust wasn't being piped into the cockpit, and that the man wasn't dead – just shitfaced – we continued on our way.

The *1812* was triumphantly premièred in Moscow's stunning, neoclassical Cathedral of Christ the Saviour on 20 August 1882. As with the Bolshoi and St Basil's, we weren't able to find our way inside, so, in search of some respite from the gutters'pother, we headed for Gorky Park, the rural idyll in the heart of Moscow where its cityfolk, bored of drinking vodka in their dreary apartment blocks, go to drink vodka on park benches instead. But it was all frozen, and full of bulldozers and men in leather jackets saying эакрыт and *nyet*. It was the most depressing park either of us had ever been to in our lives; there wasn't even anybody to sidle up alongside and whisper *the ducks are flying south* to, or prod with a poison umbrella. Owen even got temporarily stranded on a snowbank.

After a frustrating couple of hours spent sliding muckily around the deserted Gorky wastelands, we made our way back up to Маяковская and the Tchaikovsky Concert Hall for the evening's show. We'd been worried that two dishevelled Westerners, soaked to our thighs and covered with Gorky grime, might be unwelcome in such rarefied confines, but the crowd tonight was agreeably down-to-earth, the polar opposite to the cigar-puffing, style-obsessed Romans. The red-uniformed, not-so-cuddly usher matrons even allowed us to buy a programme; which we stared at uncomprehendingly for fifteen minutes over a beer in the neoclassical foyer of the concert hall, as hazy, yellow evening sunlight flooded the bright white, elegant civic space, where communism wasn't a dirty word so much as a noble concept for mankind to aspire to or recall with fondness and pride.

'Earth calling Seb,' came a capitalist pigdog voice to my right. 'The show's about to begin; we ought to take our seats.'

We did, and were transported back to an altogether more humane continuance.*

Day Three

We decided to go on a Moscow literary/musical tour. This wasn't as part of a group or with a guide, it was a walking tour itinerary provided by my guidebook that we'd need to orienteer ourselves. As, so far, Owen had taken zero responsibility for deciphering any Cyrillic lettering, or map-reading, or metro directions, or menu-decoding, or Russian speaking or anything whatsoever, it was agreed that he would

---

* The concert was fine. Owen fell asleep during the Prokofiev première – the very first piece.

take charge of this particular outing. It meant I'd be able to relax for an hour or two while Owen played mother. 'You're sure this is OK?'

'It's fine,' he said, staring at the map with horror.

'You're sure you're happy about doing this?'

'It's fine,' he repeated, defiantly cracking the spine of the book and holding it upside-down. To begin, he positioned us on a street corner facing a small square. 'Here we are. This is . . .' he said, reading from the guidebook, '. . . the Tverskoy bulvar, the most popular walking street of the nineteenth century, featured in Tolstoy's *Anna Karenina*.' We stood atop a scrawny quadrangle, belittered with slush and birdshit, and watched some paralytic homeless dudes. Owen led us down the filthy main artery. 'On the north side, you will notice a large classical Russian Empire-style mansion . . .'

'Where?'

'. . . that houses the Pushkin Drama Theatre.'

'Where?'

'There.'

'It's a housing block and a stationery shop.'

'And on the south side, you will see the salmon-coloured 26a, which now houses the exquisite *haute russe* cuisine Café Pushkin.'

There was a dirty mustard building and a fence.

'We're in the wrong park, man. None of this stuff is here.'

Owen ignored me and marched on down through the muck. 'In the middle of the boulevard is a statue of Sergei Yesenin, an early twentieth-century poet who was in and out of favour throughout the Soviet era.' And he stood and pointed triumphantly at a statue – because there was a statue, only it was of Rachmaninov.

'No, that's Rachmaninov.'

'No, it's Sergei Yesenin.'

'But it says here, on the panel – I'll translate the Cyrillic: RACHMANINOV. See?'

Owen, head-deep in the guidebook, ignored me. But Rachmaninov was cool – in fact Rachmaninov was fantastic, because he's the guy who came after Pyotr Ilyich (who died in 1893, after drinking a glass of untreated water. This was either damn foolish or suicide: forced upon him by a kangaroo court after being caught *in flagrante delicto* with a handsome young soldier). За ваше эдоровъе! And don't drink the Moscow tapwater. Drink vodka.

Rachmanenough?

Sergei (top) and Sebastian (bottom).

Rachmaninov was a tremendously serious man. And although he wasn't nearly as strung-out as Tchaikovsky, he too let some European spritzer dilute his nationalistic liquor. Rachers was born in 1873. He was good at the piano. And he was good at composing. He won Gold Medals for these things. And he was an arrogant bastard. Then, at twenty-two years old, he composed his first symphony and arranged to have it premièred in St Petersburg. So far, so yawny-yawn-yawn. Except *everyone hated it*. Oh dear. Rachers, until now an aloof and superior kind of guy, fell apart. He was so devastated by the blanket loathing of his symphony that he had a complete nervous breakdown and wasn't able to write any more music for five years. He just played the piano dejectedly. In the end things got so bad that he subjected himself to a course of hypnotherapy.

'Repeat after me,' said Dr Dahl, his hypnotherapist.

'Repeat after me,' mumbled Rachers.

'Not yet! Repeat after me – I'm going to go home, sit down at my piano and compose a masterpiece that everyone will love for ever.'

'. . . go home . . .' mumbled Rachers. '. . . sit down . . . compose . . . masterpiece . . . everyone . . . love . . . for ever.'

Dahl clicked his fingers and Rachers woke up, paid up, moped home, sat down at the keyboard and began to compose his C Minor Piano Concerto; otherwise known as his Piano Concerto No. 2 – one of the holiest, most beloved pieces in all of classical music; in fact, just this year it was officially voted Britain's favourite piece of classical music *ever*. That's right – even more popular than 'Land of Hope and Glory' – maybe there's hope for us yet. There is *none more Russian* than Rachmaninov's Piano Concerto No. 2 (which makes you wonder why they used the piece in the *none more English* 1945 romantic classic *Brief Encounter*); indeed it's so Russian that it steals melodies from Russian Orthodox church music (on which I am an expert). Had they not all been dead by the time of its composition, the Mighty Hand-ful would've hailed it a nationalistic masterpiece. Which it is, plus a helluva lot of virtuosic joanna, raging throughout. Rachmaninov's Piano Concerto No. 2 – the *Blake's Seven* music on crystal meth – hits all the right spots: it's sturdy, dramatic, it has wonderful sweeping melodies, it's passion-ate, makes your heart swell, and romanticizes the noble ideal of the potato and the peasant without resorting to being all that patronizing. Just a little. Rachers was so chuffed by the favourable reaction to the concerto that he ploughed on and composed another two symphonies, which went down much better than his first. I, too, find them both agreeable, with a golden syrupy tang.

'Are Rachmaninov's Second and Third Symphonies masterpieces?' I asked Fiona.

'They are both perfectly fine,' she replied. 'I think they're pretty exciting, but shouldn't be heard that often. Is that an answer?'

I find Fiona gets more cryptic by the day.

'I have only heard them twice, so I won't put them on again,' I wrote back. And I haven't. The CDs are just sitting here, looking at me. I'm not sure what to do with them.

Rachmaninov left Russia for Switzerland soon after the revolution, where he cemented his reputation as probably the greatest pianist since Franz Liszt. There are recordings of him – scratchy ones. Then, in 1935, he settled permanently in the United States, where he became grossly unfashionable because of his Late Romantic vision and chops. He was 'too emotional'. He died in Beverly Hills in 1943, and remains despised by critics (Fiona didn't disguise it very well) but fêted by the public. *Are you Rachmanenough?**

* I don't know what this means but it sounds quite good.

In the Kremlin

It's not easy to get into the Kremlin; you need this pass, that pass; these roubles, those roubles; this queue, that queue; this soldier's shakedown, that soldier's shakedown. Again, smile and they won't let you in. Act too surly and they won't let you in. Wave your arms in the air and speak English at them and they absolutely love it – they can't get enough of that.

You're only let into the Kremlin to look around the ancient cathedrals huddled around Sobornaya Square – the highest point in the city; from up here you (and the KGB and the Politburo and many gentlemen in dark jackets with 'bulges') can keep a beady, paranoiac eye on the entire conurbation. That the citadel's walls are between 3.5 and 6.5 metres thick and defended by twenty separate towers only adds to one's sense of security, well-being and comfort in the knowledge that dissent will lead to immediate execution and/or encouragement eastward. Owen and I strolled beleaguered around the square, laden with passes and laminates round our necks and stickers and giant audioguide walkie-talkies. It was a bit like being an astronaut. But of course, what everybody *really* wants to do is wander around the parts of the Kremlin you're not supposed to. Sod the cathedrals – give us some pasty-faced bureaucratic chills. So we tried it. Not the best idea we've ever had. From the giant Tsar Bell, we edged slowly backwards away from the square towards the cover of some scrawny trees and a parapet while the nearest cossack had his back turned. We made it to the trees and looked triumphantly over the parapet to observe some military manoeuvres taking place in a courtyard far below.

'Quick, take a photograph!' hissed Owen. But I was all tangled up in my laminated passes and walkie-talkie, so I couldn't. We scuttled along the parapet's edge towards a far bulwark that gave us cover from a narrow cobbled square that led to a fierce yellow façade that just screamed *I am a scary government building: come and have a go if you think you're hard enough.*

'Why are we doing this?' I whispered to Owen.

'Shhhh,' and he pushed me into the wall as a guard passed by on the other side of the bulwark. Flattening ourselves against the concrete, we could see the shiny black butt of the guy's submachine-gun poking out from underneath his right elbow.

'He's gone,' whispered Owen. 'Come on!'

Upon reaching the end of the parapet, we took a few deep breaths and began strolling nonchalantly across the cobbled square; I fancied we looked rather camp – *la-de-da*, not a care in the world! A long black limousine was parked outside the building's ornate black double-doors: we couldn't see inside, but its motor was running, and large Russian flags were mounted on the front corners of the bonnet.

'That's probably Putin's car,' muttered Owen out the side of his mouth, as we gradually closed in. 'Don't look surprised if he suddenly gets out.'

'Or gets in.'

'Yes, or gets in. Look as normal as you can.'

'I am.'

We'd got within about 50 yards of the doors when a skull-fucking whistle rang out. And then another, and another. There was shouting. We froze.

'Do you think they mean us?'

'They could.'

Two guys in leather jackets were screaming at us from the other end of the square. Others were blowing whistles and running. We froze even more.

'What now, do you reckon?' asked Owen.

'Look stupid and smile.'

'OK.'

We looked stupid and smiled. Fortunately we were stupid already. The leather jackets gestured at us madly. We started to walk towards them but that made it worse, so we veered back towards the trees but nope, more shouting. Our only options were either forward towards Putin's car, or off to the left back in the direction of the cathedrals again. We chose the cathedrals. The leather jackets stomped across and caught up with us and really weren't very happy at all; they even gave us a shove. We were shepherded angrily back into Sobornaya Square, where all the tourists stared at us disapprovingly.

'Good work,' said Owen.

'Excellent work,' I replied.

'Did you get a picture?'

'I sure did.'

And then the cathedrals, how exciting.

*

The Mighty Handful score:
Sex: 3. No time for that!
Drugs: 2. Evil bourgeois trickery!
Rock 'n' roll: 9. Moscow girls make me sing and shout.

Pyotr Ilyich Tchaikovsky scores:
Sex: 1. Mercilessly repressed; ultimately tragic.
Drugs: 4. Points for sheer alcoholism. ☹
Rock 'n' roll: 3. You don't know how lucky you are, boy.

The Kremlin – a naughty bit.

Sergei Rachmaninov scores:
Sex: 2. Very.
Drugs: 2. Dull.
Rock 'n' roll: 8. Let me hear your balalaikas ringing out.

Seb suggests:

Mussorgsky: *Pictures at an Exhibition* by Evgeny Kissin (Red Seal) 🚑 🚑 🚑 🚑

(Piano music. None more Russian. Superb; and Kissin's a keyboard-ticklin' genius.)

Mussorgsky: *Boris Godunov* by the Conservatoire Concert Society Orchestra and the Sofia National Opera Chorus (EMI Classics) 🚑 🚑 🚑 🚑

(Better than most opera. Overwhelmingly Russian-sounding.)

Tchaikovsky: Anything. It's like gorging on vast piles of creamy mashed potato. Soon you'll feel sick. Next you'll vomit. You won't be in the mood for mashed potato for ages but you'll always have a wee taste for it.

Rachmaninov: *Piano Concertos 2 and 3* by Sergei Rachmaninov and the Philadelphia Orchestra (Naxos Historical) 🚗🚗🚗🚗🚗

(He dedicated this piece to Dr Dahl – the hypnotist who'd cleared his writer's block. Once you get through this recording's hiss, Sergei himself is the pianist. That's pretty cool; pretty goddamn definitive.)

Prokofiev: *Romeo and Juliet* (Act One, approximately nine minutes in) by Anyone Cheap 🚗🚗🚗🚗🚗

(Overwhelmingly Russian-sounding.)

The Late Romantic era is tiring.

14. A Crack in the Cosmic Egg

Claude Debussy, a Bagpuss-like dandy from Paris with a scary, Elephant Man-esque protuberance on the front of his head, wore a white suit, carried an umbrella (occasionally a parasol) at all times, nibbled on caviar and expensive pastries constantly and hated bumping into people on his occasional shuffles along the promenade, or back down the pastry shop for, oh, what the heck, another tray of those delicious éclairs please, Monsieur le Patissier. Humanity irritated him. Claude was a typical Late Romantic devoted Wagnerian and he attended Bayreuth every year like any aspiring young Conservatoire musician ought until, one dainty Parisian afternoon, he bumped into irreverent surrealist backstreet composeur Erik Satie, who was balancing on a unicycle, reciting pre-Dadaist limericks backwards whilst juggling kittens.

'Wagner est *merde*,' announced Satie, whose career was in the doldrums following his expulsion from the Conservatoire for not taking things seriously enough. 'Wagner is too much sauerkraut. Not enough . . . *boof*.' And he extracted an egg from his mouth and barked like a dog.

Debussy, pulling his hat down over his eyes to cover his forehump, was hypnotized by this strange behaviour, and the pair headed back to Satie's apartment, where he played Debussy some of his own compositions for piano. These included *Three Pear-shaped Pieces*, *Cold Pieces*, *New Cold Pieces*, *Dead Embryos* and the definitive *Three Flabby Preludes (For a Dog)*. I don't know how, but Debussy was impressed, and he immediately disavowed Wagner (and Romanticism generally) for ever. This new, rather stupid and meaningless music sounded to Debussy like the future (and actually it *was* the future, but, as usual, no one realized).

'Merci, Satie, you have shown me ze light!' Debussy cried, tossing his Bayreuth season ticket into the fireplace and excitedly picking up the kittens. Satie did that funny mime where you pretend to be stuck inside an invisible box, then barked like a dog and said, 'I am a fish.' Everyone laughed. With him, not at him.

Back at the Conservatoire, Debussy suddenly became extremely unpopular. His new Satie-inspired compositions were unfocused, hazy – they didn't go anywhere, didn't *resolve* like everyone was taught everything had to. This was because Debussy had just invented musical impressionism; this new music was just dabs, feelings, moods, colours – dissonant harmonics, revolution! – and of course nobody liked it: it wasn't German enough.

'Music is the expression of the movement of the waters, the play of curves described by changing breezes,' Debussy wistfully mused, dozing on the banks of the Seine one lazy summer afternoon.

'We have nursed a viper in our bosom!' cried the Conservatoire, which doesn't sound like 'conservative' by accident.

Debussy's music and subsequent career were a celebration of sound for its own sake, the opposite to the self-righteous, insistent demands of Wagnerian post-Romanticism. The music had no purpose, it just floated there, shimmering prettily in the early evening sun. If a melody presents itself, then fine, but if not ... why worry? Have another cake instead! Debussy also said: 'I'm convinced that music is something that cannot be cast into a traditional and fixed form; it's made up of colours and rhythms. The rest is a load of humbug invented by frigid imbeciles riding on the backs of the Masters. Bach alone had an idea of the truth . . .'

So true. He began to describe himself simply as a *musicien français* and went out of his way to slag off anything German as heavy, bombastic, burdensome, *cabbage*, compared to the wit, élan and intelligence of your average Frenchman and your average French *sensibilité*. Though he continued to despise all forms of human contact, and two of his ex-girlfriends proceeded to shoot themselves, the rest of France began to warm to Debussy; maybe he was on to something with all this anti-German shtick. After all, you had all these French impressionist painters, so why not impressionist composers too?

In the end, Debussy's ethereal genius proved too radical to launch a whole new French school, though he did have his followers; among them Maurice Ravel, who did the same sort of thing and should not only be remembered as having composed that hackneyed ice-skating music – the Ravel piece that was on the bill at our concert at the Tchaikovsky Concert Hall in Moscow was mind-bending and propulsive, and I keep meaning to go and get hold of some more, but it always slips my mind. *Bolero* it is, then.

Maxxing Out, Baby

Back in Germany, the Late Romantics continued as if nothing was wrong, like nothing had happened. Outside Claude Debussy's Parisian piano room, the musical universe continued to expand. Everything was still getting bigger and bigger: ambition, orchestras, symphonies, egos, ideas, batons, lapels, audiences – even spaceships. Which had got as far as Jupiter. Wider, deeper, longer, grander, more lush, more tender, more sonorous, *my God, it's full of stars*. That's right, I was completely bored shitless with everything and had resorted to watching Stanley Kubrick's stoner science fiction masterpiece *2001: A Space Odyssey*.

'Why?' wrote Fiona.

Instead of reminding her that the film's famous soundtrack is actually *Also Sprach Zarathustra*, a tone poem by Richard Strauss, the (thank God) last and most successful of the Great German Romantics, I wrote back: 'It's a classic.'

'How thoroughly pointless.'

Ignoring this dispiriting message, and too frightened to confess my advancing indifference to all this ultra-orchestral sludge, I became steadily more horrified as the extent of H.A.L.'s robotic psychosis revealed itself.

'I wouldn't do that, Dave,' repeated H.A.L. like a terrifying broken record which in a way he was; but fortunately Dave shuts him down and then it all goes resolutely psychedelic and both meaningful and meaningless, depending on one's mood. As watching the film sure beat sitting in a chair listening to more of Richard Strauss's 'beautiful', 'elegiac' tone poems, I found it meaningful. But what is a tone poem? It sounds nice – but is it really? My Collins dictionary defines one as 'an extended orchestral composition based on nonmusical material, such as a work of literature or a folk tale'. So it's not that nice after all. The remainder of *Also Sprach Zarathustra* (all looming menace, bom-bom-bom-bom-bom-bom-bom-bom-crash – fake apes, monolith, dawn – you know the score) is nowhere near as good as its definitive (fake apes, monolith, dawn) first part. Though it works up a glutinous and lordly head of steam, it's nothing special – no real space vibes. Strauss wrote hundreds of (extra-schmaltzy) pieces like this, and became incredibly rich, possibly the richest composer of all. The press at the time were obsessed with how much money Strauss was earning – in Europe as well as America, where the *New York Times* maintained a rolling tally, much to the Strauss family's annoyance.

As the biggest and best-known composer during a period of wild European economic growth, writing incredibly long and convoluted pieces, perhaps also getting paid by the hour, maybe it's a little unfair that Richard Strauss's reputation is that of rich man first, composer-of-any-interest second. But then, from what I've heard of it, I can honestly say that these fiscal facts are more interesting than his music. And the man. He was industrious, he was married and he was henpecked. That's all there is to say. Except that the music goes on and on. And on and on and on and on. It really is indescribably boring. And there's always another piece lined up ready to go after that one's rewinding – for which he was paid exceedingly well. The story goes that once, upon returning to Berlin after rehearsals for a gigantic tone-poem recital in Dresden, he was met at the station by his son, who bounded up to Strauss Snr crying, 'Papa! Papa! Tell me how much you got paid for the rehearsal!'

Upon hearing these wondrous words fall from his boy's sweet lips, Strauss wept tears of joy and exclaimed, 'Now I know you are a true son of mine!'

Then he went home, and his wife smacked him around the head with a rolling pin. Then he wrote a three-hour tone poem. Then in 1949 he died. No one cared – it was 1949 and some heavy shit had been going down in the meantime.

Anton and On

I don't know how I feel about Bruckner – a bit weirded out, to be honest – maybe slightly disarmed. All I'm sure of is that I'm intrigued by him; by what he managed to do in his bottomless fathoms of chasms. Though his was a similar idiom to Strauss's, there's something in his music that gets me inside; his stuff sets off a distinct magical vibration somewhere near the intestine/bowels region; maybe slightly higher, a little to the left. What *is* that? Beats me. Here he is anyway, at various stages of his . . . progressions.

The many, myriad faces of Anton Bruckner: not really cutting much of a dash at any point.

Back in the 1870s, Bruckner was (mistakenly) considered the village idiot of the Late Romantic scene. He was a country bumpkin; he dressed like a peasant, spoke like one, had a shaved head and a 'tache and still believed in God. Hahahaha, what a twat. But Bruckner was driven to compose; and when he did compose – wow – it went on for *fucking centuries*. But I think this is actually a Very Good Thing. This is the bit where I get confused. I should hate these symphonies but I don't, and I don't know why not.

Bruckner symphonies make Wagner's *Der Ring des Nibelungen* feel like a stroll in the park. They turn Richard Strauss's symphonic poems into mere soundbites. You can fit entire Mozart symphonies into a single Bruckner movement – even his overtures take twenty minutes. He didn't compose tone poems so much as forge glaciers. Village idiots can't forge glaciers. I can only describe the whole Bruckner symphony-listening experience as akin to being lost at sea, adrift in oceanic perpetuity; you don't know where you are or which is north or south or up or down or God knows where. Yet Bruckner's rustic trust in the Lord guided him to shores of the end of the symphony every time. This stasis can feel like a good thing – not always but sometimes. Enough of the time not to destroy your hi-fi equipment or mislay your appetite for existence.*

There's a good rule of thumb to follow when choosing which of a composer's symphonies to buy or perhaps even go and see live: always avoid Symphony No. 1. The (often young and underdeveloped) composer's always going to be learning the ropes on his first one, so you're not going to get the full, mature voice at optimum mystic elevation. It's often quite shit; and rarely cheaper despite this. Most of the time I've found this rule works pretty well (Beethoven, Rachmaninov, Mozart – who, of course, didn't even write his first one); but there's one famously watertight exception:

---

* I reckon the best Bruckner symphonies for getting lost in are the Second and the Fifth. The Fourth is rather pretty – but sod pretty – let's get lost.

Gustav Mahler. So long as you've got plenty of hours to spare in your day and ears like pebbles, Mahler's First is perfectly all right; some even consider it a masterpiece; but then Mahler fans are like that – they're a strange and twitchy bunch, the classical music equivalent of Scientologists. So tread carefully when discussing Mahler; be aware that you might be in conversation with one of *them*. This is why I'm being nice about his First Symphony. And hell – all his other ones too, why not.

Writhing Existential Agonies and So On

Because they both wrote really long symphonies and worked at the arse end of the Late Romantic coal face, people tend to lump Mahler and Bruckner together. In reality, nothing could be further from the truth. Where Bruckner is stoned, Mahler is wired; where Bruckner lets be, Mahler tinkers and fiddles; where Bruckner is confident, relaxed and able to let it flow, man, Mahler's uptight, paranoid and desperate to please. Mahler was a nü-metal prog-rock bunny-boiler: Rammstein on Prozac.

This neurotic pantheism is where he gets all his legions of fans from. They're empathizing with his existential angst. And believe me, they are *legions*. And a pretty recent phenomenon. Back in the day, Mahler was famous in Vienna as a conductor; an ill-tempered, up-himself conductor. He did compose some stuff on the side, but nobody gave a damn – not even his wife.* His music was performed occasionally, but not much. If there was nothing else to play that day, they might give one of Herr Mahler's knock-offs a

* This isn't true. I don't know why I wrote that.

run-through, but only if the pubs weren't open yet. Oh, look, they are.

I remembered that my first-ever Prom had involved a Mahler symphony; his Seventh, I seemed to recall. I'd gone with Rodney – of the blazer with the gold buttons – who – it all came flooding back – was a huge Mahler fan. I immediately picked up the phone and called him.

'Please can I come round to your flat and listen to all your Mahler?'

There was a pause of medium length.

'I suppose so.'

Rodney is lucky enough to live in a brand new south London apartment block where all the apartments are named after famous composers.

'What a coincidence!' I said to Rodders as he buzzed me in.

'I suppose so,' he replied.

His flat was christened 'Elgar'. Next door was 'Haydn', only their research had been sloppy and they'd spelled it 'Hayden' by mistake.

'For a hardcore classical music lover like yourself, seeing that error outside your front door every day must be pretty galling,' I said, as he took my jacket and went to fix us some drinks.

'I suppose so.'

'It's a shame you haven't got "Mahler", though, isn't it?'

'I like Elgar. "Mahler" is a couple called Andrew and Lawrence, upstairs.'

'Lucky them!'

'I suppose so.'

We went upstairs to the mezzanine music room and took our places in two red armchairs facing an expensive music system and a high-tech pair of speakers. This was Romanticism's grand finale – its nuclear sunset. Packed CD towers, um, towered over us as we sipped at glasses of rosé on ice – that's how posh Rodney is, you see. We clinked exquisite cut-glass goblets and sat back to enjoy Mahler's Symphony No. 5 – his favourite. It was all right.* Sensing a need to up a few antes, Rodders leaned forward and skipped to the fourth movement, and *kapow*. So this is what all the fuss is about. My first major-league Mahler Moment. I flumped back in the armchair as the Mahler heroin worked its way around my bloodstream. It was rich and dark, fluid and smoky. I discerned a distinct yet profoundly existential rendering of the concept of Death. At least I think I did.

'Aha,' I whispered.

'Mmm,' Rodders replied.

The effect was ruined when Rodney – who appeared impatient to get through the Mahler as quickly as possible tonight – switched to the legendary Kathleen Ferrier singing a song Mahler wrote after the death of a child.

'This is a woman singing? It sounds like a man.'

Rodney rolled his eyes and moved onward to Mahler's Third. It lasted three minutes.

'Got that?' said Rodney.

'Erm, yes.'

'Good. Next movement.'

It was a jaunty choir. Through these snippets I was learning that there's an entire independent sound world inside Mahler's symphonies; take a trip through his looking glass and ooh, it's like *The Wizard of Oz*. You could probably spend your whole life getting to grips with its vast palate of

---

* Mahler fans prefer to witter on about its joy, love, longing, terror, bitterness, fear, serenity, hysteria and profound manifestation of the human condition. They really are very boring.

colours, its myriad Donkey Kong levels. This is probably why his fans are so evangelically loyal – they never need withdraw.

Moving on quickly, very quickly indeed actually, it was time for Mahler's Ninth, and a fascinating historical document. This performance, conducted by the legendary Bruno Walter, was recorded in Vienna on 9 January 1938, just weeks before the Nazis rolled into town and probably murdered Bruno Walter.

'This stuff freaks me well out,' said Rodney, dropping into uncommon vernacular for my sake. The recording was scratchy. It sounded like the incidental music from *The Wizard of Oz*. The Ninth was followed by *Das Lied von der Erde*, a rather dull song cycle based on Chinese poetry. I was unable to detect any further themes or metaphors involving *The Wizard of Oz* in this piece.

'For dinner, it's gammon,' said Rodney after four or five minutes. 'Is that all right for you, gammon?'

'Gammon is fine.'

We ate the gammon with some potatoes and then I was ushered out of 'Elgar' and down on to the cold and dangerous streets of Vauxhall.

'But what about Mahler the man?' I called after Rodney, who was closing the door behind me.

'I've got to be at work early,' he said. 'Look him up.' The door whumped shut.

I went home.

Look him up.

The Baton and the Damage Done: Confessions of a Conductor

Name: Stuart Stratford
Age: thirty-two
From: Preston
Occupation: freelance conductor
Location: the Blue Posts public house in Soho, London
Date: April 2005
Time: 7.30 p.m.

Me: Stuart, for Christ's sake – why conducting?

Stuart: I started off playing the clarinet. Then at university one day the college orchestra was short of a conductor, and I thought, fuck it – I'll do it; I don't mind, I'll stand up there and, you know, give it a go.

Me: Did you have any idea what you were doing?

Stu: No, but afterwards my mates said I was pretty good and that I should keep on doing it. So I did. I got some lessons.

Me: Conducting lessons.

Stu: Yeah. And I conducted the (Cambridge) university orchestra and stuff, ending up passing an audition to get into a conducting school in St Petersburg, where I studied with Ilya Musin (ninety-two) for three years.

Me: In Russian?

Stu: Of course. And if you made a mistake with your hands he'd lean across and like . . .

Stuart leaned over and slapped me hard on the wrist.

Me: Ouch.

Stu: Yeah, and so on. Very physical, very Russian – lots of abuse. It was basically a kind of conducting *Rocky*.

Then, back home, I went to the Royal Northern College of Music in Manchester, before coming down to London. Streets paved with gold ... opportunity knocks ... Dick Whittington ...

Me: Please get on with it.

Stu: And that was that. I was a freelance conductor. That's what I am.

Me: A freelance conductor? You mean you place ads at the back of *Gramophone* magazine?

Stu: Hahaha. No.

We ordered some more pints.

Stu: But when times have been hard I've had to, for example, play the Snowman in a sort of musical Christmas panto, doing an elongated mime to 'Walking in the Air' by Aled Jones.

Me: Isn't that rather demeaning for a prestigious conductor such as yourself?

Stu: [*wistfully*] Busloads of octogenarians bussed in from Rochdale. We'd come up with new moves for the Snowman each night. Moonwalking. Breakdancing. Pat-a-cake. Even some discreet simulated sex.

Me: So this is what you do when you're not conducting?

Stu: Yes sometimes.

Me: So when you're conducting for the ...

Stu: The ENO, or the LPO, the LSO, maybe the RPO.

These are orchestras, apparently.

Me: Do they just phone you up, or ...

Stu: They used to have house conductors, but now, yeah, they'd rather save money and phone up people like me who are cheaper.

Me: How come you're cheap?

Stu: Well, I'm young.

Me: Is there much money in conducting?

Stu: [*long and bitter pause*] Well, yeah. Some people get paid ten grand per concert. And other people . . . like me . . . get paid about 650 quid. Or a grand or whatever, but . . .

Me: Can you make a decent living out of it?

Stu: I make *a* living.

Me: What's the next step in your ideal career path?

Stu: Well, just keep it as it's going, but . . . do less Snowman.

Me: Is the Snowman always looming in the shadows; like a monkey on your back?

Stu: [*weary nod*].

Me: One of my perceptions about conducting is that you're actually just standing there, showing off. Is that wrong?

Stu: It's completely wrong.

Me: Because I've been to a lot of classical music concerts now, and often feel that the only reason the conductor's there at all is to give the audience something to look at. We're all just . . . watching the conductor. The musicians know their stuff, and they've got the music and so on. What are you doing then, other than just being an animated visual aid?

Stu: It's like directing a play – I'm shaping it. Sure, your Gielguds and Oliviers all know their lines backwards and have done this a million times before, but without direction it's a mess; they'll drag the thing this way and that; and I'm there to mesh them all together and, whether they like it or not, my vision is this and we're going that way together. It's about leadership.

Ooh.

Stu: And you build control. The tempo, the dynamics, everything really, come under your control. However, this is all much harder when you're conducting an opera, cos you're down in the pit and trying to control the singers as

360

well as your orchestra. But in a symphony situation, you are the driving machine – you're in charge 100 per cent.

Me: What's your average rehearsal time?

Stu: Your maximum would be three three-hour rehearsals, but often it's just two, sometimes only one. So you've only got time to run through it once, and you have to signal what you want while you're doing it. Signal with your hands – be quite physical.

Me: So you have to sort of 'tame' the orchestra?

Stu: It can be difficult. You just have to … wave your arms.

Me: Yes, of course.

Stu: And hopefully, the way you move your arms; if your technique is clear, you obviously know the piece and if they feel comfortable and you're not fucking it up, basically, then they're happy.

Me: Do you ever watch another conductor in action – say, Simon Rattle – and decide to cop a few of his licks?

Stu: His moves?

Me: Yeah, the way he moves his hand or something there is so cool, I'll try a bit of that myself next time – that'll drive 'em crazy!

Stu: Not as such.

Me: But there's an element of performance to what you do, though, right?

Stu: Yes, but all the time there should be a sort of feedback situation, between any kind of physical gesture you're giving and the sound that's coming back. You're in a constant state of modification. You know – the intensity of the second violins is slipping, so you do something to counter that.

Me: Wave your arms?

Stu: Wave your fucking arms! Or look at the players. Encouragingly. Sometimes out of politeness. I mean, if the flute player's just about to play a solo, the last thing you want to do is look at the violins.

Me: Because the flute player will be pissed off?

Stu: Yeah, and it's encouraging . . .

Me: You're making them feel a bit special.

Stu: They want to know you're looking after them.

Me: Like a shepherd.

Stu: There's a bit of that goes on.

Me: How big's your baton?

Stu: [*pause*] About a foot. That's actually a very serious question, because a lot of conductors don't use batons. I was taught without a baton.

Me: What do they use instead?

Stu: Their hands.

Me: Fingers.

Stu: Hands.

Me: Do people ever have fluorescent batons, or stripy ones or anything?

Stu: No.

We ordered some more pints.

Me: I'm interested in the pure physicality of what you do. Are there any idiot-proof basic signals that a conductor might use that everybody would understand?

Stu: Well, the obvious thing is that the bigger you conduct, the louder it'll be. The more amplitude of the beat. Generally speaking.

Me: So that's your volume control?

Stu: It could be. But the main thing is the speed control; which is quite a hard thing to do if you've got a particularly flexible piece. For example, you're conducting a piece of music with a regular beat like this . . . [*Stu begins clapping*] . . . and there's nothing marked on anyone's part, and there's sixty people playing at once, and then all of a sudden you don't want them to play the tune like this, you want them to play it . . . [*Stu claps a bit differently*] . . . going slightly faster. So what do you do?

Me: What can you do?

Stu: You move your arms slightly faster.

We giggle.

Stu: It sounds very easy . . .

Me: It sounds terrifying!

Stu: . . . but to get sixty people simultaneously to understand that, as one and identically . . . and you've got to be able to do all this to order – spontaneously. There's a lot of traffic control involved.

Me: And with a new score; do you have to learn a piece bar-by-bar, like an actor and his lines?

Stu: Yeah, supposedly. If you've got time. Often you don't. And it's a bit obvious when you don't, cos you're always looking down at the score. The musicians don't like that much; in fact they hate it.

Me: Have you ever got lost and just waggled your arms around a bit till you find your place?

Stu: [*guilty yet slightly hysterical laughter*] Yes. Absolutely. Not recently, though. I used to be a bit lazy like that, but then one day I was like – come on, you can't do this. So now I always learn the score. All good conductors do – all the famous ones know the score.

Me: 'Know the score'. Hahaha!

Stu: There's always more to discover in a truly great piece, there's always another layer of the onion, and we never get tired of peeling it.

Me: So there's no such thing as a definitive version of a great work?

Stu: No such thing.

Me: Unless you were conducting it.

363

Stu: Exactly.

Me: Is there anything you won't conduct?'

Stu: Electricity.

Oof.

Stuart and I continued to drink more pints. I was having a fabulous evening – Stuart was a complete dude. I'd been expecting a chippy nerd kind of a guy, but Stuart was utterly switched on and progressive in every sense. He was a singularly righteous motherfucker. Eventually, of course, I asked him my usual boring, stock question about whether he liked pop music as well as classical.

'No,' he replied.

'What do you mean, no?'

'I don't like pop music. What don't you understand about that?'

'What, none? You're not even going to pay this question lip service?'

'No, none. I'm classical only.'

'My God, that's so grown-up.'

'I just love classical music. I *love* classical music. It's enough for me. More than enough for me.'

I gazed at him in stunned, sober admiration.

'That is just so cool,' I replied.

'Why?'

'It's just *brave.*'

'Why?'

'I don't know.'

'Another drink?'

'I don't know. Yes.'

I also asked Stuart for his opinion on some of the world's most famous conductors. And by this time, he'd had more than just a few pints, so I hope these comments don't jeopardize any future job prospects, although half these people are dead, so presumably he's safe from those.

Conducting Hall of Fame

Wilhelm Furtwängler (dead, bald, iconic German – conducted my stepfather's Ring Cycle box-set and collaborated with the Nazis): 'Overrated. Cavalier with the piece. Messes around with the tempo and it sounds terrible.'

Leonard Bernstein (who also wrote *West Side Story*): 'A great musician and a great conductor. Great.'

Simon Rattle (English, curly hair): 'Very good. Fantastic. Excellent.'

'Great?'

'Yes, great.'

André Previn (used to do Martini adverts): [*pregnant pause*] 'Well, he's not great, is he?'

'Is he not?'

'No, he's shit.'

Herbert von Karajan (I seem to have many CDs on which he seems to be conducting): 'Do you think Hitler also closed his eyes after listening to Wagner?'

'What?'

Valery Gergiev (Russian): 'The best working conductor today.'

Yuri Temirkanov (Russian): 'Inspirational, daring, annoyingly inconsistent.'

Arturo Toscanini (could be Italian): 'Great, shouted a lot. Makes Furtwängler look like mutton dressed as mutton.'*

The conductor from the Muppets: 'See Furtwängler.'

I had become a bit bored with conductors.

Nigel Kennedy: 'He's all right. Not a great violinist. Good, not brilliant.'

---

* Yes, I had run out of conductors, so Stuart suggested these last three himself.

Nicola Benedetti: 'I've not heard her play but she looks pretty fit.'

Katherine Jenkins: 'Absolute bollocks. She sings like a fucking drain.'

I remind Stuart that he might be required to conduct buxom Katherine one day.

'All right – she's average. Actually no, no, fuck that, she *is* bollocks.'

Vanessa Mae: 'Whatever.'

But then it was closing time, and we were expelled from the pub. For a while we mooched around trying to find somewhere else that was open, but soon gave up and headed back to the Underground. We shook hands in Leicester Square ticket hall.

'Goodbye, Stuart, and thanks.'

'Goodbye. That's fine.'

I hope that one day Stuart becomes really famous, so that I can sell the taped transcription of our conversation for a load of cash.

*

Claude Debussy scores:

Sex: 5. 'How much has to be explored and discarded before reaching the naked flesh of feeling?'

Drugs: 6. 'The colour of my soul is iron-grey and sad bats wheel about the steeple of my dreams.'

Rock 'n' roll: 7. 'The century of aeroplanes deserves its own music. As there are no precedents, I must create anew!'

Strauss, Bruckner and Mahler score:

Sex: 2. Nah.

Drugs: 8. There's certainly something in their water.

Money, glaciers and existential angst: 10. I think there's a *Titanic* metaphor here somewhere, struggling to get out.

Seb suggests:

Debussy: *Piano Works* by Pascal Rogé (Decca) 🚐🚐🚐🚐

(Woozy impressionistic wonderment from the King of the Wonky Piano.)

Richard Strauss: *2001: A Space Odyssey – Original Soundtrack* by Alex North and Stanley Kubrick (Rhino / WEA) 🚐🚐🚐🚐🚐

(As well as the Strauss, you get a load of genius iron-wool pieces by György Ligeti, as well as 'The Blue Danube' again, that rotten waltz by R. Strauss's unrelated namesake, J. Strauss. One of the greatest soundtracks ever.)

Bruckner: Any of his symphonies – they're all awesome – conducted by anybody except that fascist coot Furtwängler. 🚐🚐🚐🚐🚐

(Tune in, turn on, free Tibet.)

Aled Jones: 'Walking in the Air' (*The Snowman*) 🚐🚐🚐🚐🚐

(I can't imagine Xmas without this.)

15.

Back on the European mainland in the very late nineteenth century, somebody heard a discreet coughing sound from somewhere up in the wings. A very soft and polite cough – more of a mild throat-clearance really. Up here, that's it, keep going. Further up. Now left a tad, hop over the water there, smashing, you've got it. Well, blow me down if this doesn't appear to be an *English Classical Music Renaissance*. We won't keep you, though, don't fret. Shan't be a tick. Just a mo.

Sorry.

The Boys Are Back in Town

'Listening to the fifth symphony of Ralph Vaughan Williams is like staring at a cow for forty-five minutes.'
Aaron Copland

Where had we been all this time? The Winchester Troper → John Dunstable → John Taverner → William Byrd → John Dowland → Henry Purcell → that bloke Gibbons, thingy Gibbons. What a noble line of succession. Who came next?

Nobody. We stopped. And it was all because of one man: that bloody Handel. George Frederick's eighteenth-century ubiquity meant the musical landscape after his death was like an elephant had sat on it. Him and his Italian Style operas and oratorios had been so dominant, so devastatingly successful, there weren't any healthy seeds around in his wake to grow any shit up. It was a bit like the musical oxygen shortage that took place in Germanic lands post-Beethoven, except that instead of eventually throwing up a Schubert, a Brahms or if you must a Wagner, all the UK had to show for their efforts was a perpetual welcoming party for that Germanic (but terribly well-mannered) repeat offender Felix Mendelssohn. Yes, hello again; we *know* you can speak English, yes, well done. Oh all right – have everything.

Throughout the Victorian era, English music was in the hands of above-their-station clergymen and hapless amateurs. While Europe collapsed in rapture at the feet of the Romantic Masters, the British Isles attempted to compete using the likes of: William Sterndale Bennett (1816–75); Charles Villiers Stanford (1852–1924); Sir Hubert Parry (1848–1918); Alexander Campbell MacKenzie (1847–1935).

You haven't heard of any of these because they were useless (although Sir Hubert Parry did compose 'Jerusalem', if you think this makes him less useless. I think it probably might do). Aside from the fact that these (beneath minor) composers weren't especially talented, another barrier was that the very act of composing music – and especially acting like you were a full-time composer – was considered ungentlemanly: rather coarse, distinctly base, come off it, old bean, one's not a gaylord, eh what? Thus, when a moustachioed visionary Catholic grocer's son arrived on the non-existent scene in 1890, everybody ignored him – and rightly so, you weedy blinking blighter, pull yourself together – what's wrong with Charles Villiers Stanford?

With zero folk influences and all the swing of an arthritic Norris McWhirter (1925–2004) doused in concrete and starch, Elgar's music appeals to a particular kind of an ear

I say.

– a decrepit one emitting steam sitting on a settee reading a copy of the *Daily Mail* in Royal Tunbridge Wells.

Elgar liked fox-hunting, fishing, golf, bowls, Gordon's Gin, cock-fighting, bear-baiting, seal-clubbing, butterfly-wing-pulling, the *Daily Telegraph* and moustache wax, of which he got through many tins over the course of his seventy-seven dignified years. It would be impossible to imagine a more clichéd idea of a typical, straight-backed, establishment Edwardian gentleman than Elgar, so instead, revel in 'Pomp and Circumstance March 1', Elgar's best-known tune, for one final time.

Bizarrely, 'Pomp and Circumstance' actually ruined Elgar's career. It was first performed at the Proms in 1901 and proved so immediately popular (three rapturous encores) that King Edward VII (1841–1910) rushed backstage to demand

Elgar turn its stirring central melody into a patriotic song *right this very minute*. Elgar called his friend the poet A. C. Benson (1862–1925), who came up with some pompous lyrics and lo, 'Land of Hope and Glory' was born. Elgar was hurriedly knighted.*

But 'Land of Hope and Glory' soon became so popular that its reputation began to eclipse Elgar's other achievements – his groovy variations, plangent symphonies and a disastrous première of a piece entitled *The Dream of Gerontius*. He went on a victorious tour of America, and everyone waved their flags and sang enthusiastically along to 'Land of Hope and Glory' (we hadn't fully concreted its ownership yet), and thus grew his unfair reputation as a jingoistic one-trick pony. The waxed 'tache definitely wasn't helping at this point. Yes, but, said Elgar, 'The people all rose and yelled – I simply had to play it again!'

Fame and riches inevitably followed. Poor Elgar; he was terribly misunderstood – he wanted to be an English Brahms, not some Edwardian Robert Kilroy-Silk (1942–). He became depressed, disillusioned, never left his house. Bitter. So bitter that after years of receding fame and sulky inaction, he eventually gave in and composed his bleak, black Cello Concerto. It was mournful and juddery. It's great. Everyone went *whoah*. Then he died, having bitterly failed to finish an opera that he'd said (lied) he'd almost finished and a (third) symphony commissioned by the BBC. There is a statue of him in Worcester town centre; its moustache is *incredible*.

Composing around at the same time as Elgar was Bradford's atheist dandy dilettante Frederick Delius (1862–1934).

---

* And on the back of the (old) twenty-pound note. Fish into your (grandfather's) wallet and check him out!

Fiona sent an unexpectedly brutal email saying Delius was a substandard composer who wrote 'English cow-pat music',* and whose operas were 'perfectly horrible', and that it was 'music to kill yourself by'. But then the Maddocks/Delius family feud dates from all the way back to 1924, so I thought I should probably ignore her frenzied malevolence and give Delius a fair shake of the maracas. I listened to *Brigg Fair – An English Rhapsody* (1907) 🎵🎵. It sounded like pollen. I didn't mind bits of it – the shame hit me full-on. But then, fortunately, I fell asleep, disgracing myself no longer.

I had similar problems with Ralph Vaughan Williams (1872–1958). I listened to his *Sea Symphony* and then his *London Symphony* and dozed off during each. I clearly needed to buck my ideas up, pull myself together, get to grips with these minor (to the rest of the world, but major to us) English composers' œuvres – this stuff is an important part of our isles' cultural heritage. So what better way to imbibe these swollen draughts of ancient Albion lore than to go on a sunny spring outing in my motor car? And not just in silence on my own, but with CDs of these guys' music too. And no emergency pop CDs. *None.*

Motor Car Sunny Spring Outing

London's M25 Orbital Motorway, May 2005

From my local library I'd borrowed two Elgar CDs (by the look of them, both much-borrowed), one Delius (less so), two Vaughan Williams (somewhere in between) and one various artists (virginal), featuring William Walton, Frank Bridge and Ethel Smyth (a woman?). On another disc I'd

* There's a definite cow-pat theme emerging here.

burned a selection of English classics, such as Hubert Parry's 'Jerusalem', Holst's 'Jupiter', Thomas Arne's 'Rule Britannia', Bull's 'God Save the Queen', Vera Lynn's 'We'll Meet Again' and 'Roll out the Barrel' by someone called Trad Arr. I also had Classic FM's *Best of British* CD, which Darren had given me, and a bottle of Robinson's Lemon Barley Water and an ivory ingot of Milky Bar. The petrol was fresh from a British Petroleum forecourt. Oil by Duckhams. My car is German, so I won't be mentioning that.

It was a spectacularly fresh and sunny day, and I made cheerfully slow progress around the North Circular road (A406), grinding through Ealing and up towards the Hanger Lane gyratory system while the car's CD player delivered Elgar's 'Nimrod'. The nice, leafy trees swayed around in the wind most charmingly. I was so happy. This, I thought to myself, is the life. And this, I thought to myself, is 'Nimrod'. The royal family aren't so bad. Soon, to my left, I spied the new Wembley Stadium building site and was cut up by a filthy yellow van. I waved a bright 'never mind' as its weathered driver deftly flicked a cigarette butt across two stationary lanes of traffic at the lights right before the Ikea exit. Then we all roared past Ikea. On came 'Jerusalem': *And did those feet in ancient time / walk upon England's mountains green / and was the holy lamb of God / on England's pleasant pastures seen?* Is it a riddle? Everyone braked madly ten yards before a speed camera before lurching on towards the M1 turn-off. A minor phalanx shot off; most of us accelerated up on to the flyover, to hell with braking distances – I must get to the A1 junction before you and him and that fucker especially. I was too busy struggling with a bastard BMW to notice the coming and going of the William Walton and Ethel Smyth (good for her, though, eh?). Stuck outside Tottenham for twenty minutes, I paid some vague, irritated attention to

Vaughan Williams' something or other. There was no falling asleep this time, just sweaty, simmering biting-point at the injustice of further blatant lane-cutting, barging BMW/Mercedes/Lexus bastards. Beyond Walthamstow, there was a consensual 65 mph surge away as the lanes widened out to four-ish. Overtaking, undertaking, Elgar's *Variations*, cut-up, give a guy the finger, screw you, defending my lane, defending my lane, defending my lane, no, you fool, don't let him in, *don't let him in, Jesus*. She let him in. Scream out north-east on the M11. Slice through to the slip for the M25, which was the same, except faster. Milky Bar hurt my teeth. Driving's great, isn't it?

Exciting live action dangerous in-car widescreen photography: the M25.

I was heading for Suffolk. To be precise, Aldeburgh, just down the coast from Sizewell nuclear power station and home, muse and ultimate resting place of possibly the most respected of all of these English Renaissance composers (his music features no cheese), Benjamin Britten (1913–76). I wasn't there yet, though; bugger me, the A12 is a seriously hairy rail of bitumen – a hellriding dragstrip of death. All these cars and lorries plus the reversing tractors – well! – I had no idea tractors could go so slowly, and in directions like that. I discovered that I do like Vaughan Williams' *Sea Symphony* – racked-up full volume, just about audible over the roaring engine. Woof. It didn't sound much like the sea, though – it sounded like choral racing stripes. I stopped for a wee outside Ipswich and felt calmer. By the time I arrived in sleepy Aldeburgh, my road rage/terror had all but evaporated, and the sight of the crashing East Anglian waves bolstered my sagging spirits to the point where I was almost enthusiastic at the prospect of chasing down the author of *The Burning Fiery Furnace*, *Albert Herring* and *Noye's Fludde*. First, though, I sat in the car for fifteen minutes and had a nap and a small cry.

Britten was born in Lowestoft – a few miles up the coast – in 1913. He began to compose aged five and was discouraged by all of his teachers. '*Desist*, Benjamin,' repeated his music teacher, sinister Walter Greatorex. 'You are not in possession of what this sort of thing takes.' But young Benny was determined to succeed and, at sixteen, escaped Suffolk to study at the Royal College of Music, soon thereafter hooking up with young tenor (Sir) Peter (Neville Luard) Pears (1910–86). Britten considered handsome Pears' voice perfect for the music he was writing: the annoying opera *Peter Grimes* and another, Morrissey-inspired, opera, *Billy Budd*; thus the pair entered into a friendship that would last for the rest of their happy, suspiciously wife-free lives.*

Though his music became increasingly popular, Britten didn't get quite the establishment support he required up in London, and so, in 1947, he and Pears moved back to Suffolk – and windy, isolated Aldeburgh – to found their

---

* Yes they were gay lovers. Not that you'd ever know that from anything in Aldeburgh. Aldeburgh prefers the term 'companions' or 'good pals'.

own company, the English Opera Group, in a sort of low-key, modest seaside version of Wagner's Bayreuth festival idea, only with tea and cakes instead of fame and sausages. The prodigal son and his lover, damn, had returned. They would remain here until death.

Down the deserted, flapping high street I strolled; past meagre handfuls of daytripping pensioners popping confusedly in and out of competitively twee tea shops. Aldeburgh was sunbleached, empty, windswept and comfortably precious. I ducked into a tiny record shop; its Britten racks were strung out by the doorway; I nodded hello to the proprietor, who stood semi-suspicious behind the counter in thick glasses and bulbous headphones. There was so much Britten for sale that I fast became overwhelmed by it.

'Can I be of assistance?' slimed the proprietor.

'No, no thanks, I know exactly what I'm doing.' I boldly shuffled over to the World Music section by accident, and then boldly shuffled quickly back again. I started to pick up random Britten CDs, blankly stare at the back and then put them back again. I could feel him staring at me and began to feel horribly self-conscious. Sweat began to prick my forehead – I knew I'd have to shit or get off the pot, and quickly, before I knocked everything over or looked at something *absurd*. I pulled out a CD at complete random and gave a 'that's what I was looking for' cluck and delighted-sounding sigh. It was Britten's *Simple Symphony*. I was thrown into immediate panic. I can't buy *that*, my brain whirred – well, it slowly turned-over – he'll think I've chosen it because I think it's simple enough for me! Shit, why couldn't I have picked out one of his complicated symphonies? Instead of just putting it back, I lunged for another. Yeah, multi-buyer – music lover! My sweaty grasp came back with something called *Sinfonia da Requiem*. That's better,

I breathed out, that sounds significantly cleverer. I did the same happy cluck of recognition and approached the counter with a minor swagger.

'These please,' I said, and smiled horribly.

He took them. 'Benjamin Britten,' he replied.

'Yes.'

And then he said it again. 'Benjamin Britten.'

'*Yes.*'

Finally, thank God, he went to get the CDs for the empty cases. Laid out on the countertop were more Britten CDs. And, worse, these all had way-cool covers, much better than the austere, minimalist ones I'd unwittingly selected. When the proprietor returned, I snatched one up. It had a dramatic, abstract oil painting on the front; and I could see he was impressed by my choice. He went to get it. My card wasn't rejected. I walked back to the car and sat and listened to them with the warm dregs of the Lemon Barley Water. Inevitably, the oil painting one was the worst.

A few hours later, after I was done, I wandered around town some more – along the seafront, past Britten's big old house and up the lane to the town's big squat wistful church made of flint, in whose graveyard Britten and Pears are buried, side by side, their tombs exact replicas of the monolith in *2001: A Space Odyssey*. Is this a clue that Britten and Pears were fans of Richard Strauss; perhaps even György Ligeti?*

One thing Britten (and Pears) and Strauss share is a distinct lack of melody in their music. They were both short on tunes/something to whistle. Instead, Britten's compositions are all texture; his music is architecturally satisfying; gritty, crunchy, it sounds darn fine even if a tune's not forthcoming; lost somewhere in construction. His music is

* Seriously though, Ligeti rules.

muscular; its tone precise; it's not sentimental, nor atonal, nor self-indulgent or mawkish. Yet it can only be British; it has that thin, stand-alone asymmetry; a beanpole reach and cocksure modesty. If your ears were colourblind, this would be the music for you – I'd call it richly monochromatic. This is fine by me – I'm a Bruckner fan, I likes them glaciers.

Britten was passionate about East Anglia and Aldeburgh; and it was passionate about him (and Pears) in return. Britten was also passionate in his keenness for his young male singers (he became infatuated with the young David Hemmings before his acting fame), though this potentially unsavoury side of his character has been airbrushed out of history somewhat. But his modest local music festival continued to grow through the years until it became a kind of low-key seaside version of the Proms. It's still going strong today, both in the town centre and a few miles down the road in the charming village of Snape. 'I belong at home – there – in Aldeburgh,' said Britten. 'I have tried to bring music *to* it in the shape of our local festival; and the music I write comes *from* it.' The queen made him Lord Britten in 1976, shortly before he died of heart failure. I hope the two incidents weren't related.

I left my car and attempted to find some more things to do on the Aldeburgh-Britten trail. Unable to find a single other thing, I went to ask in the Tourist Information Centre.

'Have you been up to the church and seen the stained-glass window and the grave?' suggested Captain Bird's Eye.

'Yes.'

'Have you seen his old house?'

'Yes.'

'Have you been up to the Peter Pears Gallery?'

'Yes.' Unfortunately. It was contemporary local artists.

'Have you had a nice wander around?'

'Oh yes!'

'That's all, then. Art and crafts for sale over here.' The captain gestured toward the arts and crafts. 'Aldeburgh pencils are on special, only fifteen pence, all different colours.'

I think Aldeburgh could do a bit better, to be honest. A small museum or a statue or something would be nice – after all, he is one of our greatest-ever composers, and we don't have that many to begin with. I hope the lack of stuff hasn't got anything to do with his sexuality; that would be rubbish. I suppose they have the festival. Let's give them the benefit of the doubt and have a nice stroll past his house again.

An hour or so later, trying to find the main road on my journey back to London, I became confused and took a wrong turning. I got quite badly lost. I drove through several strange, *Straw Dogs*-like villages in the low, crystalline evening sun, each with its own chunky, staring skinhead standing outside the local stores with his dog in long shadows. The flat, endless, winding country lanes at least finally made sense of Britten's music for me. It really did feel like what I was listening to had come directly out of this local soil. Landscape and sound. They really matched. I'd got it at last. I pulled over into a brambly passing point and sat listening to *Sinfonia da Requiem* as low sunbeams split the fields into blinding prisms. It was elegiac, proudly parochial, sophisticated yet straightforward. I drove on with the sun in my eyes, feeling like something of critical importance had just been revealed to me.* But then a Land Rover came burning round the corner behind me and gave a nasty great unnecessary honk as it overtook. It was the skinhead from the previous village, his dog giving me the evil eye through the rear windscreen. I thought it might be best to turn around and see if I couldn't get back the way I came somehow.

It all got fighty again on the southbound A12.

*

The Gentlemen of the English Classical Music Renaissance score:
Sex: 1. Hmmm, no thanks.
Drugs: 1. Hmmm, no thanks very much.
National Pride: 10. *Trembling knee; rheumy eye.*

Benjamin Britten scores:
Sex: 8. Yes, please.
Drugs: 5. I don't know whether Britten took drugs or not, so I'll score him neutral.
Peter Pears: 10.

Seb suggests:
Elgar: *Enigma Variations and Cello Concerto* by Mischa Maisky and the Philharmonia Orchestra (DG) 🚐🚐🚐🚐

* It hadn't. I'd just had too much Barley Water.

(Each variation is meant to represent one of Elgar's friends. Variation 1 is Alice, his wife; 2 is David Steuart-Powell; 3 is Richard Baxter Townshend; 4 is William Meath Baker; 5 is Richard Arnold; 6 is Isabel Fitton; 7 is Arthur Troyte Griffith; 8 is Winifred Norbury; 9 is A. J. Jaeger; 10 is Dora Penney; 11 is Stephen Hendry; 12 is Basil Nevinson; 13 is Lady Mary Lygon; 14 is Elgar himself. The 'enigma' is that there's supposed to be a 'missing' main theme, of which the variations are but a shadow. The consensus nowadays is that this was all just a merry jape by Elgar, and that there isn't a main theme after all. Golly, what fun. The most popular variation is 9 – A. J. Jaeger – 'Nimrod'. I expect I'll win the Nobel Prize for Literature for this masterly piece of research. The racked, popular Cello Concerto is perfect for when feeling sorry for one-self and perhaps slightly drunk. Or, if you like, just drunk.)

Holst: *The Planets* by Sir Adrian Boult and the London Philharmonic (EMI Classics) 🚐🚐🚐🚐
(Hey, it's *The Planets*. No one knows anything about Holst, but everyone loves *The Planets*.)

Vaughan Williams: *A Sea Symphony* by the BBC Symphony Chorus (Free with BBC Music Magazine, sorry) 🚐🚐🚐
(Wet, salty, fresh. Imagine a trawlerload of twitching mackerel. Just imagine.)

Britten: *Sinfonia da Requiem* by the London Symphony Orchestra (Naxos) 🚐🚐🚐
(Harsh. All Britten is harsh, unless you're from Suffolk.)

All this music is sterling. If you like rugby, you'll love all this shit.

16. Sheer Fucking Carnage

And then BANG. It was all over. Two bald and dismal men whose photographs always imply rain and the smell of ink dismantled 500 years' worth of steady progression: Igor Stravinsky (RUS) and Arnold Schoenberg (AUT). They said, forget this overloaded, Andrex Puppy, weepy chocolate-box, bloated, self-indulgent Romantic bullshit – *let's get real*.

Stravinsky (an ex-lawyer) took out rhythm.

Schoenberg (an ex-painter) offloaded tonality.*

What was left? Nothing that made any sense.

'The Emancipation of Dissonance'.

Stravinsky's *The Rite of Spring* 💣💥💣💣💥💣 and Schoenberg's *Pieces for Piano* 💣💥💣💣💣💥and *Pierrot Lunaire* 💣💥💣🚒

CLANG.

The First World War helped demolish any remaining expansionist aspirations Romanticism still clung on to. Nobody felt like being terribly Romantic after that; they just felt hollow. And that was OK, because the new music was hollow too. When I say hollow, I mean *skeletal and way off-balance* and with nothing in the middle, obviously. After WW1, music's previous ongoing evocation of the rich, bottomless soul of humanity was revealed as a sham, bitter conceit, outdated, passé wishful thinking. The harsh new Modernist reality was manifested through dissonance

* Music that sounds like it's moving in the right direction.

and neoclassic Expressionism: exploration of emotion through subjective, warped distortion. The new music was stripped back, asymmetrical, discordant and difficult as hell. The centuries-old touchstones of harmony and tonality and sonority had been torched. This was classical music's *Wicker Man* moment, with Schoenberg as Christopher Lee, Stravinsky as Britt Ekland, and Strauss, Mahler and Bruckner as, erm, Edward Woodward. People were playing whatever they liked – just whacking their instruments randomly while sarcastically shouting: 'Is *this* what you wanted? Is *this* how you wanted things to turn out? *Happy now?*'

WANG.

At the world première in Paris of *The Rite of Spring* (subtitled *Scenes from Pagan Russia*) on 29 May 1913, there was a riot. An actual *riot*. (*The Rite of Spring* is a ballet, not a hip-hop guns, pimps and bitches throwdown.)

'I dreamed of a scene of pagan ritual in which a chosen sacrificial virgin danced herself to death,' explained a taken-aback Igor afterwards in his Yoko Ono glasses, cigarette holder in hand. 'And, strange as it may seem, I was entirely unprepared for such explosive reactions. The uproar continued and I left the hall in a rage; I remember slamming the door behind me ... I loved the music, and couldn't understand why people who had not yet heard it wanted to protest in advance.'

It premièred in London five weeks later to a similar, albeit more polite, reception. As one critic put it: 'This has no relation to music at all as most of us understand the word.'

DANG.

Hearing *The Rite of Spring* for the first time is like being mugged. Hearing *The Rite of Spring* a second time is like being mugged and chucked in a river, because you've forgotten how much of a shock it was the first time. Third time around I was able to actually listen to it rather than feel like my ears were being poked unnecessarily. I'm really not surprised about the riot – I nearly rioted in my front room myself. It's the rhythms; they ain't normal. They're all spooked and twisted; they jump out like Tyrannosaurus poltergeists and disappear as soon as they've bitten. This is true edge-of-the-seat stuff. Or rip-your-seat-up-and-throw-it stuff. It's spell-bindingly magnificent. Instead of 'Allegro', 'Scherzo', etc., its movements are called things like: 'Mock Abduction', 'Mystic Circles of the Young Girls' and 'Glorification of the Chosen Victim'. It's so hardcore that I can't actually type while it's on; I can only sit here dumbly, waiting for it to end. As did its audiences. Eventually. It's not surprising music took fifty-odd years to recover.

SWEET POONTANG.

Stravinsky was pals with Picasso; they were similar in many ways – both short, bald, dominators of their respective fields; dominators of the first half of the whole of the twentieth century; and they went through their various periods hand in hand: blue (Pablo), primitive (Igor), rose (Pablo), neoclassical (Igor), cubist (Pablo), serialist (Igor). *Et tu, Igor?* Yes, even dogged Stravinsky fell in line with Schoenberg's dogma in the end.

Arnold Schoenberg was dour and self-taught. (He had to be really – who'd have taught him that?) He grew up in Vienna, ironically, as an arch Romantic, but soon became disgusted with music – which he had learned anyway, just so's he could ruin it. Unlike Mussorgsky, he wasn't modest; his CV contained the line: 'Composer of *Pierrot Lunaire* and other works that have changed the history of music.' Schoenberg didn't respect anything or anybody, not even

Stravinsky, whom he considered an idiot (Stravinsky thought Schoenberg was an idiot too).

Schoenberg ← idiot → Stravinsky

Most of all, Schoenberg disrespected music itself; it's Schoenberg who's to blame for atonality. 'In ten years' time, all good composers will be writing this way,' Schoenberg boasted. And he was right. Old-fashioned music fans settled down for a very long wait. Some are still waiting. Schoenberg and Stravinsky continued to control the twentieth century in this way because no one else knew what the devil was going on, so nobody dared challenge them.

Meanwhile, everyone pretended to like it.

Concert hall audiences declined.

Lesser atonalists followed tentatively in their wake, like Sergei Prokofiev, who fled Russia after the Kremlin smelled a rat in this new and suddenly unrevolutionary-sounding music. America will understand me, he thought, but was gravely mistaken. America was showtunes, and ignored him.

Paris will get it, he rationalized, but Paris already had its own pretentious atonalists in *Les Six*,* and didn't care for another – especially after what happened the last time a Russian came to town. Instead Prokofiev moped back to Moscow, where, although he was banned from composing the kind of music he wanted to, at least he was famous. I apologize for this not being a very inspiring tale.† Dmitri Shostakovich was forced to tread a similar Soviet tightrope, but he dealt with these restrictions by carefully parodying the establishment, under the permissible heading of 'social realism'. He was rumbled, however, by Stalin, after a performance of his sarcastic opera *Lady Macbeth of Mtsensk*, whose bitter irony was clear, unfortunately, to all present. Stalin responded by executing a number of Shostakovich's family and friends; then most of his income vanished after his works were placed on the banned list. Shostakovich eventually got his revenge with his bombastic nationalist parody Symphony No. 5, which the proud authorities officially declared 'a Soviet artist's practical creative reply to ideologically just criticism'. Unfortunately, a Second Official Denunciation soon followed in 1948, and his works were all banned again. As a result of these many ironic machinations, Shostakovich became deeply fucked up and suicidal; so much so that in 1960 he even joined the Communist Party before, in 1975, dying of non-ironic lung cancer. His hobby had been football refereeing. Was that a cruel joke too?

Europe's atonal anarchy had become extremely tiresome for everybody. Though no one was suggesting a return to

---

* Poulenc, Milhaud, Honegger, Auric, Durey and Tailleferre. Significantly less fun than the Handful.

† Unwatered-down, communist-propaganda-free early Prokofiev is aces, though. It's right up there.

Romanticism, they at least wanted some kind of system to work within. Otherwise, everybody agreed, all this would end in tears, of which there were plenty enough already. Schoenberg claimed to have invented a solution. He was told to *shut the hell up, you've done enough damage as it is.*

In around 1945, after everybody had calmed down in a number of ways, Schoenberg calmly explained his new compositional technique: it was called serialism. Magic numbers. Maths. The bitterest pill. Yes, even bitterer than the last one.

Serialism

'Serialism?' I emailed Fiona.

Nothing. A few days later I emailed her again.

'Serialism?'

Then it clicked. Instead, I wrote: 's r m e s l a s i ____ m a ssss mismmims i s a l s e m r s –'

'Ah, serialism!' replied Fiona. 'You ought to get out more. Try an Andrew Lloyd Webber musical or something.'

I have a sneaking suspicion that nobody knows what serialism actually means. I even suspect that Schoenberg didn't know either, and he invented it. My own glossary was no use, so I went in search of an understandable definition; one that wasn't going to bamboozle me with jargon. Much to my surprise, I discovered that serialism is actually so simple you can go straight past it without even noticing. Unless you really want to go past it without noticing, in which case you'll have no problems either, unless you accidentally read the next paragraph.

Serialism is an extremely rigorous system for writing music that uses tone rows. A tone row is a permutation of the twelve notes of the chromatic scale (i.e. the twelve tones and semi-tones that you get going from, say, C to C). Serialism involves starting on any note at random and playing all the other notes in that tone row in any order, just so long as the note cycle is completed (i.e. every note touched upon). Why you'd want to do something like this I do not know. People like working within strict parameters – systems – I guess; especially miserable-looking bald men in tight suits. If you're a real tosser, you can refer to serialism as dodecaphony instead – you'll certainly give yourself some elbow space in the pub. So after you've sorted out your tone rows, you can then begin plenty of atonal variations upon your original, probably atonal, theme; including Bach's old trick of turning them upside-down, playing them backwards, and playing them backwards and upside-down both at the same time. Carry on like this for ages for no particular reason.

The first completely serialist work was Schoenberg's *Suite for Piano*.

It's weird.

I think I like it, but I'm not sure. This is the whole point about serialism: the music is meant to be mysterious, jagged, unpredictable; it never resolves. It's unashamedly intellectual music, and this is why so many people reject it – they can't stand the idea of music being intellectual – it ought to be felt, not rationalized, they protest. Hell, I can see both sides: Bach was maths; Bruckner is guts; both are good gods.

But here in the mid-twentieth century, guts were grossly unfashionable, so maths it remained. The young, post-war composers (and Schoenberg disciples) Berg and Webern enthusiastically spread serialism as a cunning – and cruel – way to merge the rhythmic chaos of Stravinsky with yer twelve-tone technique (like serialism except a bit easier) of early Schoenberg. This became known as the Second

Viennese School. You think you've got a headache now? Wait till you hear the fucking music!

Yes, but what headaches.

Escape from Darmstadt

Ah, Darmstadt, Darmstadt – how beautiful you are; how stochastic are your group theory combinatorics. How integrally $n$factorial your recursive gamma function parameterization of tetrachords. What time is love?

Darmstadt is a small town in the south-west of Germany whose city centre was destroyed in a British bombing raid on 11 September 1944, killing approximately 11,000 (the town's 3,000 Jews had been shipped out and executed a few years previously). The war finished, and the city lay in ruins. Darmstadtians were either dead or disheartened. However, one of the few structures left standing was a large laboratory building in some woodland in the town's outskirts. This building was commandeered by a group of musicians and hastily converted into a summer school for new music; or to be more precise, the *Internationale Ferienkurse für Neue Musik*. Young musicians began to gravitate around Darmstadt as word got out that here was a refuge in war-torn Europe for those proto-serialist Schoenberg disciples, scattered all over the face of the earth. Included in the summer school's ranks were the following young composers:

Olivier Messiaen. Likes: God, birdsong, organs, modes of limited transposition. Dislikes: rude people, snakes.

Karlheinz Stockhausen. Likes: electronics and helicopters. Dislikes: royalties.

Pierre Boulez. Likes: tunelessness and shouting. Dislikes: litterbugs, *Pop Idol*.

Messiaen was one of the school's teachers, a radical organ-ist from Paris who'd been captured by the Germans in 1941 and placed in a prisoner-of-war camp. While incarcerated he ingeniously premièred his quasi-tonal piece 'Quatour pour le fin de temps' in Stalag VIII-A before a sub-zero audience of frozen Polish paratroopers. They liked it but couldn't clap in case their fingers fell off. After that, the whole Darmstadt malarkey was a piece of chilly piss for Messiaen, whose approach to music was more eclectic than most of the other pupils' (hence his music's still played today). Messiaen's in-spirations were 'birdsong, Shakespeare, my mother, Debussy, plainsong, Indian rhythms, Russian music, more birdsong, the mountains of Dauphiné, indeed from everything that is stained glass and rainbows'. The hardcore serialists gathered in the shadows and conspired to kick his head in.

Darmstadt's pupils were encouraged to forget the tonal heritage of the piano; instead to treat it as a mere sound-producing box. The sounds that emerged were

I n t e r e s t i n g.

Patterns, shapes, systems, clusters, no melody, no coherent rhythm. National musical identity vanished – everything sounded like everything else, borders became irrelevant.

'Any musician who has not felt the necessity of the serial language is USELESS,' pounded Boulez, before question-ing serial language's insistence upon playing all twelve notes. 'Hold on. It is cumbersome!' he wrote. 'Why can't I just use four notes, or, say, six?'

That's a shocking thing to say. No, in serialism you have to use all twelve notes. It's hard to overestimate how incredibly confused everybody was at this point. The musicians who were instructed to play it all, especially.

The Darmstadt school dominated the remainder of the twentieth century in classical music. Stockhausen took serialism and added electronics; he was more interested in the acoustic and psychological aspects of music than the melodic – or even notational. The result was usually a sparse cacophony that nobody liked. It was perfect; this was the sound of *now*.* This racket was the final straw for weary concert-goers who, in between deafening blasts of random percussion, pounding electronic glitches and backwards tape recorders, remembered the good old days, when composers wrote music for them rather than against them. The serial composers were bitterly contemptuous of their new, non-existent, audience; they talked of 'cultural lag': the time it would take for the public to catch up with their ultra-modern future music. Sadly the public never did catch up, which is why you rarely hear any of this material in concert halls any more. And because they have been banned.

Forget tonality and rhythm, Stockhausen even considered gravity restrictive to his art. He had dreams about flying, which eventually turned into his *Helikopter-Streichquartett*, where each of the four members of a string quartet go up in their own helicopter and play the same piece simultaneously with the aid of a click-track. The audience down below hear the merged instruments, plus not-so-subtle chopper ambience, through four giant speakers below. This piece has been performed on a number of occasions – at air shows, oil rigs, Noel Edmonds' house – and you can buy it on CD, except on the recording I've got they cheated and added the helicopter noise on separately, afterwards. Harrumph. 🚁🚁

Boulez was the arch serialist – the one who stuck at it for the longest, its philosophical leader. Now in his eighties and

* The 1950s, the 1960s.

considered the cuddly grandfather of Modern classical music (in the 1970s, they even invited him to Bayreuth to conduct the Ring Cycle – they regretted it at their leisure), it's easy to forget quite how austere his reputation – and music – really was. Like Stockhausen, Boulez used electronics in conjunction with orchestras; and, like Stockhausen, his frightening reputation precedes him. Yet general knowledge of their works remains virtually non-existent. People talk of the influence of Stockhausen, Boulez, Varèse (helped invent the theremin), Schaeffer (pioneer of *musique concrète*) et al. constantly, but their popular appeal is extremely limited; their curatorship lies in the hands of leftfield esoteric specialists; it's hard to get your hands on any of this stuff. Today's mainstream audiences consider this postwar esoterica at best dry and academic and at worst deeply suspicious, fundamentally risible – you'll never hear a single note (nor even a small klang) played on Classic FM. Which is a shame – this music is inspiring, challenging, even fun, and delivers as much of a physiological punch as any other music; it's just coming at you from a different angle, that's all. Sideways. In an aleatoric helicopter. Have I not mentioned aleatorics? Oh.

UnCaged

John Cage was born in Los Angeles in 1912. He went to Pomona College in Claremont, California. On campus one afternoon, Cage entered the library and was shocked to see all the other students reading exactly the same textbook. I don't know why he was shocked exactly, as this is what students tend to have to do occasionally. Cage went directly to the bookshelves and took out the first book written by an author whose name began with a Z, and received the highest grade in the class. This single incident inspired him to drop out of college and try and become a composer. Stranger things had happened – Berlioz, for example. Cage composed a few small pieces but soon became bored and decided to put a load of screws, bolts and strips of rubber and plastic inside his piano. This made the piano sound strange – glottal and percussive, pained but oddly emotive. He had invented the prepared piano, which he began to compose music for, which turned out to be uncommonly brilliant. His reputation grew. Over in France, Boulez heard about what was going on and got in touch, asking if Cage wanted to join his gang of serialists over here in Europe, where all the real action was, only sadly no audiences for it. Cage said, sure, but I want to use a few of my own techniques, if that's OK?

'You mean your prepared piano? Sure!' replied Boulez.

'No, I'm talking about indeterminacy.'

'What's that?'

'Music where the compositional and performance parameters are left to chance.'

'You mean *complete randomness*?'

'Well, I've got some charts and stuff, but that's about the gist of it.'

Boulez slammed the phone down. Such insanity, plus Cage's obvious disrespect for the twelve-tone system, plus an inordinate love of mushrooms meant that Boulez never spoke to Cage again. The offer of collaboration was fiercely withdrawn. Instead Cage got to work writing indeterminate (aleatoric) music and became super-famous and super-cool. He was worshipped by students all over the world. Everyone else thought he was terrible. Some of his more infamous pieces include:

Music for Changes. A piece based on random patterns taken from the *I Ching*, and coin-tossing.

Imaginary Landscape 3 was constructed from random variable-speed turntables and oscillators.

Imaginary Landscape 4 was written for twelve radio receivers, each manned with two people, one controlling the frequency, one the volume. Cage scored their actions but the emergent sounds depended on what was on the radio. They still do, of course.

Water Music was composed for (specifically): piano, radio, three whistles, water containers, a deck of cards, a wooden stick, four objects for preparing a piano and a stopwatch. So far, solar system.

Then came the notorious *4'33"*.

On 29 August 1952, a young pianist named David Tudor strode out on to the stage at the Maverick Concert Hall in Woodstock, New York, and placed Cage's brand new, handwritten score on the piano. The audience hushed. Tudor lowered the lid of the piano and, holding a stopwatch in his right hand, proceeded to do nothing. After exactly thirty seconds he raised the piano lid to indicate the end of the first movement. There was some confused muttering from the auditorium. The second movement passed in a similar fashion, with some raindrops being discerned on the faculty roof, plus more whispering than was usual. As did the third movement, with Tudor methodically turning the pages of the score as he sat, counting out the minutes. At the end of the fourth and final movement, throughout whose duration the audience had become distinctly uneasy, Tudor opened the piano lid, stood and turned to the audience for his ovation, or otherwise. He received the otherwise. There was uproar; not quite a riot, but not far off.

4'33" is often mistakenly referred to as Cage's silent piece, when of course it's not about silence (there's no such thing), but the ambient acoustics of the venue, the audience and any extraneous sounds from outside. And taking the piss. It's as much a reflection on the listener as a statement by the composer; it's about the nature of hearing. Of course, everybody complained that he'd gone too far – beyond a joke; but it was a historic and definitive moment in music, a turning point, a point of no return. After *4'33"*, music would have to reinvent itself somehow – build itself back together, towards something else, something new. Which, of course, it did (in the end). Even that repellent bourgeois cliché tonality made a comeback – and melody and rhythm and all these cheesy things that make music easier to listen to. Contemporary composers are gradually clawing their land back – clawing their old audiences back, man by man, woman by woman, child by poor bitter bloody child – as we speak, gently asking them not to.

'Try as we may to make a silence, we cannot,' wrote Cage, who'd given it a damn good try. 'One need not fear for the future of music.'

*

Seb suggests:

The Firebird / The Rite of Spring by The Columbia Symphony Orchestra and Igor Stravinsky (Sony Classical)

(Stravinsky was commissioned to write *The Firebird* in 1909, and it established him immediately as a force to be reckoned with. It's clearly an early work, as it is melodic and relatively easy on the ear. Thus Stravinsky despised it, and it has remained his most popular piece. *The Rite of Spring* follows. This CD's like a starter and a main course; and all conducted by Igor himself. I don't know when, though – it doesn't say, I've checked.)

Piano Music of the Darmstadt School, Volume One by Various Artists (DG)

(*plinkety*   )

Piano Music of the Darmstadt School, Volume Two by Various Artists (DG)

(*plonk*   )

Messiaen: *par lui-meme* by Olivier Messiaen (EMI Classics)

(This is a four-CD box-set of Messiaen's complete organ works, played by his nibs on the organ in La Trinité in Paris, where he played – on and off – from 1931 until his death in 1992. These recordings date from 1956. Over four discs, this can be heavy going, but you will never hear anybody play the organ in this way ever again. I had no idea you could make an organ sound like this! There is a lot of

deep, mystical stuff going on in here; it gives me the mofin'
shivers. Essential unless you can't afford it or think four
CDs of organ-playing is three-and-a-half too many.)

Schoenberg: *Piano Music* by Paul Jacobs (Apex) 🚐🚐🚐
🚐🚐

(This CD features all the music Schoenberg wrote for
piano. Takes Debussy a couple of steps further down the
line. Arguably over the edge of a cliff, but that's all right.
There's really nothing to be afraid of here. Whatever you
might think of atonal piano music, it's difficult to argue
when it's as beautifully played as this. Hearing this, it
all makes sense; this isn't gratuitous, wilful, destructive
randomness – it's explorative and sincere and big-hearted
and profound. You could even go so far as to call it . . .
Romantic. Oh, Jesus!)

Stockhausen: *Kontakte* by David Tudor, Christoph Caskel
and Karlheinz Stockhausen (Wergo) 🚐🚐🚐🚐🚐
(For electronics, piano and percussion. Colour-merge;
lightning; tension. Who knows what's going on here, but
it's one of my favourite favourite pieces of music none-
theless.)

Cage: *Indeterminacy* by John Cage and David Tudor (Smith-
sonian Folkways) 🚐🚐🚐🚐🚐
(Cage reads ninety one-minute anecdotal stories at varying speeds, depending on the story's individual length.
In another room, David Tudor triggers various random
samples of Cage's *Concert for Piano and Orchestra* and *Fontana
Mix*. Double CD. Playful, profound, and a strangely
satisfying experience all around. A must-buy. Zen as you
like!)

17. Composers of the Undead

Post-Cage, there's been a breakout of a New Eclecticism, in the hope of undoing the commercial damage done by Darmstadt and Boulez, and because there are no giant Stravinsky/Schoenberg figures towering over everybody making sure their tone rows resolve. Except Boulez himself, of course, but he's old and probably can't punch as hard as he used to. There isn't a pervading stylistic school at present; you're pretty much allowed to do whatever you want, within reason. McCartney, for one, should know better.

But then it takes a while for a composer to make a mark. It's not like the hype, hype, first album, hype, whoops, *you're dead* culture of popular music. These days you have to be pretty old before you're allowed to even claim to have composed something; seventy might be a good age; or eighty-five.

Some of the more high profile contemporary composers include:

Sir John Tavener. Depressive, weird Munster-like figure referred to in chapter three. My Tavener CD hasn't improved in the intervening chapters.
Music sounds like: dying.

Henryk Gorecki. Mystic Polish minimalist, responsible for some genuine classical crossover back in 1993 when his *Symphony of Sorrowful Songs* captured the public imagination to such a degree they bought two million copies

of it. Has been happily living off the royalties ever since.
Music sounds like: dying.

György Ligeti. Mystic Hungarian avant-gardist who specialized
in soundtracking films by Stanley Kubrick but hasn't so
much since Kubrick died. Or indeed since he himself
died, in between editions of this book.
Music sounds like: being born.

Philip Glass. Famous American minimalist who specializes
in suspiciously similar film soundtracks and repetition.
Music sounds like: bubbles that go on for ever.

John Adams. Famous American minimalist who specializes
in operas.
Music sounds like: opera.

Steve Reich. Famous American minimalist who specializes in
rhythm, phasing and tape loops and being namechecked
by hip young electronica kidz.
Music sounds like: drumming, especially *Drumming*.

Arvo Pärt. Mystical Estonian minimalist who specializes
in Estonian mystic minimalism. His choral works are
particularly esteemed.
Music sounds like: reggae party.

Sir Peter Maxwell Davies. Prolific English eclecticist, who
likes to compose using 'magic squares'. His music features elements of plainsong, jazz, schmaltz, serialism,
raga and bagpipes. He smiles a lot.
Music sounds like: bagpipes being jammed down a waste
disposal unit in Southall.

Harrison Birtwhistle: Quite tricksy, complex English Modernist, whose première, at the Last Night of the Proms

in 1995, of his piece *Panic* – featuring drumkit and saxophone – went down *extremely badly*, as it was not in the slightest bit nationalistic.

Music sounds like: bloody nonsense.

Joby Talbot. Much-too-young (my age)* English composer who used to be in pop group the Divine Comedy, and in whose capable young hands rests the entire future of classical music.† Has recently been made Classic FM's first-ever composer-in-residence.

Music sounds like: the theme music from *Terry and June*.

Ellen Zwilich. A post-modernist female composer from the United States.

Music sounds like: I have no idea.

Pierre Boulez. Is still hanging on in there – in case you'd forgotten.

Music souCLANG.

As we can see, classical music appears to be neither dead nor planning to die any time soon. OK it's hardly setting the world on fire or raking in mountains of cash (Nigel Kennedy arguably excepted), but it's not the force it once was – this is a specialist market now, firmly outside the mainstream. Apart from the sterling populist job being done by Classic FM, the BBC Proms and all those at the rough and tumble marketeers' frontline, it exists in a civilized, just about self-supporting cul-de-sac, perpetually looking over its shoulder in fear of becoming engulfed by the unholy tsunami of popular culture's all-powerful shitstorm. So far it has continued to survive; but the true test will surely arrive when the previous generation has passed away, and all that's left are those whose

* *So* young.
† Possibly.

lives have been lived through an entirely post-Elvis prism. Will the new generation be able to hold it up by themselves? And will there be anything left for them to hold up anyway?

The answer is surely yes. Pianos are darned heavy.

Some Conclusions

Before I started this, classical music seemed to me like a self-satisfied clique of bow-tied aesthetes, frugging, cod-rapt, around a foetid canon of preordained costume jewellery, with the sound of everyone patting everyone else's back drowning out the endless banality playing out in the hallowed, creaking, crushed red velvet auditoria. I realize now that I was mistaken – it's not costume jewellery, it's real. And that they're not patting each other on the back – they're just old, and helping each other to the exits. And you don't spell foetid like that any more either – you spell it 'fetid'.

Just how wrong could I have been?

As a final attempt at an interesting experiment, I ventured downstairs in HMV on Oxford Street one last time; I wanted to see how the two names at the top of their respective cultural fields fared in a contemporary retail face-off: Mozart vs the Beatles. How many racks did each of these giants command in one of the biggest record stores in the world? Who'd come out on top on sheer volume of discs stocked? And would my maths up to the task?* First, I went to the ground floor to count the Beatles. There were four of them. Hahaha. Including 'interview' CDs, the Fab Four took up an impressive twenty-seven compartments (each compartment holds about ten CDs), plus an additional eight racks of

* No.

tribute CDs by other artists. Other artists, you should be ashamed of yourselves.

Downstairs in the familiar glassed-off section of the basement (which nowadays holds almost no fear for me – indeed, I've begun to swagger) I began to work through the Mozart, but kept losing my place. Taking out a pen and paper, I counted each vertical and horizontal column, multiplied them and then did the same on the other side of the unit. Altogether I counted 208 compartments for Mozart alone. Then on top of that was the 'sale' area (there was no Beatles in the sale bit upstairs), in which I counted a further forty-one. Plus the separate Naxos zone: another twenty-eight. Then in the opera section: a further twenty-five-odd. This means that in just one single store, and without including box-sets or various items on display elsewhere, there were a mammoth *306* compartments just for Mozart alone. *Over ten times as many as the Beatles.*

I appreciate this statistic is relatively meaningless – that hundreds of recordings of Mozart exist compared to the singular recorded output of the Beatles; but it's still quite interesting – that classical music survives almost entirely on these multitudinous cover versions, all competing to be the one-off, definitive recording of a piece. Or, should I say that all these orchestras, conductors, singers and dancers never tire of peeling back the layers of the onion to reveal . . . they hope, something new. I mean, Christ, *how many more times?*

The answer appears, for now, to be endless. But will it be for ever?

Throughout the course of this book, I've missed out a lot of stuff. I'm sorry about that. If I'm honest I've barely scratched the surface. If you take the Pacific Ocean as representing all classical music, this book is an ugly steamer puffing across a B-road shipping channel. If classical music is an Olympic-sized swimming pool, this book is the urine in the toddlers' paddling pool. If classical music is the Royal Albert Hall, we are the Feltham Tramshed. If classical music is an elephant (which actually it is), this book is a mere flea on its big grey arse. Or perhaps a tick is more accurate, as I feel I have penetrated the elephant and had a damn good poke around its elephantinnards before being burned off with the hot tip of a scalding baton. There have been positives:

No longer am I afraid of the violin.

No longer do I blanch before a flute.

No more tremors outside concert halls.

No more blazer panic.

No more basement cower.

No more avoidance of Radio 3 – at least not all that much.

No more shame; less ignorance; I am nicer to old people.

I'm going to miss classical music. For some months now, I've dared to excitedly anticipate the end of this whole thing so I can go back and wallow in listening to nothing but pop again, but now I'm not so sure I'm ready to. The thought of no classical in my life makes me feel a bit panicky, bereft, a little agoraphobic. I've got so used to it over these (almost) two years, I can't imagine returning to a life without it. After all, this journey was supposed to be – in some respect – about accumulation – of knowledge, information, passion, revelation and most of all education. And I have achieved some of these things; I know that I'll listen to much of this music now for the rest of my life; and I know there's still loads more fantastic stuff beneath the surface that I can explore and swim through for years to come. It's been worth it just for that, I reckon. I would definitely call myself a classical music fan now; if only such a definition didn't sound quite so trite and meaningless. I hope this might mean I've got somewhere.

Twelve Classical Commandments

When Darren unexpectedly asked what I'd learned in his office that sunny afternoon, the real answer wasn't just my spontaneous yet profound statement that 'people are nice'. Though it's true, and they are (nice), I have also learned the following. Consider these my twelve classical music commandments; my dozen stone tablets carried down from the heights of Mount Furtwängler. If you, too, want to explore the world of violins, sonority, tone rows and David Mellor's teeth, maybe you can cut these out and carry them in your wallet or your purse. You never know when you might need them (indeed, I required Commandment 8 a mere fifteen minutes ago).

1) The absolute key to listening to classical music – the most difficult thing of all – is *concentration*. We music fans under forty are weaned on music that demands a very short attention span. You must attempt to unlearn this some-how.* Your unlearning will probably involve a lot of falling asleep. Do not worry about this. Consider it power-napping.

2) *Get past the first movement.* It doesn't really count as listening to the whole piece if you've only made it to the end of the first movement. Maybe next time start on a movement other than the first. Mix it up, (attempt to) keep things inter-esting. I have never done this because I enjoy the comfort

---

* Early Tangerine Dream is very good for practising with.

of first-movement recognition, yet I ought to have done. And remember, you're meant to be listening, not just hearing – there's a big difference between the two.

3) *Don't feel guilty* about not liking something, especially if it involves operatic singing. But then, on the other hand, don't just dismiss a piece of music because it features operatic singing. Persevere. For a while. Then turn it off and go out to play.

4) *Go to a Prom.* If you can't get to a Prom, go to any classical music concert – the cheaper the better. Have a beer. Enjoy it. Remember Commandment 1.

5) *Trust Bach*, not Beethoven. You can trust Mozart too if you're feeling bright. If someone comes up and tells you to trust *anybody else* – often it will be Wagner – they're not your friend: they have ulterior motives.

6) Go to your local CD emporium and *buy £10–20 worth of random, cheap classical music*. Something might spark. If it doesn't, give it to your family for Christmas.

7) If in doubt, *go with the piano music*.

8) *Opera is stupid.*

9) You might be thinking that a lot of classical music sounds exactly the same. Well, it does. *Trust your ears* – if you're sitting there, bored out of your mind, trying hard to get to grips with a piece but all you can hear is your life slipping further and further away, then turn it off and replace it with Wagnerian opera. That'll teach you to be such a shallow prick, won't it? Not really. Turn it off; and why not destroy it?

10) *There aren't any secrets*; there's no club-class enlightenment zone waiting for anybody anywhere except, for when you hit seventy, *Gramophone*. Many people at a classical music concert will have even less of an idea of what's going down musically than you do. There are lots of

defensive smoke and mirrors – ignore them, because at the end of the day, Brian . . .

11) *Classical music loves you*. It really does. To keep going it needs your support and approval and your bum on the seat. And your money. See Commandment 6.

12) Remember these wise words from that fat man with the make-up, Luciano Pavarotti: '*You don't need brains* to listen to music.' Remember also these words from pianist and composer Oscar Levant: 'Mine was the kind of piece in which *nobody knew what was going on* – including the composer, the conductor and the critics. Consequently I got *pretty good notices*,' i.e. nobody holds the key to ultimate truth, nobody really knows anything, except Fiona, who knows it all. And if you ask her nicely, she'll tell you.

No Sleep till Wigmore Hall

There was one final, mythic piece of my jigsaw remaining: a trip to London's ultimate purists' haven, the Wigmore Hall, halfway down Wigmore Street, deep in the heart of central London. There was no way I could call myself any sort of classical music fan without coming here at least once. This place eats Classic FM listeners for breakfast; seasoned Prommers for lunch. For dinner it entices the crème-de-la-crème of classical aficionados into its hallowed portals to worship before the Holy Grail of internationally renowned chamber music quartets, quintets, troupes, groups and solo performers, most of whom are elderly and Russian; sometimes actual corpses. The Wigmore Hall is the architectural manifestation of *Gramophone* magazine – you just don't mess about with it; it's not funny; it makes a gold leaf-bound

King James Bible look like a knackered, charity-shop Jeffrey Archer. It's famed for its near-perfect acoustics, which they recently spent £3m making even more perfect. I think they put a new carpet in too, and cleaned the chandeliers and light fittings. None of these things are cheap.

As a Friend of Wigmore Hall, Rodney had agreed to take me along on one of his regular outings. And before you all rush to become Friends too, you don't actually receive any discounts for this status (discounts are vulgar), but you do get 'priority booking', a regular Friends newsletter and a sumptuous membership card that you can have fun flashing at lesser folk.

'Are we "priority booked" tonight?' I asked Rodney, as we stood outside, flicking through the glossy programme and drinking in the vibes, of which there were none except a mild, late spring breeze. Though this was my official 'farewell' concert, I was unable to muster up much profundity or excitement; all I felt was numb, exhausted, ready for a holiday and some death fucking metal.

'Yes of course.'

'So this is all pretty special, yeah? Being priority booked here at the Wigmore Hall is a pretty special thing, right?'

'Oh yes. This is . . .'

'Is it *sublime*?'

'I suppose so, yes.'

'Thank God.'

Otherwise what was the point in being their Friend?

Tonight's was the oldest audience of all – most of these babes and dudes were as wizened and delicate as bark from an old silver birch. We'd come to see the Borodin Quartet, a famous Russian chamber orchestra; and the programme was eclectic: Rachmaninov, Schubert, Debussy, Dvořák – the usual suspects. The auditorium was lush and compact;

the seats were deep and wine-coloured, as was the special new carpet; the atmosphere was thick and deeply respectful. At seven o'clock precisely, the quartet emerged from the wings in skewed ducktails to ripples of educated applause. They smirked, took their seats and shuffled their music a little. One had to pop backstage to get some more. Rodney and I smiled at one another and leaned back into our soft, soft chairs. Following nods and raised eyebrows, the quartet at last began, and after approximately nine minutes of sublime tonality, sonority and some damn good bowing technique, I fell fast asleep. What must have been a good hour later, Rodney tapped me gently on the shoulder.

'Seb?' he whispered.

'Mmm?'

'It's over.'

Acknowledgements

Thank you!

Fiona Maddocks; Neil Taylor; Rowland White, Becke Parker, Rob Williams, Carly Cook and all at Penguin; Owen Oakeshott; Small, Pete and Mel; Drew Fud Dunn; Sir Rodney of Troubridge; the inferior two-thirds of Crater: Turf and Snaggers; Christian 'Goatfucker' Misje; Trapper Ragg and family; Craig Leon; Pauly Fop Twat Erdpresser; Amy Roach; Jill and Dennis; Anne Bourgeois-Vignon; David Watson; Stuart Stratford; Peter Skuce; Mike Sargeant; Darren Henley; Emma Oxborrow; Giles Pearman; Michelle Kane; Knut Ellingsen; Somerfield in Brentford; Annie; Claus Lundekvam, and everyone else who has given me support and encouragement. And *hope*.

No thanks to: Glenn Collins.

Extra special thanks to: Faye Phillipa Brewster, for putting up with all my bullshit.

And a big hello to: Reuben!

MY TOP 15 CLASSICAL MUSIC PIECES, IN NO
PARTICULAR ORDER

Bach *Mass in B Minor*
Bruckner *Symphony No. 2 in C minor*
Debussy *Les Préludes*
Palestrina *Missa Sine Nomine*
Mozart *Requiem* (but not all of it thanks)
Mussorgsky *Pictures at an Exhibition*

Stravinsky *The Rite of Spring*
Machaut *La Messe de Notre Dame*
Bach *The Art of Fugue* (played on piano)
Liszt *Piano Music*
Handel *Messiah* (see *Requiem*)
Messiaen *Le Banquet Céleste* (for organ)
Stockhausen *Kontakte*
Elgar *Cello Concerto*
Schoenberg *Piano Music*

FIONA MADDOCKS' TOP 10 CLASSICAL MASTERPIECES, IN ALPHABETICAL ORDER

Bach *Chorale Preludes*
Bach *St Matthew Passion*
Bach *Well-tempered Klavier* (played on piano)
Beethoven *String Quartets* (all)
Brahms *Symphonies* (all)
Byrd/Tallis *Cantiones Sacrae*
Cage *Sonatas and Interludes*
Elgar *Violin Concerto*
Josquin *Missa Pange lingua*
Purcell *Funeral Odes for Queen Mary*

FIONA MADDOCKS' TOP 5 OPERAS, IN ALPHABETICAL ORDER

Beethoven *Fidelio*
Debussy *Pelléas et Mélisande*
Mozart: all operas written after 1785 plus *Idomeneo*
Tchaikovsky *Eugene Onegin*
Wagner *Dwarfs' Ring*

OWEN'S TOP 5 CLASSICAL PIECES, IN ORDER

Fauré *Requiem*
Tavener *Eternal Sunrise*
Prokofiev *Romeo and Juliet*
Handel *Zadok the Priest* (The Champions League music)
Hubert Parry *I Was Glad When They Said Unto Me*

ANDREW'S TOP 5 CLASSICAL PIECES

MY MOTHER'S TOP 6 CLASSICAL PIECES

Gounod *Faust*
Vaughan Williams *Fantasia on a Theme by Thomas Tallis*
Brahms *Symphony No. 4*
Schubert *The Shepherd on the Rock*
Allegri *Miserere*
Sibelius *Symphony No. 2*

RODNEY'S TOP 5 CLASSICAL PIECES

RICHBORNE TERRACE
LONDON SW8 IAS
020-7793███

Sir Rodney Top 5

1 ~~Chopin~~ Schubert
Die Schöne Müllerin

2 Parsifal by Wagner
Whole Opera!

3 Bach - Goldberg
Variations

4 Dvorak - String Qt
"American"

5 Sinfonia ~~Domestica~~ Concertina
by Mozart

17th May '05

STUART STRATFORD'S TOP 5 CLASSICAL PIECES

Stravinsky *Les Noces*
Verdi *La Traviata*
Beethoven *Symphony No. 9*
Mozart *Don Giovanni*
Chopin *Ballades*

Glossary

A Capella unaccompanied.

Accidental by mistake.

Adagio slow/prolonged.

Aleatory random.

Allegro zippy.

Alto in a high voice.

Andante chewy.

Anthem *classic*.

Antiphon a reply to a hymn in a hymn-like style.

Aria a vocal solo in an opera.

Arpeggio pluck like a harp, like a *harp*.

Atonal like Simon le Bon.

Aunt Sally Wurzel Gummidge's straw-filled love interest.

Ballad an emotional song like Bryan Adams' 'Everything I Do (I Do It for You)', or Meat Loaf's 'I Would Do Anything for Love (But I Won't Do That)'.

Ballet dancing for no good reason.

Barcarolle very sweet, parallelogram-shaped Turkish dessert.

Baritone male voice in between tenor and bass.

Bass a fish, or beer, or what Kiss's Gene Simmons plays while sticking his tongue out in silver boots made from dragons.

Basse danse 'I was made for loving you'.

Bel canto literally: 'beautiful song' – e.g. 'Venus as a Boy' by Björk.

Blue notes those nice notes; missing from classical music.

Cabaletta overrated bread. Also might be a horse or a Spanish toilet.

Cadence the closing sequence of a phrase.

Cadenza improvised showing off.

Canon Japanese camera maker that used to sponsor Nigel Mansell. Also a type of priest.

Cantus firmus virgin bride.

Castrato child/man hybrid with high singing voice due to testicular desecration.

Chaconne sausage.

Chamber music intimate music written to be performed in a room rather than a concert hall, e.g. Chas 'n' Dave.

Chanson French song, e.g. 'Joe Le Taxi'.

Chorale a French ranch.

Chord some examples of chords are: E, A, D, G, F and C Minor.

Chromaticism a deep love of things made of chrome.

Coda the not-very-good outtakes album Led Zeppelin released not long after John Bonham's death.

Combinatorics a complicated branch of mathematics.

Con brio spunky.

Concertante a command to *concentrate*.

Concerto a work where a solo instrument plays on top of an orchestra.

Concerto grosso a concerto that's been *ruined*.

Continuo you're doing fine, son, keep it up.

Contralto contrition/guilt/failure.

Contrapuntal *extremely naughty*.

Counterpoint ubiquitous chain of currency exchange outlets.

Countertenor the highest male voice (apart from castrato).

Crescendo the money shot.

Da Capo Love's rubbish second album.

Diatonic sports drink endorsed by Alan Shearer.

Diminuendo lacklustre remix of the last Queen album to feature Freddie Mercury.

Discant South London slang, *trans.*: 'this particular gentleman'.

Dissonance if you don't like something it's because there's too much (or not enough) of this.

Dodecaphonic dinosaur hip-hop.

Dynamics dynamics.

Empfindsamkeit type of German empathy involving not much empathy at all.

Étude practising in a good mood.

Expressionism gratuitous clapping between the movements.

Fantasia a dream in which you're listening to something else.

Finale WAKE UP.

Fret has it been worth the money? No.

Fugato a short fugue, outside of a fugue.

Gavotte Belgian profanity.

Gesamtkunstwerk German profanity.

Gigue French gig.

Glissando Italian shampoo.

Gruppo a bear.

Harmony I think one of the female fighter plane pilots in *Captain Scarlet*.

Hocket sports wine.

Homophony what castrati get up to on their days off.

Hymn a song you sing in church.

Intermezzo although occasionally used by pretentious Italians, nobody really knows what this word means.

Interval time to neck as much booze as is humanly possible.

Inversion it's upside-down!

Key which note to start on.

Key Largo a place to go diving in Florida.

Koechel numbers oh, for God's sake.

Largo instruction to play slowly.

Legato make good use of your leg.

Lento grinding.

Libretto the text in an opera, often written by a poet.

416

Mezzo Mediterranean snacks, e.g. marinated anchovies.

Minuet I think it's a waltz.

Mode a feeling you get inside.

Modulation fickleness.

Monody a boring bit in the middle.

Movement the noisy bit straight afterwards that jolts you back awake.

Musique concrète music that's trying really hard to make you angry.

Naxos devilishly affordable.

Neoclassicism new classicism.

Nocturne music played at night.

Obbligato Portuguese for 'thank you'.

Octave surely this is the same as a scale?

Ornament unnecessary vocal or instrumental trill.

Overture won't go on too long.

Pedal point the point is to use the pedal.

Pitch chuck.

Pizzicato one of five members of kitsch Japanese pop group.

Pointillism technique utilized on Harry Nilsson's 1970 *Yellow Submarine* rip-off album.

Polytonality the use of two keys simultaneously; spreading your bets.

Prelude the bit that comes before you dribble down your chin.

Presto lucky surname of unusual female magician Faye.

Prince Charles much-respected future King of England.

Rallentando slow down; prepare for a nap.

Recitative plagiarism.

Repertory any classical music piece that gets a regular airing.

Rhapsody ostentatious display of self-satisfaction.

Romanticism lovely, pretty things of tender love.

Rondo Beckham child.

Rubato Venezuelan nickname for Rubens Barrichello.

Scale climb.

Scherzo e.g. Robert de Niro in *Cape Fear*.

Sequence a hymn sung by a Catholic in the olden days.

Serenade see 'ballad', only with candles and a rose.

Serialism frequency.

Sonata form many claim that knowledge and understanding of sonata form leads to the unlocking of the secret of life itself. Others say it's just a three-part musical model that consists of an exposition followed by a development and then a recapitulation. My own – third – way boils down to: *who gives a toss?*

Sonority anything David Mellor says – the most serious thing of all.

Soprano a singing lady. When she stops singing, you can leave.

Sprechgesang deadly poison made out of old bassoon casing.

Staccato jerky.

Stretto a soprano's throat lozenge.

Strophic orchestral suffix for *cata*.

Suite Nigel Kennedy's contract rider demands one, bedecked in expensive bunches of flowers and a champagne bucket.

Suspension a note left hanging in the air.

Syncopation a way to keep time when your metronome is broken.

Tempo measure of hurtle.

Tenor one of either Luciano Pavarotti, Placido Domingo, or the other one.

Tessitura anxiousness.

Timbre firewood from France.

Time signature instructions as to whether something goes 1–2–3–4, 1–2–3–4, or 1–2–3, 1–2–3. Or maybe something completely new.

Tonality the system of major and minor scales and keys that forms the basis of all Western art music from the seventeenth century until Schoenberg.

Tree house a good song by a band called Buffalo Tom.

Triad a three-note chord consisting of a root note plus the intervals of a third and a fifth.

Trio the above only multiplied by three.

Triplets as above, only *divided* by three.

Tutti spitting footballer.

Vibrato annoying warble of the voice favoured by boybands.

Wagner Nazi midget, composer of fourteen-hour Ring Cycle.

Waltz a group of men named Walter who prefer to be known by the shortened form of their first name.

Xylophone important percussion instrument, especially on children's television.

Zarathustra thus she spake.

Zither a popular, value-for-money, multi-stringed instrument that sounds cool even when you just kick it.

Zymurgy fermentation.

Picture Credits

He just wanted a decent book to read ...

Not too much to ask, is it? It was in 1935 when Allen Lane, Managing Director of Bodley Head Publishers, stood on a platform at Exeter railway station looking for something good to read on his journey back to London. His choice was limited to popular magazines and poor-quality paperbacks – the same choice faced every day by the vast majority of readers, few of whom could afford hardbacks. Lane's disappointment and subsequent anger at the range of books generally available led him to found a company – and change the world.

'We believed in the existence in this country of a vast reading public for intelligent books at a low price, and staked everything on it'
Sir Allen Lane, 1902–1970, founder of Penguin Books

The quality paperback had arrived – and not just in bookshops. Lane was adamant that his Penguins should appear in chain stores and tobacconists, and should cost no more than a packet of cigarettes.

Reading habits (and cigarette prices) have changed since 1935, but Penguin still believes in publishing the best books for everybody to enjoy. We still believe that good design costs no more than bad design, and we still believe that quality books published passionately and responsibly make the world a better place.

So wherever you see the little bird – whether it's on a piece of prize-winning literary fiction or a celebrity autobiography, political tour de force or historical masterpiece, a serial-killer thriller, reference book, world classic or a piece of pure escapism – you can bet that it represents the very best that the genre has to offer.

Whatever you like to read – trust Penguin.